The Better Photo Checklist

If you're getting ready to go out on a photo safari and wondering what you may have forgotten, use this list.

- **Check your batteries.** Make sure they're all charged up and carry a spare.

- **Check your memory cards.** Make sure you've downloaded old images and formatted your cards.

- **Clean lenses and LCDs.** Ensure your lens is clear of dust and smudges.

- **Bring a tripod.** Try to shoot all your photos with one.

- **Always carry a cell phone.** Let someone know where you're headed, too.

- **Bring Twinkies.** Have some bottled water on hand, too.

- **Make camera settings ahead of time.** Set your white balance, shooting mode, aperture or shutter, and file size.

A Photoshop Workflow

Assembled here are the critical steps needed to consistently process quality digital photographs using Photoshop.

1. **Calibrate your monitor.**

   Use Gamma or a colorimeter.

2. **Apply color settings.**

   Use the correct color space for your images.

3. **Load images to your computer.**

   For faster downloads, use a card reader to load images from a memory card to your computer.

4. **Back up your images.**

   Save backup copies of all your images to CD or DVD.

5. **View images with Bridge.**

   Use Bridge as your file management program.

6. **Save the file in Photoshop PSD format.**

   Never apply corrections and edits to original files.

    Keep your original and working images separate by first saving the file in PSD format in a working images folder.

7. **Apply overall corrections.**

   Apply auto-corrections or create separate adjustment layers to adjust Levels, Brightness/Contrast, and Saturation.

8. **Apply image edits.**

   Apply individual edits such as burning and dodging or removing blemishes and red-eye.

9. **Save the corrected and edited image**.

   Save this image to a working images folder, retaining all your adjustment layers.

10. **Prepare the image for output.**

    Resize the image and use the Unsharp Mask filter to sharpen your image. Then flatten the layers.

11. **Save the image as an output file.**

    Include the words "print" or "Web" in the filename.

     Descriptive names help you figure out if the output file was for your printer or for the Web.

12. **Print the image.**

    Use the Print with Preview command to make sure you are selecting the right color management options for printing.

For Dummies: Bestselling Book Series for Beginners

The Photoshop Window

Click to close

Click to maximize

Click to minimize

Palette well

Image window

Option bar

Toggle Bridge

Toolbox   Menu bar

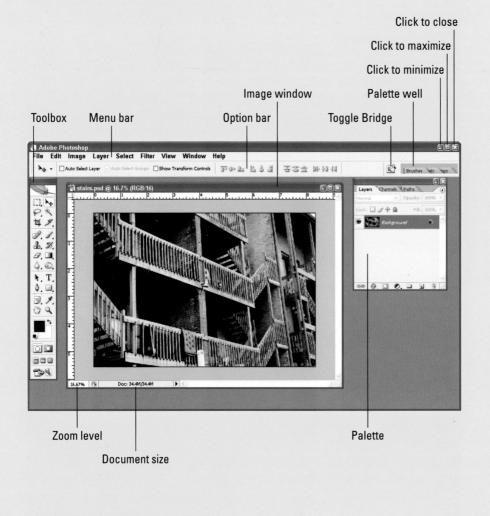

Zoom level

Document size

Palette

Wiley, the Wiley Publishing logo, For Dummies, the Dummies Man logo, the Dummies Man logo, the For Dummies Bestselling Book Series logo and all related trade dress are trademarks or registered trademarks of John Wiley & Sons, Inc. and/or its affiliates. All other trademarks are property of their respective owners.

Copyright © 2005 Wiley Publishing, Inc. All rights reserved. Item 9580-6.
For more information about Wiley Publishing, call 1-800-762-2974.

For Dummies: Bestselling Book Series for Beginners

Photoshop® CS2 and Digital Photography

FOR

DUMMIES®

by Kevin L. Moss

WILEY

Wiley Publishing, Inc.

Photoshop® CS2 and Digital Photography For Dummies®

Published by
Wiley Publishing, Inc.
111 River Street
Hoboken, NJ 07030-5774
www.wiley.com

Copyright © 2005 by Wiley Publishing, Inc., Indianapolis, Indiana

All photographs copyright © 2005 Kevin L. Moss

Published by Wiley Publishing, Inc., Indianapolis, Indiana

Published simultaneously in Canada

No part of this publication may be reproduced, stored in a retrieval system or transmitted in any form or by any means, electronic, mechanical, photocopying, recording, scanning or otherwise, except as permitted under Sections 107 or 108 of the 1976 United States Copyright Act, without either the prior written permission of the Publisher, or authorization through payment of the appropriate per-copy fee to the Copyright Clearance Center, 222 Rosewood Drive, Danvers, MA 01923, 978-750-8400, fax 978-646-8600. Requests to the Publisher for permission should be addressed to the Legal Department, Wiley Publishing, Inc., 10475 Crosspoint Blvd., Indianapolis, IN 46256, 317-572-3447, fax 317-572-4355, or www.wiley.com/go/permissions.

Trademarks: Wiley, the Wiley Publishing logo, For Dummies, the Dummies Man logo, A Reference for the Rest of Us!, The Dummies Way, Dummies Daily, The Fun and Easy Way, Dummies.com, and related trade dress are trademarks or registered trademarks of John Wiley & Sons, Inc. and/or its affiliates in the United States and other countries, and may not be used without written permission. Photoshop is a registered trademark of Adobe Systems, Inc. All other trademarks are the property of their respective owners. Wiley Publishing, Inc., is not associated with any product or vendor mentioned in this book.

LIMIT OF LIABILITY/DISCLAIMER OF WARRANTY: THE PUBLISHER AND THE AUTHOR MAKE NO REPRESENTATIONS OR WARRANTIES WITH RESPECT TO THE ACCURACY OR COMPLETENESS OF THE CONTENTS OF THIS WORK AND SPECIFICALLY DISCLAIM ALL WARRANTIES, INCLUDING WITHOUT LIMITATION WARRANTIES OF FITNESS FOR A PARTICULAR PURPOSE. NO WARRANTY MAY BE CREATED OR EXTENDED BY SALES OR PROMOTIONAL MATERIALS. THE ADVICE AND STRATEGIES CONTAINED HEREIN MAY NOT BE SUITABLE FOR EVERY SITUATION. THIS WORK IS SOLD WITH THE UNDERSTANDING THAT THE PUBLISHER IS NOT ENGAGED IN RENDERING LEGAL, ACCOUNTING, OR OTHER PROFESSIONAL SERVICES. IF PROFESSIONAL ASSISTANCE IS REQUIRED, THE SERVICES OF A COMPETENT PROFESSIONAL PERSON SHOULD BE SOUGHT. NEITHER THE PUBLISHER NOR THE AUTHOR SHALL BE LIABLE FOR DAMAGES ARISING HEREFROM. THE FACT THAT AN ORGANIZATION OR WEBSITE IS REFERRED TO IN THIS WORK AS A CITATION AND/OR A POTENTIAL SOURCE OF FURTHER INFORMATION DOES NOT MEAN THAT THE AUTHOR OR THE PUBLISHER ENDORSES THE INFORMATION THE ORGANIZATION OR WEBSITE MAY PROVIDE OR RECOMMENDATIONS IT MAY MAKE. FURTHER, READERS SHOULD BE AWARE THAT INTERNET WEBSITES LISTED IN THIS WORK MAY HAVE CHANGED OR DISAPPEARED BETWEEN WHEN THIS WORK WAS WRITTEN AND WHEN IT IS READ.

For general information on our other products and services, please contact our Customer Care Department within the U.S. at 800-762-2974, outside the U.S. at 317-572-3993, or fax 317-572-4002.

For technical support, please visit www.wiley.com/techsupport.

Wiley also publishes its books in a variety of electronic formats. Some content that appears in print may not be available in electronic books.

Library of Congress Control Number: 2005923211

ISBN-13: 978-0-7645-9580-6

ISBN-10: 0-7645-9580-6

Manufactured in the United States of America

10 9 8 7 6 5 4 3 2 1

1K/QT/QY/QV/IN

WILEY

About the Author

Kevin Moss is a photographer, author, and expert in digital photography, personal computing, and the World Wide Web. An early adopter and long-time user of Photoshop, Kevin has specialized in combining traditional photography and the latest in computer and digital technologies. He is the coauthor of *50 Fast Digital Camera Techniques,* 2nd Edition.

Kevin specializes in fine art landscape, abstract, and portrait photography. For more information about Kevin's photographic work or to contact him regarding this book, visit his Web site at www.kevinmossphotography.com.

Dedication

For my beautiful wife, Amy, whom I've been madly in love with *all* my adult life. Together, we dedicate this book to our equally beautiful children, Amanda, Emily, and David. You have all given me the ability to complete this project by keeping me fed, rested, and, best of all, loved.

Author's Acknowledgments

I can't thank the people enough who helped make this book possible. Writing a book isn't the effort of the author only; there are a number other important people involved who make it all happen. I especially want to thank Laura Lewin from Studio B and Tom Heine at Wiley for believing in me and in what I wanted to accomplish. You two helped me make this project a reality. I would like to personally acknowledge project editor Sarah Hellert, who provided guidance to me when needed, helped me keep on schedule, and was always there when I had a question.

I would also like to acknowledge the rest of the team that get things done behind the scenes: copy editor Jerelind Charles, technical editor Ron Rockwell, and project coordinator Shannon Schiller. Thank you all for your efforts in making sure my writing, images, and figures are all formatted, arranged correctly, and understandable.

Special thanks for those who agreed to model for me throughout the project. To my family, you no longer need to run when you see me coming with my digital camera! To the Atkinson and Casadei families, thank you for letting me use the portraits I've taken of you for this book.

Publisher's Acknowledgments

We're proud of this book; please send us your comments through our online registration form located at www.dummies.com/register.

Some of the people who helped bring this book to market include the following:

Acquisitions, Editorial, and Media Development

Project Editor: Sarah Hellert

Acquisitions Editor: Tom Heine

Copy Editor: Jerelind Charles

Technical Editor: Ron Rockwell

Editorial Manager: Robyn B. Siesky

Media Development Manager: Laura VanWinkle

Media Development Supervisor: Richard Graves

Editorial Assistant: Adrienne D. Porter

Cartoons: Rich Tennant, www.the5thwave.com

Composition Services

Project Coordinator: Shannon Schiller

Layout and Graphics: Lauren Goddard, Melanee Prendergast, Kathie Rickard, Heather Ryan, Janet Seib

Cover Art: Daniela Richardson

Proofreaders: Betty Kish, Carl Pierce, Dwight Ramsey, Sossity Smith

Indexer: Sherry Massey

Special Help
Rebecca Huehls, Paul Levesque

Publishing and Editorial for Technology Publishing

    Richard Swadley, Vice President and Executive Group Publisher

    Barry Pruett, Vice President and Publisher, Visual/Web Graphics

    Andy Cummings, Vice President and Publisher

    Mary Bednarek, Executive Acquisitions Director

    Mary C. Corder, Editorial Director

Publishing for Consumer Dummies

    Diane Graves Steele, Vice President and Publisher

    Joyce Pepple, Acquisitions Director

Composition Services

    Gerry Fahey, Vice President of Production Services

    Debbie Stailey, Director of Composition Services

Contents at a Glance

Table of Contents

Introduction

· ·

*D*igital photography is something everyone seems to be getting into these days. Sending out film for processing is becoming a thing of the past, and so are film cameras. When they're not buying iPods, more and more folks are buying new digital cameras, photo printers, and the latest version of Photoshop. What a great way to spend the day, jamming to some music with your digital music player while taking digital photos! Using a digital music player is easy, but taking great photos with a digital camera takes an understanding of camera settings, composing shots, and transferring your photos from camera to computer. This book will help you do all of those.

After you download your photos from your digital camera to your computer, you next enter the "digital darkroom." Unlike the old days, when the photographer's darkroom was set up with unwieldy equipment and chemical trays, your digital darkroom is a computer and Photoshop CS2. Photoshop CS2 lets you do everything a photographer could do in the old chemical darkroom, and much more: Photoshop includes effects and image adjustment capabilities that were impossible in the old days. The book shows you how to use your digital camera to take great photos, download and organize your image files, and then use Photoshop CS2 to create your work of art, the final print!

About This Book

The purpose of this book is to provide an easy-to-use reference to those who want to find out how to take better pictures with their digital cameras, manage the huge numbers of image files they produce, and "develop" their images in Photoshop. You'll also find out how to produce stunning prints or Web images to share among family and friends.

I've spent years working on my shooting and Photoshop processes, and this book gives me the opportunity to share that knowledge with photographers, hobbyists, and those that just want to quickly get up to speed with the new technology. The book isn't intended for you to read from the beginning to the end, but to use as a reference for subjects you need to be shown how to do. To make things even easier, processes are broken down into step-by-step instructions with actual Photoshop screens and photos to provide a visual guide to how things are done.

What's unique about this book compared to other books on the subject of digital photography and Photoshop is the *workflow* approach I've presented. There are many steps between setting up your digital camera on a tripod and printing out your masterpiece. *Photoshop CS2 and Digital Photography For Dummies* provides a number of step-by-step workflows that can help you master each of these processes. For example, you can apply a workflow to something you've probably done many times before, take pictures. You'll be surprised at how the "best practice" steps can improve your photos. Printing is a workflow itself, and applying a workflow to your printing can improve your skills to where you can produce gallery-quality prints.

Foolish Assumptions

Here is a list of what I assume you already have or will add to your collection shortly:

- **Digital camera:** If you have a digital camera, you need a memory card to store your photos in the camera and a card reader or USB cable to transfer your images to your computer.

  For digital photographers, having a digital camera is a good idea, but believe it or not, you can still use your film camera! If you have a flatbed scanner you can scan your negatives or photos to your computer and open the files in Photoshop for editing. Don't forget those old negatives and photos!

- **Computer:** To work with Photoshop, you need a computer with enough memory and a decent monitor. Digital photos take up a lot of disk space, and Photoshop CS2 requires that your computer have at least 384 megabytes of memory.

- **Photoshop CS2:** Just like Windows or the Mac OS is your computer's operating system, Photoshop CS2 is your digital photography operating system.

- **Photo-quality printer:** I spent over $500 on my first photo-quality inkjet 10 years ago. You can get superior photo quality printers these days for under $100. Even if you are primarily making photos for use on the Web, having a printer on hand helps if you want to print a photo for framing or for keeping in your wallet.

How This Book Is Organized

This book is divided into parts that address general areas of shooting better photos and working with Photoshop. Within those parts you'll find chapters that get more specific, covering topics such as using natural light for portraits, or using Bridge to browse files. Skip around, or, if you have the time, read the book from beginning to end.

Part I: A New Way to Play

The best way to start with digital photography is to jump right in. This first part of the book introduces you to your digital camera, Photoshop CS2, the digital workflow process, and all the equipment and software you'll need to get started. Chapter 1 gives you a general overview of digital photography, Chapter 2 introduces you to your digital camera, Chapter 3 shows you Photoshop CS2, Chapter 4 explains what digital workflow is, and Chapter 5 describes the toys you'll use to produce digital photos.

Part II: Shooting for Quality Images

If you normally turn your digital camera on, point it at something, and then click the shutter, this part's for you. Chapter 6 explains commands you can use and adjustments you can make with your digital camera to get great portraits or nature photos in many different light conditions. Chapter 7 helps you shoot sharper photos.

Part III: Setting Up a Photoshop Workflow

There is a lot to about setting up Photoshop for use with photos. Chapter 8 shows you how to set up Photoshop to work with photos in a workflow. Chapter 9 explains how to match the color you see on your computer to what comes out of the printer. Chapter 10 dives into your file manager, Bridge. Chapter 11 is dedicated to raw file formats and to getting those raw files corrected and into Photoshop. Chapter 12 shows you how to set up your files for correcting and editing in Photoshop.

Part IV: Working with Images in Photoshop CS2

Getting to the heart of the matter, this part is dedicated solely to working with images in Photoshop using concise step-by-step workflows. Chapter 13 shows you a color correction workflow. Chapter 14 shows you how to correct smudges, blemishes, and red eye using an image editing workflow. Chapter 15 is a ton of fun using Photoshop filters. Chapter 16 shows you how to automate tasks such as creating slideshows, Web pages, and panoramas. Chapter 17 shows you how to prep your corrected and edited files for output, and Chapter 18 provides a step-by-step set of instructions for printing.

Part V: The Part of Tens

Always the favorite part of any *For Dummies* book, this part provides you with a few chapters that add to your growing technical knowledge. Chapter 19 lists 10 digital photography Web sites with even *more* about digital photography. Chapter 20 gives you 10 cool things to with your digital photos, such as creating an abstract or a gallery poster.

Icons Used in This Book

This icon alerts you to new features that are available in CS2. Adobe has added some great new features; look for this icon for more about them throughout this book.

Use this icon as a guide to doing something better. I'll often add tips to the step-by-step instructions to give you some good ideas for working with digital cameras and Photoshop CS2.

This icon is used to alert you to a topic that's important for you *not* to forget. Commit these to memory. (Just kidding!)

This icon helps explain technical topics in easy-to-understand terms. The information provided may not be critical, but these nice-to-know technical facts can make you look smart in front of you friends.

When you see one of these, don't run! This icon will help you to properly complete the steps being explained. Use the warnings to stay out of trouble: Bad things may be lurking around the corner.

Part I

A New Way to Play

*T*he days of shooting a roll of film, taking it to the drugstore for processing, and getting your prints three
days later are over. The new photography is all about
instantly viewing what you have photographed and changing the original image to get it to print the way you envi-
sion it. That means new ways of capturing images, working
with image files on the computer, and printing.

The chapters in this part get you jump-started in digital
photography. I'll show you the basics: messing around
with your digital camera so you feel more comfortable
using it, finding out about gizmos and gadgets you can add
to your equipment collection, getting to know Photoshop
CS2, and using a digital workflow to get things done. You'll
be taking and processing stunning photos in no time at all!

Chapter 1

Jumping Right In

*I*n the past year or so, just about everyone I know has gone out and purchased a digital camera. If you haven't noticed, all the consumer electronic circulars in the Sunday paper have entire sections dedicated to digital cameras, accessories, and printers. Yep, right next to the cell phone page. Digital cameras may be the latest rage, but unlike the iPod, I bet that most digital cameras end up like old film cameras, collecting dust on the shelf.

I know people who purchased their digital cameras two years ago and never bothered to learn how to transfer images to their computer. After filling up their memory cards, they display the pictures they took by turning on the camera and reviewing the pictures on the 1½ inch LCD. Funny thing is, these are the same people that are planning on buying the latest and greatest that is available on the market! The point here is to figure out the basics about how to use your camera, load images to your computer, and then go out and have some fun. Don't forget to make a few prints, by the way!

Using Your Digital Camera

Though all the hundreds of different digital camera models that are available today look different from one another, they all have the same basic operation. All run on batteries that need charging from time to time. All need some sort of memory card inserted. (Do this properly: They only go in one way!) They all have an on-off switch and a shutter button. The most important part of your digital camera is the user's manual that comes with each one. Don't forget to read yours!

Using your digital camera is as easy as 1, 2, 3. . .

1. **Learn how to turn on your camera.**

   This step may seem a little basic, but each manufacturer does it differently. Don't be embarrassed: I admit I've fumbled a few times with new cameras finding out where the simple buttons and gizmos are. See Figure 1-1 for the on/off button on a digital camera.

Figure 1-1: Power switches are located in different spots on different cameras.

2. **Get comfortable with your lens.**

   Play around by zooming in and out. Most digital cameras come equipped with a zoom lens with which you can zoom out for wide-angle shots or for some cool landscape shots. Zoom in to the image of a person for a great candid portrait.

3. **If you are shooting indoors, turn on the built-in flash.**

4. **Make sure your shooting mode is set correctly.**

   Automatic mode, surprisingly, works for many shots you take. Automatic mode is great for now until Chapter 6 covers more advanced shooting modes.

5. **Compose your subject.**

   Make sure you're not shooting into the sun: You don't want your subjects dark with a light background. Look for things in the scene that will detract from your shot, like power lines running across the horizon or telephone poles sticking out of a person's head. Make sure your scene is square and not tilted. Try to get in the habit of taking the time to compose your shot: You will be surprised how much of a difference it makes!

6. **Depress your shutter halfway to focus, the rest of the way to take the picture.**

   On most digital cameras, pressing the shutter half way focuses the shot, and pressing the shutter the rest of the way opens the shutter and takes the picture.

Get out and shoot

The way to become a better photographer and get the most from your digital camera is to just use the thing. Take it with you wherever you go. Get used to carrying it around and shooting some photos like the one shown in Figure 1-2, which I shot in a parking garage. After parking my car, I looked around, grabbed my digital camera, and shot the skyline. Get over that embarrassed feeling of taking pictures of things when other people are around. Just ignore them, or better yet, take their picture! As a bonus, you then have more images to play with when you begin to edit them in Photoshop, later in this book.

Figure 1-2: Take your camera wherever you go: You never know what you can find!

For one week, take your digital camera with you wherever you go. Take pictures that week of everything and everyone interesting to you. You'll be amazed at how many photos you would have missed if you didn't have your digital camera with you!

Copying your pictures from camera to computer

Every digital camera is packaged with a CD that includes software utilities for your camera. Before you can transfer pictures from your camera to your computer, you need to install the CD on your computer. The other item you need is that USB cable that came with your camera. It's that cable with the big thingy on one end and the little thingy on the other. Refer to your owner's manual to locate the cable connection on your camera: It can be hard to find!

The easiest way to transfer images to you computer is to use a card reader, shown in Figure 1-3. Card readers are devices that connect to your PC via USB cable. These devices often accept multiple memory card formats, such as CompactFlash and Memory Stick.

Figure 1-3: Think of your camera or card reader as an external disk: Your computer does!

The common process for transferring images from your camera to computer is:

1. **Make sure you turn your computer on.**

2. **If transferring directly from your camera, make sure you turn your camera off.**

3. **Plug the camera or card reader into your computer by inserting the camera end of the USB cable into your digital camera and the computer end of the USB cable into an available USB connection on your computer.**

4. **Turn on your digital camera if transferring directly from the camera or plug in a memory card into the card reader.**

   After a few seconds, your computer should recognize the camera or memory card and prompt you to choose your next step, as shown in Figure 1-4.

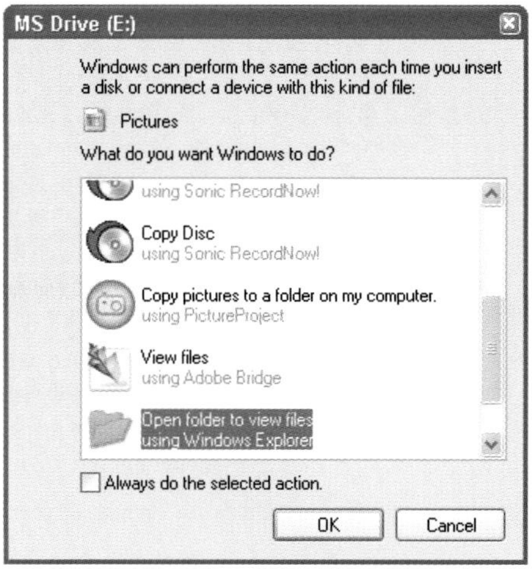

5. **Your computer will prompt you to choose the method to copy your images, or your camera's software prompts you.**

6. **Choose to either copy the images to the default folder on your computer or better yet, choose a specific directory you created to copy these images to.**

Figure 1-4: You're prompted for the next step.

Create a folder on your computer where you can copy all your images to. This way your folder won't be buried in the default images folder.

Your camera's software may automatically assign a folder name each time you copy images to your computer. Get familiar with the way your folders are set up. After your images are copied safely to your computer and they are backed up, as discussed in Chapter 4, you can then reformat your memory card in your camera to make room for more pictures.

Always make sure you have a backup of the images that are copied to your computer before you reformat your memory card. You want to make sure that these images are not only on your computer, but backed up to CD for safe-keeping. If you accidentally delete the images on the computer or the hard disk fails, at least you still have the images on CD.

Invest in a USB card reader. Prices for these devices have come way down and most of these can read multiple memory card formats. Using card readers to download images is quicker and safer. Some computers even have these built right in!

Playing with Photoshop CS2

Now that you took some photographs, copied them to your computer, and backed them up to CD, get on Photoshop and do some messing around.

Select Photoshop from the Windows Start menu, or double-click the icon on your Windows or Mac desktop.

Photoshop CS2 presents you with the Welcome screen (see Figure 1-5) every time you start up Photoshop. This screen provides you with an easy way to view help documents and other information about Photoshop CS2.

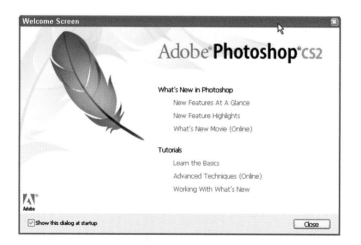

Figure 1-5: The Photoshop Welcome Screen.

You can deselect the Show This Dialog at Startup check box in the lower left of the Photoshop Welcome Screen if you don't want to see this window every time you start Photoshop.

Browsing for images

One of the biggest improvements to Photoshop in CS2 is Bridge, shown in Figure 1-6. An update to the File Browser, Bridge provides you with a powerful file management tool that allows you to visually select images you want to edit as well as organize and catalog these images.

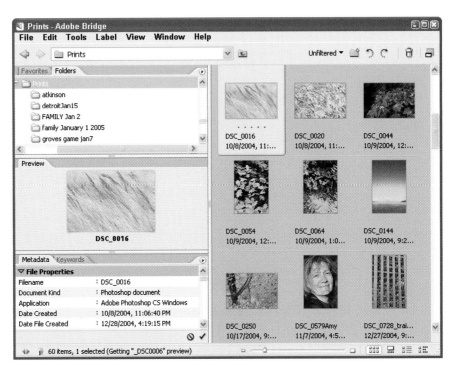

Figure 1-6: Bridge is an easy way to view, open, and organize files.

To open an image in Photoshop:

1. **Select File ⇨ Browse.**

2. **Select the folder you copied images to by using the Folders palette located within Bridge (see Figure 1-7).**

   Adobe did a nice job keeping the Folders palette functionality similar to Windows Explorer, only more tailored toward working with images.

   When you start Bridge, it will display images in the browser from the folder you last visited.

3. **Double-click the folder you want to view, as shown in Figure 1-8.**

4. **Select an image that you want to open in Photoshop by double-clicking the image.**

   You are ready to perform plastic surgery on your photos . . . I mean edit your photos!

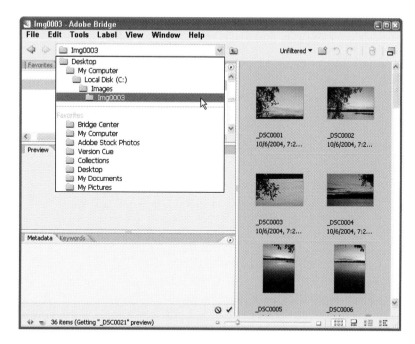

Figure 1-7: Bridge works like Windows Explorer: You drill down to your folder.

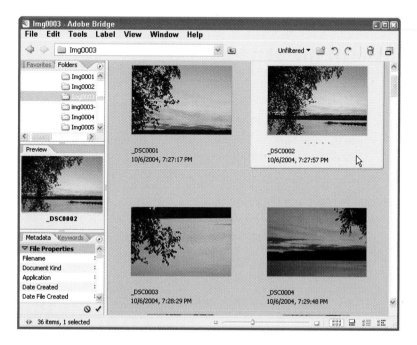

Figure 1-8: Viewing images in Bridge.

A little tweak here, a little tweak there

Without spending the next few hours going through some elaborate steps to make edits to the image and print, I leave the heavy editing stuff for later.

For now, you can do some quick edits and see how the image you choose prints out.

1. **Make a copy of the original image.**

   As a rule of thumb, I never make edits to original images: I always work on a copy. As shown in Figure 1-9, the first thing I do is save this image under another working directory. Choose File ⇨ Save As to do this. Make sure you save this file into a new or existing folder where you store your working images.

2. **Make a backup of the background (original image) layer.**

   Another rule I have in my digital workflow is to never work on the original layer. Duplicate the background copy of the original layer by choosing Layer ⇨ Duplicate Layer. You can now safely tweak without working on the background image.

3. **Tweak Brightness/Contrast and Hue/Saturation by choosing Image ⇨ Adjustments.**

   Go to Brightness/Contrast and in the Brightness/Contrast window, and move the Bright-ness and Contrast sliders to your desired look, as shown in Figure 1-10.

4. **Choose Image ⇨ Adjustments ⇨ Hue/Saturation and move the Saturation slider to the right until you see the desired colors pop out, as shown in Figure 1-11.**

   Don't overdo it, just enough until you see the colors as you want to see them.

Figure 1-9: Never work on the original: Save as a working image.

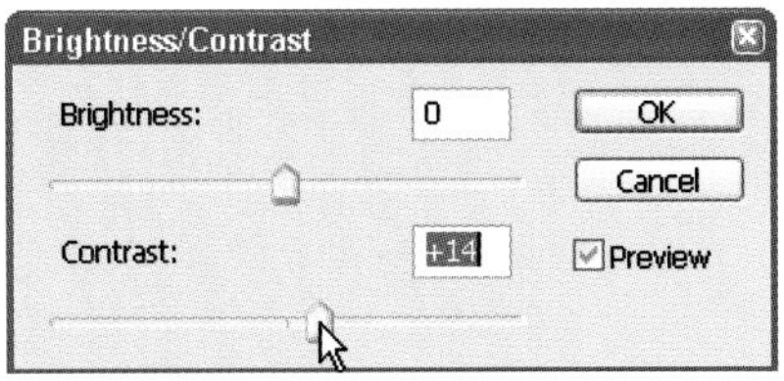

Figure 1-10: Increase contrast by moving the Contrast slider to the right.

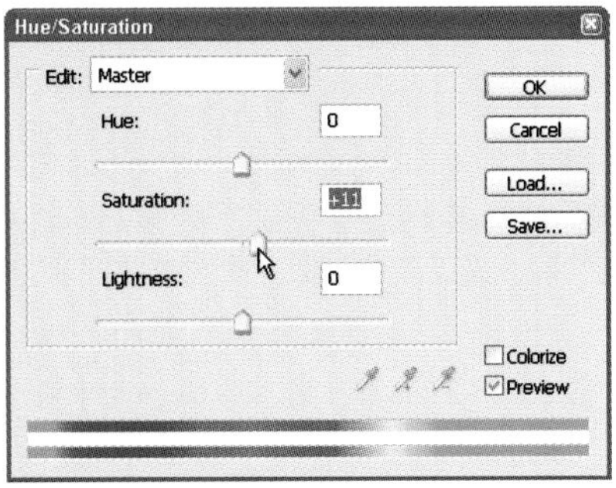

Figure 1-11: Increase color by moving the Saturation slider to the right.

5. Sharpen the image.

Sharpening usually does not happen inside the camera and has to be performed in Photoshop. Sharpen the image by choosing Filter ➪ Sharpen ➪ Unsharp Mask, as shown in Figure 1-12. Set the Amount to 150 by moving the Amount Slider to right. Set the Radius to 1.5 and the threshold to 8. These settings are pretty safe unless you have your camera sharpen settings turned up. If the photo appears weird, turn the Amount slider down until the photo looks normal and sharp. Another option is to choose Edit ➪ Fade Unsharp Mask to soften the effects of sharpening.

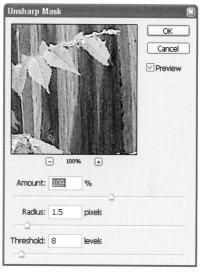

Figure 1-13 shows the original image in Photoshop and then the image with the Brightness/Contrast and Hue/Saturation adjustments made.

Figure 1-12: Unsharp Mask settings for your first photo.

Figure 1-13: The original image and the image edited in Photoshop.

Print, save, score!!!

Printing in Photoshop is a process upon itself. Chapter 18 provides you with extensive information on printing. For a quick introduction, I take you through the quickie-printing process here.

1. **Print your photo by choosing File ➪ Print with Preview.**

   The Print windows appears, as shown in Figure 1-14.

2. **Click Page Setup and indicate whether the photo is portrait or landscape orientation.**

3. **Select the correct paper size for your printer and then click OK.**

4. **In the Scaled Print Size area of the Print window, select Scale to Fit Media.**

   This automatically sizes your photo for the paper you have loaded in your printer.

5. **Click Print and then OK.**

   Watch your work of art magically appear on your printer.

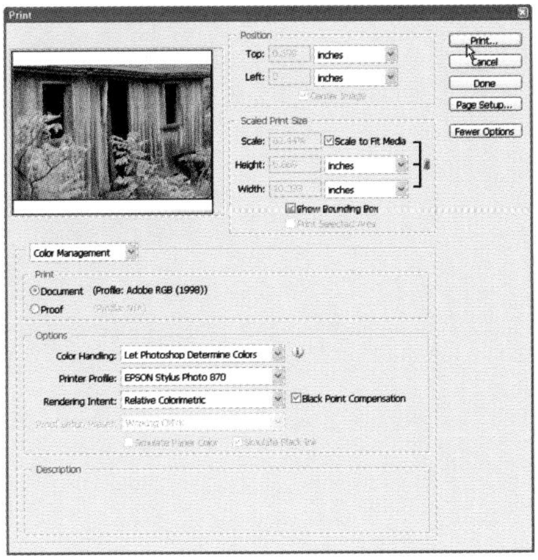

Figure 1-14: The Print with Preview window.

Consider this a quick preview: There are going to be many more steps in this book to help you in making dynamic images you can be proud of.

Get with the Flow: Digital Workflow

Everybody has a daily ritual. It usually starts getting out of bed, maybe grabbing some breakfast, and then heading out to do what people do during the day. The rest of the time is spent on similar rituals. For the most part, most days start out the same and end the same. Hey, it works for most people!

Creating great looking photographs and organizing an ever growing number of images requires the same process any successful outcome requires. Digital photographers call this digital workflow. Digital workflow is a step-by-step progression of best practices that, if followed faithfully, can absolutely make you a better photographer.

In tech-weenie talk, digital workflow starts with "proper image capture techniques." Translation: good shootin'. The workflow continues with downloading images and backing up. Setting up images with proper color settings and making sure your equipment and Photoshop are set up properly are part of the digital workflow. The order of adjustments you make to an image is important to your digital workflow as are the procedures you use for sizing, sharpening, printing, and saving. Phew! That's a mouthful! The bottom line is that digital photography is a complex process: The more disciplined you are with best practices, the better your photography will become.

The remaining chapters in this book not only show you how to use this wonderful image-editing software called Photoshop, but also provide the best practices of digital photography and how all this relates to the overall digital workflow.

Chapter 2

Getting to Know Your
Digital Camera

igital cameras have hit the mainstream around the world. Recently digital camera sales were tops among holiday items purchased. Close to half of all homes have replaced their film-based cameras with digital. Many consumers are even on their second or third and still going.

Unlike their film counterparts, digital camera technology is advancing rapidly and will continue to advance at a fever pace until the end, which, by the way, is not in sight. Currently, the top digital camera manufacturers are waging megapixel wars. Yesterday's top megapixel model is today's entry model. Today's standard memory card size is tomorrow's entry-sized card. It seems that every year the latest high resolution models increase one or two megapixels. Seven or eight megapixel high-end models, (also called *prosumer* models) are now considered the norm.

If you are into whiz-bangs and gizmos, this chapter's for you. The basics include the major features of digital cameras, how digital cameras differ from film cameras, what you need to know in setting up your digital camera, and finally some tips on shooting pictures.

1 Camera

Some folks that are into digital photography are pure gearheads. A *gearhead* is the digital photographer who spends enormous amount of free time (or time at work courtesy of your boss) cruising the Web for information on the latest digital cameras. Gearheads always have a stack of the latest digital camera magazines on their coffee table, too. They really know their stuff! It's even better if they have a digital camera and use it on a regular basis.

Unlike gearheads, some into digital photography just want to take photographs, and that's cool, too. Regardless of which type of digital photography geek you are, a good understanding of the important parts of a digital camera always comes in handy.

All the different models, shapes, and sizes of digital cameras have some basic parts in common. All digital cameras have either a built-in lens or use interchangeable lenses. All are powered by a battery: Zeros and ones need some juice to travel around the circuitry! All contain an image sensor. Most come equipped with a built-in flash, and all require a medium to store images, the memory card.

Eye to the world, the lens

The most important part of every camera is not the sensor, megapixels, or how it fits in your pocket. What's important is the lens. You can have the most awesome sensor, six, seven, or eight megapixels, but all that resolution doesn't do diddly squat if you don't have a quality lens to get the most out of that sensor.

Don't be fooled by how a camera is marketed. Lens statistics can be deceiving. You see digital cameras advertised as 2×, 3×, or even 12× zooms. Though impressive, read the fine print. You want to make sure they are talking about optical zoom range, not digital zoom range. If your lens is rated at say 10× digital, it's really not 10×. The camera is actually cropping the image and blowing it up to appear 10×, with a drop in quality. If your lens is actually rated at 10× optical, you are actually capturing the entire frame. When looking at digital cameras, ignore the digital zoom specs, and never use digital zoom on the camera. Remember the word "optical."

Figure 2-1: Digital camera models change every four or five months, usually for the better.

Today's consumer and prosumer digital cameras often come equipped with excellent quality lenses that approach or exceed 10× or even 12× optical zoom reach. See Figure 2-1 for a current (at this writing) model Nikon. Today's lenses are faster and sharper. All the major manufacturers offer excellent higher end cameras that include high resolution sensors coupled with professional quality lenses. These cameras can even come equipped with anti-shake or vibration reduction technology that greatly improves optical sharpness at high-zoom focal lengths.

Digital cameras should be rated first by the quality of the lens that is included, and then the other features, such as megapixels, startup times, and other technical buzzwords. As shown in Figure 2-2, the lens is the window to all your future great images. Make sure it's sharp and the best quality you can afford. You won't be sorry when you base your camera decision on the lens it comes with.

Figure 2-2: Lenses make the difference. This picture was shot with an older five megapixel model that just happened to have an excellent pro-quality lens.

Making sense of sensors

Digital camera *sensors* are electronic devices that collect photons (light) that travel through your camera's lens when you take a photograph. The sensor collects these photons, which convert into digital information that's processed by the camera and poof, makes up your digital image.

Consumer or prosumer digital camera sensors are usually similar across brands. A five megapixel sensor from one manufacturer is of similar quality to a five megapixel sensor from their competitor. The difference in the quality of images that are produced from make/model to make/model comes from two fronts: the software algorithms used and the quality of the lenses. The ability to make larger high quality prints corresponds with the amount of pixels contained in the sensor. The higher the megapixel size of the camera, the more photons can be collected, converted, and processed, which creates more information to print. The more pixels, the bigger the print.

Crop factors

Digital sensors are typically smaller than the standard sized 35mm film frame and are important in choosing lenses for digital SLRs in an equivalent focal length. (SLR stands for *single lens reflex*.) A crop factor of 1.5 is essentially the ratio between the sensor's size compared to a 24×36mm size of 35mm film. To make sense of this, no pun intended, on a digital SLR with a 1.5× crop factor, a 100mm lens in the 35mm world actually has a focal length of 150mm on the digital SLR.

Bigger is better: sensor size and resolution

Digital SLRs use sensors that are somewhat larger than the typical consumer or prosumer camera model. Professional photographers choose to use digital SLRs for the reason of quality. The sensor size is larger, and the quality of images is greater compared to identical megapixel count of a smaller sensor. If you print a 13×18 inch print from a six megapixel digital camera and compare it to a 13×18 inch print from a six megapixel digital SLR camera, the print from the digital SLR will be greater in quality with less noise. If cropping is needed for images, digital SLR images often maintain their quality, as shown in Figure 2-3. The good news is that the major manufacturers are now offering digital SLRs at a more affordable price than in years past, and if you are only printing up to 8×10, the quality of consumer and prosumer cameras are still excellent and getting better.

Figure 2-3: Digital SLR sensors show great quality at large reproduction sizes.

Memory cards

One of the greatest advantages of using digital as opposed to film is the cost. With digital cameras, you don't have to buy film: You just need a large enough memory card, also referred to as flash memory, to store your images. After a few hundred shots taken with your camera, your memory card pays for itself.

Rabid photographers such as myself can't have enough of these cards. I want the fastest and largest capacity cards I can find. For the typical photographer, two or three cards may be enough. Compared to figuring out crop factors and pixels, calculating the size of memory card is a little easier.

I personally like the 512MB size cards. I can fit over 90 five-megabyte raw images per card. After downloading the images to a folder on my computer, the 512MB card backs up nicely to CD with room to spare. If I used a 1GIG-sized memory card, I would have to divide the images up to get them to fit on a CD when I back them up. The advantage to using the larger cards is, of course, being able to store more images, which has its good points, too!

As shown in Figure 2-4, the most popular cards used by different camera manufacturers are CompactFlash, Secure Digital (SD), Memory Stick, and xD. Some of these cards are cross-platform between electronic devices such as cell phones, PDAs, and digital cameras, allowing you to use these cards in any of those devices. If you are wondering which brand is better, there really isn't an answer. All are commonly used and standard in the industry. Concern yourself more with the capacity of the card and its write speed. You want to make sure your camera is not waiting to write to the card so make sure you choose your cards well. Like running backs, get them big and fast.

Figure 2-4: Analog versus digital.

Flash

Almost all digital cameras come equipped with a built-in flash, such as the one shown in Figure 2-5. These onboard flashes are getting better and better every year and are usually sufficient for quick snapshots.

Figure 2-5: A built-in flash is included with most digital cameras.

If you are serious about taking the next step to high quality portraits, still life or action shots, you may want to consider purchasing an external flash that is compatible with your camera. Not only is the difference in your photographs noticeable, but the actual flash unit looks cool on your camera. Image is everything!

Good-bye Film, Hello Zeros and Ones

Developing photographs in the darkroom is one of the coolest experiences you can imagine. Seeing your photographs suddenly start appearing as you view that 8×10 soaking in the developer chemical tray really is a lot of fun, but not very efficient. Plus, spending hours inhaling fumes from those caustic chemicals can't be very good for your health or the environment. Since the advent of digital photography, those days are over for many photographers.

The reason to be excited about digital photography? For geeks like me who have been photography junkies for years and computer geeks to boot, this is the jackpot! East meets west, ying meets yang (whatever that means), the Red Sox beat the Yankees, computers and cameras collide! Today's digital cameras are meeting or exceeding the image quality and dynamic range offered by film. Another factor to be excited about? Saving a ton of money on film and processing and spending the money saved on more electronic toys for ourselves. I haven't bought a roll of film in years and looks like I never will again. Figure 2-6 shows the results of shooting six rolls of film to get only a few acceptable photos. If I had used digital, money saved on film and processing would have paid for a high-end flash card or a wild night at the casino.

Figure 2-6: It took six rolls of film to get this shot.

How Do I Work This Thing?

Like I said earlier, reading the manual usually helps. The manual is that little white book that came in the box when you bought your camera. Please don't get mad at me, but you really do have to read the manual to learn the basics about your camera. Really, I'd read the manual for you, but there are literally hundreds of different makes and models on the market now and they all do things a little differently. What I can do for you though is list the items that you need to know in order to get started with your camera.

Setting up

A brand-spanking new digital camera doesn't do much out of the box. One of my favorite rituals when I get home from the camera store is to unpack all the contents, lay them all out on the table, and open the manual. At this point, I'm ready to start putting all the pieces together. I love the smell of new plastic and electronics!

- **Charge the battery.** When you purchase the camera and get home with it, the first step (after worrying about what you are going to tell your spouse about how you are going to pay for the new toy) is to charge the battery.

- **While your battery is charging, read the manual.** If the battery is charging for a few hours, you can't play with your camera anyway. Put the time to good use: Open up the manual and read it. Even experienced photographers are lost when starting out with a new camera. All those knobs and buttons. With the most recent digital camera I purchased, I spent three hours reading the manual while I charged the battery, so listen up: If you are from a western country, read the English version. If you are Japanese, flip the book over and read the Japanese version. (I never figured out why they left everyone else out.)

- **Getting around the setup menus.** As shown in Figure 2-7, this is the hard part. Every digital camera has a menu system that you have to navigate through. This menu system is important because it's in these menus that you set your ISO speed and image resolution, format memory cards, and set white balance and flash modes.

Figure 2-7: Setting up your camera for use.

- **Care and feeding of your camera.** All manuals have sections concerning do's and don'ts of your digital camera, such as the dangers of taking pictures while climbing a mountain. Lawyers make them put that in the manuals. (I don't know about you, but at 2,000 feet, I'm hanging on to the rope for dear life and don't care about shooting technique.) You may want to refer to your manual to make sure you don't damage something while cleaning sensors, attaching accessories, and so on.

- **Check online resources.** If after reading through the manual you still don't understand a few features, go to the Web! Some great digital camera resources are out there, such as the Digital Photography Review Web site, www.dpreview.com. Thousands of people just like you and with the same questions participate in Web forums specifically for your brand of camera. Chapter 19 lists these Web sites.

Ready, go!

Now that you have completely read your manual from cover to cover and memorized it in its entirety, make some initial settings before you capture those breathtaking images.

1. **Set the date and time.**

   This is like setting up the time and date on your VCR or DVD player. Your images save to the memory card as a computer file with a typical time and date stamp. The correct time and date helps you later when you manage the massive amount of image files you will accumulate!

2. **Turn file numbering on.**

   This one is important. Digital cameras automatically assign a sequential number to each picture you take. Each image is numbered as something like DSC0001, DSC0002, DSC0003, you get the idea. When you change memory cards, the camera remembers the numbers and continues naming each picture in order. If you don't turn this feature on, the numbering will restart at 1 each time you insert a new memory card, which is not a good thing. You don't want to use the same file name for different pictures. Because I'm human, I admit I did this recently with a new digital SLR. I didn't notice the mistake until three Compact Flash cards into a shoot. After I noticed the oversight, I set the camera to file numbering on. It took me an hour to rename the images on the first three cards, though.

3. **Set ISO sensitivity.**

   Many ask the question "What's an ISO?" If you remember the days of film, this indicates the film speed. To start, shoot at the lowest ISO setting your camera allows. This ensures best possible image quality. Digital camera image quality decreases as you increase your ISO setting. Most digital cameras have ISO settings starting at 50 or 100 and increasing from there. Try not to exceed ISO settings above 200, where image noise begins to appear. Figure 2-8 shows the moon during a recent lunar eclipse photographed at high ISO of 1600, resulting in high image noise.

Figure 2-8: The higher the ISO, the more image noise.

For best image quality, use the lowest ISO setting on your camera. For indoor shooting without flash, you can increase this setting a few increments.

Remember, quality usually decreases at ISO 200 and above. You start seeing color noise in the shadow areas of your image as you increase the ISO settings. You can find out more about reducing color noise in Chapter 15.

4. Set file format.

If you are shooting primarily to print pictures, choose the highest setting to start. Though higher quality means bigger files, memory cards are cheap these days.

Downsizing photographs later in Photoshop is easier than trying to upsize your images later. Make sure you guarantee yourself the best image quality by choosing the highest file quality setting your camera has to offer. On most cameras, this would be the Fine or raw setting.

5. Be careful setting sharpness, contrast, and saturation.

Digital cameras usually have settings that let you increase or decrease the sharpness, contrast, and color saturation of your images. Be careful with making any adjustments here: You usually want to make these adjustments in Photoshop after you take a photograph. You do not want to adjust your originals from the camera: You'll have a harder time correcting a poor quality original image in software. For now, stick with the camera's default settings for these and use Photoshop to make these adjustments.

6. Choose a shooting mode.

That big dial on the top of your camera is used to choose what mode you want to shoot in. Digital cameras offer a number of ways to shoot certain types of images. If you are just starting out, choose automatic mode. This is usually indicated by a green icon on this dial. Many digital cameras offer different scene modes, such as landscape, portrait, sports, and macro. If I am shooting some quick portraits of the family, choosing the automatic mode for these shots is easiest. In automatic mode, the camera automatically adjusts the shutter speed and aperture setting for me so I can just go ahead and point and shoot. More advanced options such as A for aperture priority and S for shutter priority are available so you can freeze which shutter speed or f-stop (aperture) to use for a particular scene. For example, if I am shooting a landscape, I might choose aperture priority to set a deep depth of field for my shot: If my camera is set to A, it will automatically set the shutter speed for me. If you choose M, you are setting your camera for manual mode, where you actually choose the shutter speed and aperture, skipping the excellent metering your camera has to offer.

I Shoot, Therefore I Am

You read the manual twice, you took dozens of practice shots of your significant other, much to their disdain, and now you're ready for the big time. With all this preliminary stuff out of the way, it's time to get some images.

- ✔ **Take the time to plan your shot.** Look around and see if you can make the shot more interesting by using different angles.

- ✔ **Make sure you are shooting in the correct mode and your white balance is set.**

- ✔ **Use a tripod if you have one and it's convenient for the shot.**

- ✔ **Make sure you compose the scene carefully in the viewfinder or on your LCD.** Zoom in to the subject and be aware of other elements that are in the frame. You don't want power lines in a landscape or telephone poles sticking out of the head of the person in a portrait.

- ✔ **Try both orientations, landscape, or portrait.** Check out Figure 2-9: it's a portrait, but it's in landscape orientation.

Figure 2-9: Landscape orientation fit this photograph best. Try both orientations and see which is best for the shot.

- ✓ **Use your feet!** Close in on a subject and don't rely on your zoom for every shot.

- ✓ **Review the shot on your LCD.** If it's not right, recompose the shot and retake it until you are satisfied.

- ✓ **Enjoy yourself!** Half the fun is shooting. Learn to enjoy it.

Get the best image possible out of your camera. Make sure all your settings are properly set, you have focused properly, and zoomed in or out on the subject until the image is framed properly. Getting the picture right the first time in the camera is easier than trying to fix it in Photoshop.

An Introduction to Photoshop CS2

*P*hotoshop is the top photo editing software used by professional photographers, graphic artists, and serious enthusiasts. Photoshop can do many things many different ways. The program offers a multitude of commands and processes, which for the beginner can be somewhat intimidating. Kind of like the first day at a new school or first day on the job. Where's the break room?

Photoshop is designed with a broad range of uses for different types of applications. It's a great program for graphic designers producing print or Web material. For the photographer, Photoshop is as important as your camera. For those of you who used to develop film and print in the darkroom, it actually replaces the black-and-white or color darkroom as well as the light table you viewed your negatives and slides with. All that on one CD: How's that for technological progress!

If you are a newbie to Photoshop or a casual user, this chapter starts you off with a tour of the facilities. A walk-through of Bridge, the negative and slide table viewing area, is next. Next stop, the digital darkroom. No funny orange lights here. Like traveling to a new city or country, it sure helps having a map to help get you to where you want to go.

Photoshop in Your Face

After countless years working with computers big and small, I get a little tired of technical terms, such as *interface*. (I think *in your face* is more understandable and less technically intimidating.) If you are new to Photoshop or not very comfortable with computer programs, it's time for a walkthrough of the Photoshop program, as shown in Figure 3-1.

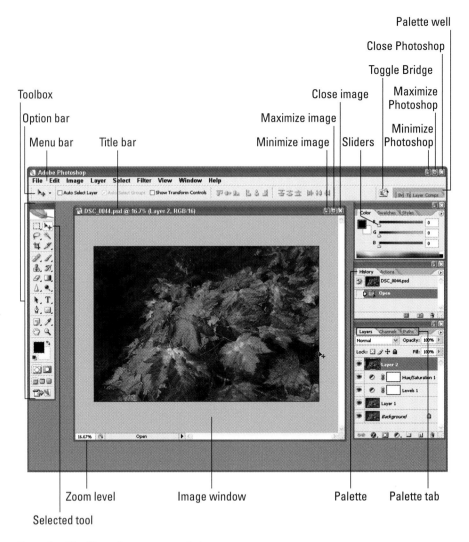

Figure 3-1: The Photoshop program window.

- Start Photoshop from a shortcut on your desktop or choose Start ⇨ All Programs ⇨ Adobe Photoshop CS2.

- Like all computer programs, you can close, maximize, or minimize the Photoshop program window. You find these controls located in the upper-right corner of your Photoshop program window in Windows and on the upper-left corner of the window if you're using a Mac.

- By default, the Photoshop Toolbox is located in the left side of your Photoshop window. Think of the Photoshop Toolbox as any other toolbox. In it you find the tools you need to edit your photos. Instead of grabbing a screwdriver or hammer, you grab photo editing tools, such as the Marquee tool, Paint Brush tool, Cropping tool, Text tool, and Healing Brush tool, among others.

- On the right side of the Photoshop program window, you find the palettes. These windows contain their own specific operations, while providing you with image information needed in the editing process. Among the most often used palettes are the Layers, Histogram, and History palettes.

- After you open an image to edit in the File menu by choosing File ⇨ Open or File ⇨ Browse, you are presented with your image window. Just like the Photoshop program window, you can close, minimize, or maximize your image windows.

Your Digital Light Table: Bridge

After going ape with your digital camera, within a short period of time you can have hundreds or thousands of images to manage. Every time you download images to your computer, you create a new folder. Pretty soon, those folders add up. Even the best photographers in the world struggle daily with managing huge numbers of images, whether negatives, slides, or digital files. Quite often, great shots get buried and never used.

Think of Bridge, shown in Figure 3-2, as your file management system. CS2 offers Bridge, a completely revised and enhanced file browser. Start Bridge from the File menu by choosing File ⇨ Browse or click the Toggle Bridge button on the Photoshop Option bar. Bridge is kind of like an Explorer or Finder for Photoshop, only you can do a lot more with Bridge, such as:

- **Navigate your hard disk.** Additionally, you can view images stored on other media, such as CDs or external disk drives.

- **View images stored in individual folders.** As you click through the file tree in the Folders palette, thumbnails of images appear as you click the folders that contain them.

- **Open images.** Double-click the thumbnail of the image you want to open. You can also click the file once and open the image by then choosing File ⇨ Open.

Right-click (Control+click on the Mac) the image thumbnail to view a menu of the most popular Bridge functions that you can use for that file. This method is good to open images in ImageReady, Photoshop program for editing images for the Web.

- **Rename images.** You can rename an image by clicking its name directly below the thumbnail. Another capability of Bridge is batch renaming.

- **Delete Files.** I'm always careful with this command. If you delete any images, you can be throwing away the only copy of it. Make sure you have a backup or a copy of that image in another folder.

- **Sort Files.** Sort files in a particular folder by choosing the Sort menu from the Bridge window. Presented to you are 15 different sorting methods, including filename, rank, size, color profile, or customer.

- **Rank images.** No, this doesn't mean your images stink. Rank images by applying a numerical ranking of your choosing to an image. For example, you may rank all your top images at a five, printable images at a three, images good enough for the Web at a three and so on. Come up with your own ranking system if you want!

- **File Info.** One of the most powerful functions of Bridge is the File Information function. For each image you can enter important cataloging information (see Figure 3-3) which you can use later to organize, retrieve, and sort. The File Info function appends Metadata information to your image. This information is stored in a sidecar file that accompanies your image rather than modifying it. For professionals or advanced enthusiasts, using the File Info function allows you to manage your ever growing image inventory.

Close Bridge

Maximize Bridge

Minimize Bridge

Delete image

Rotate clockwise

Rotate counterclockwise

Create a new folder

Selected folder　　Selected image　　Filters

Menu bar　　Image preview　　Thumbnail

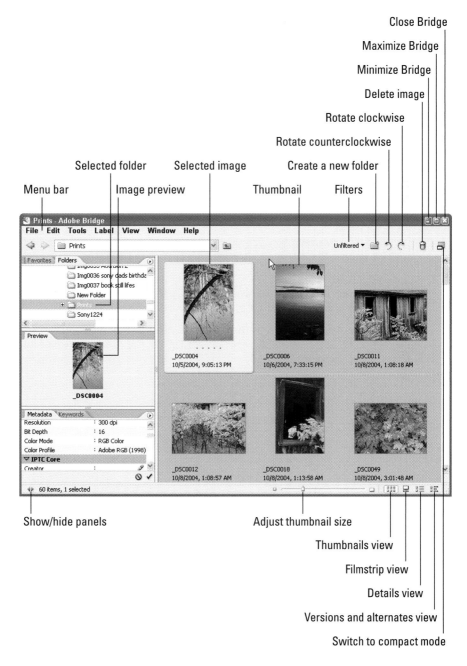

Show/hide panels　　Adjust thumbnail size

Thumbnails view

Filmstrip view

Details view

Versions and alternates view

Switch to compact mode

Figure 3-2: Bridge.

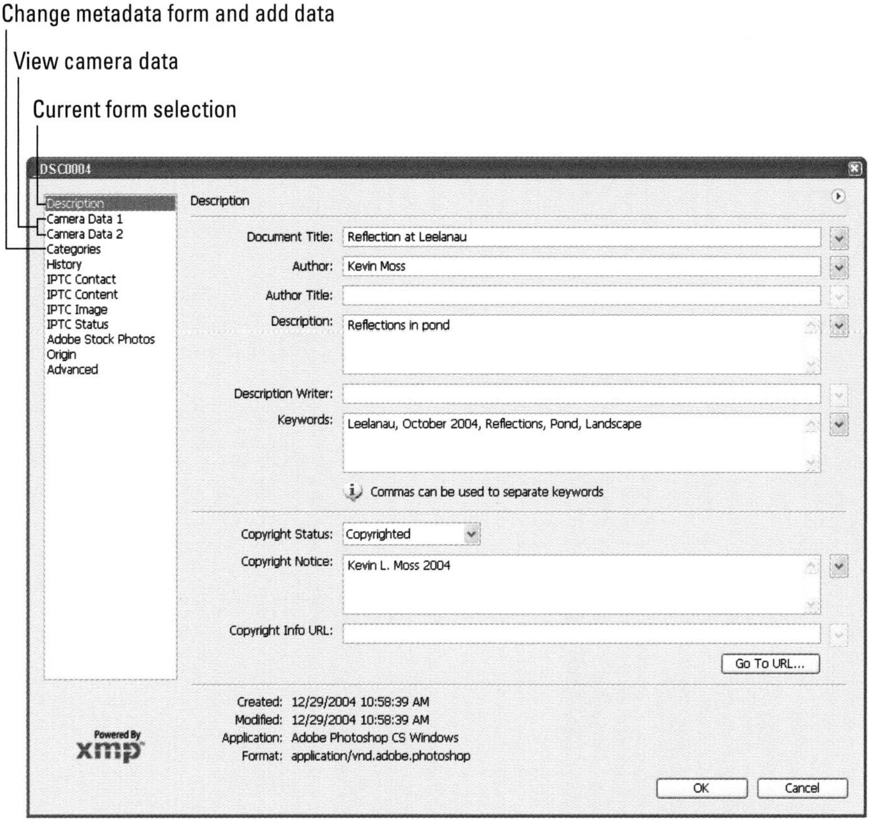

Change metadata form and add data

View camera data

Current form selection

Figure 3-3: A powerful feature to catalog and manage images is adding file info to images.

Menu Madame? Menu Sir?

Like all other computer programs, Photoshop CS2 offers the standard Menu bar to navigate through file and edit operations. To access any of the menus, just choose the menu name. A drop-down menu appears for you to choose the desired command. I explain each menu and major functions here.

File menu

The File menu in Photoshop CS2 contains the functions that allow you to perform image-related functions. Typical commands allow you to create a new file, open an existing file, browse, close a file, add file information to a file, save a file, and access the nifty Automate menu.

Edit menu

Typical commands, such as undo, cut, copy, and paste are available here. Important functions, such as Color Settings and Preferences are also available in the Edit menu.

Photoshop enhances their Edit menu by adding a helpful command called Step Backward. Step Backward is handy when you need to reverse your steps while editing images. This command is even more helpful when you are applying enhancements using brushes, the Blur tool, and the Sharpen tool, or burning, and dodging.

Image menu

The Image menu is where I really start addressing image information. Photoshop has flyout menus for Mode, Adjustments, and Rotate Canvas. As shown in Figure 3-4, the Adjustments flyout menu is where you can find common image adjustments functions, such as Hue/Saturation, Brightness/Contrast, and Levels.

Levels...	Ctrl+L
Auto Levels	Shift+Ctrl+L
Auto Contrast	Alt+Shift+Ctrl+L
Auto Color	Shift+Ctrl+B
Curves...	Ctrl+M
Color Balance...	Ctrl+B
Brightness/Contrast...	
Hue/Saturation...	Ctrl+U
Desaturate	Shift+Ctrl+U
Match Color...	
Replace Color...	
Selective Color...	
Channel Mixer...	
Gradient Map...	
Photo Filter...	
Shadow/Highlight...	
Exposure...	

Figure 3-4: The Adjustments flyout menu.

Layer menu

Layers is where you manage your image-editing workflow. Think of layers as a stack of transparencies that make up one image. For example, if the first transparency contains your image, the second transparency might add color correction, the third transparency could add brightness and contrast, the fourth increased color saturation, and the fifth might add sharpness. As you proceed with editing your image, each step in the process can be contained in an individual layer.

Many of the functions in the Layers palette can also be executed from the Layer menu. The advantage to using layers is that it makes it easy to backtrack later and make minor tweaks without undoing the rest of your image adjustments. The Layers menu is where some of the real power of using Photoshop resides and what separates Photoshop from other image-editing programs. Power to the layer!

Select menu

The Select menu contains commands having to do with, you guessed it, selections! When you use tools from the Photoshop Toolbox such as the Magic Wand tool, Marquee tools, Pen tools, and the Lasso tools to make selections, additional commands to work with those selections are available in the Select menu.

Filter menu

If you are wondering where the real fun begins, look no further. As shown in Figure 3-5, the Filter menu contains all the really cool processes for transforming your photo to a work of art. Want that picture of your wife to appear as if it were a fine-art glamour shot? Try the Diffuse Glow filter. Want your scenic photo to appear like a true watercolor painting? Just try the Watercolor filter.

One other important filter to remember is the Unsharp Mask filter, located within the Sharpen flyout menu. The Sharpen function is located among special effects in the Filter menu because it is considered a filter.

| Colored Pencil... |
| Cutout... |
| Dry Brush... |
| Film Grain... |
| Fresco... |
| Neon Glow... |
| Paint Daubs... |
| Palette Knife... |
| Plastic Wrap... |
| Poster Edges... |
| Rough Pastels... |
| Smudge Stick... |
| Sponge... |
| Underpainting... |
| Watercolor... |

Figure 3-5: All the cool filters reside in the Filter menu.

View menu

The View menu maintains the functions that relate to how images view on your computer monitor. Guides, rulers, and zooming in and out are all included in the View menu. Proofing setups also reside in the View menu for those who prepare images for press work.

Window menu

The Window menu presents you with the wonderful world of Photoshop palettes. Has your Photoshop Toolbox or Layers palette vanished? Just go the Window menu and reselect the palette to bring it back to your workspace.

To be safe, you can set the palettes that appear on your screen every time you start Photoshop by choosing Window ➪ Save Workspace.

Help menu

Photoshop offers the best help menu I have ever seen in a software program, and I'm talking about over 20 years of using computer software. For almost any procedure you want to perform in Photoshop, you have either a reference or a tutorial available to you, as shown in Figure 3-6. More than 50 How to. . . links are in the Help menu: they link you to HTML-based tutorials that are loaded on your computer (not the Web) when you install Photoshop. Sort of like having a quick-reference right on your computer!

How to Create Web Images ▸
How to Customize and Automate ▸
How to Fix and Enhance Photos ▸
How to Paint and Draw ▸
How to Prepare Art for Other Applications ▸
How to Print Photos ▸
How to Work with Color ▸
How to Work with Layers and Selections ▸
How to Work with Type ▸
How to Create How Tos ▸

Figure 3-6: Help menu How to. . . links.

Need to look up your Photoshop Serial Number? Choose Help ➪ System Info. This feature provides you with more system information about your computer than you probably care to know, but this information can come in handy when troubleshooting issues about your computer and Photoshop.

Need to look up available Photoshop software updates? Choose Help ➪ Updates. This option takes you directly to the Adobe Web site Photoshop download section.

Playing with the Toolbox

Where in your art studio can you find a toolbox that contains over 60 tools you use in your everyday work and is only a couple of inches long? The Photoshop Toolbox, shown in Figure 3-7. Name another program that packs all these handy artistic tools in one box!

The Photoshop Toolbox provides a number of tools you use to edit images. Among the 60 or so tools offered in this window are brushes, lassos, burning and dodging tools, marquees, erasers, healing brushes, and so on.

Toward the bottom of the Toolbox, you find commonly-used color selection, masking, and viewing icons.

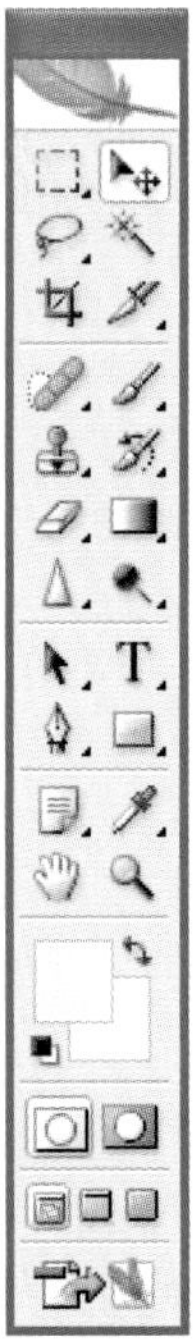

The tiny triangle in the bottom right of an icon represents a flyout menu that contains similar tools. Right-click the icon to bring out the flyout menu for that icon.

Try the two new tools located in the Healing Brush tool. New to CS2 are the Red Eye tool and the Spot Healing Brush tool.

Figure 3-7: Your Toolbox.

Wet Your Palette

One of the most powerful features of Photoshop is the ability to display and hide a number of tool options and functions in the form of floating and dockable palettes. As explained previously in the Window menu section in this chapter, these palettes are accessible through the Window menu.

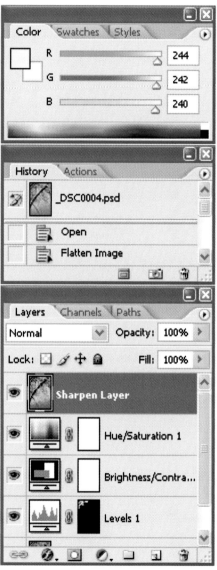

As shown in Figure 3-8, each palette displays as a group of tabs. When you click a tab, a function of the palette appears. For example, the Layers palette includes tabs for Channels and Paths. The Color palette includes tabs for Swatches and Styles.

Like the Toolbox, palettes are an important part of your Photoshop arsenal and assist you in customizing your Photoshop interface (remember, in-your-face). Here are some tips about palettes you may find helpful:

- Open palettes by choosing Window ⇨ (palette name).

- Click the palette tabs within the palette to show that palette.

- Close a palette by clicking the Close button.

- Hide a palette by clicking the Collapse button.

- Dock individual palette tabs by dragging them to the palette well.

- Create your own palettes or break out any tab to its own palette by dragging a palette tab to the Photoshop Workspace or by dragging palette tabs to other palettes.

- Reset your palettes and locations by choosing Window ⇨ Workspace ⇨ Reset Palette Locations.

Figure 3-8: Palettes are a major part of your Photoshop arsenal.

Chapter 4

Digital Workflow Is Free

*W*hat is a digital workflow? you ask. Is this something else I need to buy to be a better photographer? Jeepers, I already invested half my life savings into this stuff. I never heard of this in my high school photography class, am I missing something? Digital photography was *supposed* to be easier than film photography!

Digital workflow isn't something you forgot or need to buy. Workflow is simply the steps you follow to make your photography better. Think about the steps you take to drive your car. First, you walk to the car and unlock your door. Next, you get in the car. Then, you put on your seatbelt, check the rear view mirror, insert the key in the ignition, and start the car. Turn on the radio, pop in a cool CD, turn your head to make sure nobody is behind you, put the transmission in reverse and lightly step on the gas. After checking for traffic on the street and backing out of the driveway, you brake, put the car in drive and begin your journey. Digital workflow is the same concept: a number of steps you faithfully take to arrive safely at your destination, the killer-print!

If you want to read the best practices from preparing for your shooting all the way through to printing and archiving your images, this chapter's for you. I cover the basic components of a proper digital workflow by breaking down each part in easy-to-understand steps that you can practice to create perfection. Best of all, workflow doesn't cost anything. Let the flow begin!

Prepare, Prepare, and Prepare

Most casual photographers just throw the camera in the car and let things happen. Hey, it works for them and that's cool. A lot of professionals are like that. Other photographers, like myself, prepare every time they venture out to shoot photos. I am not the type to leave things to chance. I want to make sure that I cover any contingency that may arise. Like most people, I want to make sure that I get the most out of the time I spend capturing images.

If I am scheduled to do a two-hour nature hike to photograph landscapes, on location portraits, or a drive into the city for a morning of urban landscapes, I spend time going through my equipment checklist. Charged batteries? Enough memory cards? Are my lenses clean? Is my sensor clean? I even turn on my camera, set my aperture priority ahead of time and review all my menu settings. If I'm shooting a high school basketball game, I make sure I bump up the ISO setting and attach a fast lens to my digital SLR. I call this my preparation workflow.

Figure 4-1: Preparing for location shoots gives more time to concentrate on your subjects.

On location for portrait sessions, I follow an entire checklist to make sure not only my camera gear is in order, but also strobes, backgrounds, stands, umbrellas, soft boxes, tripods, tape, and aspirin are all accounted for. I want to make sure I can concentrate on the subject I am photographing instead of looking for batteries for an external flash. Figure 4-1 illustrates how having the right equipment helps make an on-location portrait session successful. Follow this list when preparing for your photo shoot:

- **Check batteries.** Make sure your digital camera battery is charged and ready to go. Carrying a spare battery is always a good idea. Most digital camera batteries provide a full day on one charge, but performance declines as the batteries get older. Always have a charged spare in your camera bag.

- **Check memory cards.** You never know when you may come across a subject that you take 50 shots of just to get it right. If you figure you're going to take 100 photographs during your shoot, take enough memory cards to shoot 300 photographs. Make sure your memory cards are for-matted and ready to go. That means that you previously downloaded images and archived them to CD or DVD!

✔ **Clean lenses and sensor.** Make sure your lenses are clean and free of dust before venturing out. If you are using a digital SLR, make sure your sensor is clean. Check your user manual to find out the correct procedure for cleaning your sensor.

✔ **Camera setup.** If you are setting out on a landscape trip or a portrait shoot, make sure your shooting mode, white balance, exposure com-pensation, and ISO speed are set.

✔ **Camera bag.** Before you leave, make sure your camera bag is properly packed. Dust removal equipment, lenses, flashes, batteries, memory cards, user manual, and your tripod should all be packed up and ready to go. I always have a small flashlight with fresh batteries packed just in case I am shooting night scenes and need to see camera controls in dark places. Don't forget the aspirin, Twinkies, and some bottled water for the trip.

Always keep safety in mind. When venturing out on a nature shoot alone, let a family member or someone at your hotel know where you are going and how long you will be. Additionally, take a charged cell phone with you at all times. Figure 4-2 shows the results of a photographer traveling to a remote location to get the shot.

Figure 4-2: Keep safety in mind when traveling to locations.

Digital Capture

Recently, I braved sub-zero degree temperatures to shoot moving traffic from a highway overpass. I wanted to get one of those cool streamer shots of the cars going 70 miles per hour. I parked the car, walked a few blocks, and crossed a busy intersection in the dark and set up my camera and tripod on the overpass sidewalk.

Fifteen minutes and near-frostbite later, I ran back to my car and its heater. When I finally got feeling back to my extremities, I turned the camera back on to view my images. Upon closer inspection, the taillights didn't appear blurred like I had planned. Upon further inspection, I realized my camera was in manual mode, not the aperture priority I thought I was using! This resulted in faster shutter speeds that didn't create the effect I wanted . Poor planning led to a useless shoot and some frostbite.

The list that follows explains the shooting workflow that can help you be more prepared when taking photos. Going through the same process every time you take photos helps you increase the quality of your photographs and reduce the number of images that you'll have to throw out later.

- ✔ **Check focus.** It's easy to turn auto focus off, and then shoot a number of photos thinking they are in focus. Before shooting, check that your auto focus is turned on or off. For action shots, make sure you are set to continuous focus mode.

- ✔ **Set white balance.** Many photographers do not use auto white balance for a reason. In some lighting situations, auto white balance does not always work. Make sure you set your white balance for the particular lighting situation you are shooting in. If it's outdoors and cloudy, set your white balance for cloudy. If it's sunny, set white balance for sunny. If you are indoors under fluorescent lighting, set your white balance for fluorescent.

- ✔ **Check settings.** Check that your camera is set up properly for the type of photography you are about to begin shooting. Make sure your exposure compensation, file size, ISO setting, and other customizable features of your camera are properly set.

- ✔ **Shoot and review.** After taking photographs, review each shot on your LCD. Is the white balance correct? Overexposed or underexposed? Review the histogram: It can tell you if your exposure is correct.

- ✔ **Review orientation.** Review your subject and determine if it would look better in portrait or landscape orientation. To be safe, shoot your subjects in both portrait and landscape orientations, as shown in Figure 4-3.

Figure 4-3: Shoot your subjects in both portrait and landscape orientations.

✏ **Delete unwanted shots.** Sometimes you'll want to delete shots you've taken when you review your digital camera's LCD. It does save some card space if you're in a jam for image storage while shooting. In most cases, try to be careful when deleting unwanted shots while you are taking pictures. You can always delete these after you download the images to your computer. If you're going to delete some images in your digital camera, first make sure you don't want the image. Ask yourself if a shot can be salvaged in Photoshop or by cropping.

Transferring and Organizing Images

One of the advantages to using digital cameras is that you can take as many photographs as you want without paying a cent more. Not unlike an all-you-can-eat buffet, but too much food and you get indigestion. Too many images and your files become unmanageable. Following a simple image transfer, storage, and organizing workflow like the workflow described here can save you a lot of headaches down the road and make you a much more efficient photographer. You will have more time to head down to the all-you-can-eat buffet!

✔ **Set up folders.** Set up a folder system that best fits your photography work. I personally have a folder set up on my hard disk that contains all my original images transferred from my memory cards. In this folder I have subfolders that contain all the images per card download numbered IMG001, IMG002, and so on.

✔ **Transfer images.** Using a card reader that is directly connected to your computer to transfer your images is best. This method is more desirable than connecting your camera directly to your computer and transferring your images. Cameras have a tendency to run out of battery charge while transferring images: Card readers are faster and easier anyway. If you're using a transfer program that came with your camera to transfer images, never let the transfer program delete images from your memory card after the transfer. You want to make sure your images are backed up to CD or DVD first.

✔ **Back up originals.** Before you open Bridge to begin organizing and glorifying your images, back 'em up. Whether you are using CDs or DVDs to archive, as shown in Figure 4-4, get this step out of the way now or you'll never do it. Write the date or dates of the images, filename range, and a description of the subject matter. I make two CD copies of all my originals: one for my image library and one for my fire safe. If one CD gets damaged, I always have a backup of my backup to rely on. Remember, the original images are your digital negative. Photographers working with digital photos make duplicates (dupes) of everything, even dupes of dupes, just like they did when they worked with film.

Figure 4-4: Always make backups of your images to CD or DVD.

✔ **View and organize.** Now that you have a backup and a backup of your *original* images out of camera, you can safely reformat your memory cards and dive into Bridge. As described in Chapter 3, you can use the Bridge to view, sort, rename, rank, and delete images. If there are images in the download folder that you know you will never use, now is the time to delete them.

Backups are part of my life and with good reason. Years ago, when I was a college student majoring in photography, an unfortunate event took place back home: A fire nearly destroyed my parent's house. We rebuilt the house, but the fire destroyed my darkroom and the archival box where I stored *all* my negatives (this was years before digital photography). I'll never be able to scan those negatives into Photoshop now, and some were award-winning photographs. Lesson learned? Make backups to CD or DVD of all your digital images, scanned negatives, and slides.

Keep two copies of your original images on CD or DVD. One for your image library and the other stored either in a fire safe or even better, locked up in a safety deposit box.

Messing Around with Images

As you can tell by now, this workflow matter has a lot of steps! Digital workflow is actually a set of individual workflows. When you put all these together, your work improves, and you are more organized, less stressed, and more efficient in your photographic work. The next and most involved part of the overall workflow is image editing in Photoshop. I really dive into Photoshop image editing in Parts III and IV. For now, I provide you with an overview of the Photoshop workflow. Figure 4-5 shows you the Photoshop Layers palette and also an example of an image editing workflow being applied to an image. The list that follows provides details of the image editing workflow.

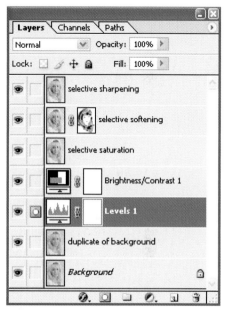

Figure 4-5: This Photoshop Layers palette shows an example of an editing workflow. The steps start from the bottom of the palette, one step per layer.

✔ **Convert raw images.** If you are not shooting your images in raw format, skip this step of the workflow. Using Bridge to open raw images in Camera Raw, adjust your images for correct color temperature/white balance, exposure, shadows, brightness, contrast, and color saturation. Save the sharpening for later. When your initial adjustments are made, save your raw image in the Photoshop native PSD format into your working folder.

✔ **Plan your edits.** Take the time to view your image in Photoshop. Carefully plan what image edits you think you want to perform before you dive in. Planning makes for better photographs!

✔ **Perform overall adjustments.** Make adjustments by removing color cast using levels, adjusting brightness/contrast, or by increasing or decreasing color saturation.

✔ **Perform targeted adjustments.** Targeted adjustments is a fancy way to adjust only certain areas of your image. Use dodging, burning, healing brush, and other Photoshop tools to make local adjustments. Remember, do not sharpen your image until resizing and printing.

✏ **Save the master file.** After you make all your overall and targeted image adjustments, save the master. Make sure you save this file with a unique filename, such as dsc0204_master. This file contains all your adjustments and layers that can be retained or modified for future work.

✏ **Save a flattened file.** Before printing or preparing an adjusted image for the Web, I always flatten my adjusted image and save it as a unique name, such as dsc0204_flattened. This file becomes my output file. Before printing, I first resize this file to the desired output size and then sharpen the image using Unsharp Mask.

Printing and Output

Output is a computer term that is older than almost everyone, except maybe me. For digital photographers, this usually means printing. Everything I do and every workflow I adhere to has one destination in mind, the fine print. Today's technology offers you other means of displaying your work: Prints for family and friends from your inkjet printer like the one shown in Figure 4-6, or prints for books, magazines, the Web, or e-mail. To establish best practices in outputting images, I provide an example of my Printing and Output workflow in the following list.

Figure 4-6: Printing is a workflow all by itself.

✏ **Choose output format.** Photographers have to prepare their output for a number of different media types: prints for display, magazines, newspapers, and the Web. The output type determines the size and resolution in your flattened version of the image. I usually output my images for three different media types: print, my Web site, and publication. I save all these files in a folder I create specifically for that image. I store a copy of the original edited and flattened image, my image for print, and the version I use for my Web site.

✏ **Size the image.** For each type of output, you need to size your flattened image. Images I produce for Web sites get sized usually at two to four inches at 72 PPI (pixels per inch). For prints, I usually size my photographs for the paper I am using and set the output at 300 or 360 PPI.

✔ **Choose paper.** Assuming you are going to print your photographs, take care in selecting a good paper to match your printer. You can find many options out there. For me, I usually prefer the photo quality paper supplied by my printer manufacturer. I also stay away from third party inks. Make sure you tell your printer driver (the Print dialog on the Mac) which paper you are using.

✔ **Use correct color management.** Make sure your printer driver is set up correctly. Be careful not to apply color management twice. Chapter 18 covers these details.

✔ **Let prints dry.** Like the old-fashioned chemical darkroom, inkjet prints need to dry after printing. Letting the print dry overnight on a flat surface is best. Don't stack multiple prints on top of each other until they are dry.

✔ **Archiving.** There are two types of people: those who have lost their data, and those that will. Hard disk drives have only so many hours of life. If you're lucky, your computer hard disk will never fail or get corrupted by a computer virus or Trojan horse. To be safe, I always archive my edited images along with my output folders to CD. It may seem excessive, but it saves a lot of work when my hard disk does fail me. CDs and DVDs are cheap, but time is not!

Chapter 5

We're All Gearheads and Geeks

This chapter is the digital photography State of the Union. There are no red states, there are no blue states, just the digital RGB of red, green, and blue. Face it. We are indeed digital photography geeks. We buy expensive digital cameras. We spend the extra few bucks on software and color management tools. Serious geeks buy tripods and tripod heads, all essential gear. We need to buy the best we can afford. We have more memory cards than we usually need. And I don't know about you, but I have my eye on that new portable storage thingamajig.

Having the latest and greatest in digital gear is always nice, but not practical for most of us. Many of the best photographers will tell you this: It's not the equipment that makes for good pictures, it's the photographer. The best way to improve digital capture is by perfecting techniques and spending the time to figure out how to maximize the equipment you already have. After you do master your digital camera, carefully choose the next addition for your collection, an addition that will enable you to improve as a photographer.

If I had a million dollars, I would probably have no problem finding enough goodies to spend it on. Unfortunately, most of us need to choose carefully and try to get the most out of each dollar we spend on our craft. This chapter is dedicated to those who, like me, scan the trade magazines and Internet for the latest trends and gear for digital photographers.

Hitting a Moving Target

Reporting on what is going to be the latest trend in digital photography is like hitting a moving target. I would be hard pressed to tell you what you could expect in one year, or even six months. In the computer world, Moore's law states that the technology will double every 18 months. Digital photography cameras and sensors often approach just that.

Think back 18 months ago when three or five megapixel cameras were considered state of the art and produced some great photos. One year ago? Six megapixel cameras were the norm. Today's prosumer (professional/advanced consumer level digital camera) standard sits at seven or eight megapixels. Pro level full frame (equivalent in size to 35mm film) sensor model megapixel sizes are now in double-digits. Digital SLR manufacturers offer professional digital SLRs with up to 12 or 16 million effective pixels. Eighteen months from now? It's hard to tell. I'm not even sure if I would ever need anything beyond 16 megapixel at the size of the traditional 35mm frame. I thought my three-year-old five-megapixel prosumer model gave me better images than I ever shot with film, such as the one shown in Figure 5-1, but you know that something more advanced is coming soon!

Figure 5-1: My four-year-old five-megapixel digital camera still kicks out the jams.

Evaluating the most recent trends and anticipating digital photographer's needs for equipment and software, the following list provides a Digital Photography State of the Union:

- **Digital cameras are now emerging with faster startup times than earlier models.** That split second can make a difference when trying to get that once in a lifetime candid.

- **The problem of long shutter lag finally is starting to disappear.** If you've been using digital cameras for a while you know all too well the problem of the lag between the time you press the shutter button and the time the camera actually takes the picture. Action shots were almost impossible due to this time lag. Cameras now typically have a lag time of a fraction of a second. As new cameras are announced, the speed increases.

- **Digital camera liquid crystal displays (LCD) monitors are getting larger.** 1.8" LCD monitors are common on most digital cameras. Mid-range and higher end models are now sporting LCD monitors up to 2.5", such as the one shown in Figure 5-2. LCDs have a tendency to draw power, but advancements in the technologies that go into camera batteries are allowing for these larger LCDs.

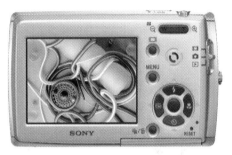

Photo courtesy of Sony Electronics, Inc.

Figure 5-2: LCD displays are getting bigger and better.

- **Vibration reduction or "antishake" is becoming much more prominent in higher end digital cameras, and the trend will likely continue with more mid-range models.** Recent to the market are digital cameras sporting zoom lenses at a 35mm equivalent of 35mm to 420mm. Cameras, such as the Panasonic shown in Figure 5-3, have long telephoto ranges and need built-in capability to reduce vibration. This feature is very welcome.

Figure 5-3: Vibration reduction is becoming common in large zoom digital cameras, such as this Panasonic.

✐ **Software is always getting better.** With each new version, capabilities increase and the bugs decrease. A recent trend is the availability of some great Photoshop plug-in filters. Look for more color management utilities and equipment as well. These are welcome friends to an already pretty good lineup of software tools.

✐ **Digital printing is evolving.** Almost half of prints made from digital cameras are being done at the corner pharmacy or warehouse store. Online digital printing leaders are emerging, offering unique printing services. This trend will continue into the foreseeable future.

Love Story: My Digital Camera

Nothing can be better than to get comfortable in front of a nice fire and read a good novel. Digital camera manuals are dry compared to mindless entertainment, but you have to read them if you want to know how to work the basics of your camera. Every digital camera is different from the next. These digital cameras are much more complex than the old film cameras, and the only way you can keep up is by reading the manuals, checking the Web, and asking the gearhead camera guy you know technical questions.

Reviewing a few technical aspects you need to know about your equipment is important. The list that follows provides a list of controls and procedures that allow you to become, let's say, more *intimate* with your camera, such as the guy in Figure 5-4. Remember, in digital photography, everyday is Valentine's Day.

Figure 5-4: Care for and love your digital camera.

- **On/Off switch.** It helps knowing these minor details. Go to the camera store and play with 10 digital cameras. I bet you figure out how to turn on only half of them.

- **Charging batteries.** Some batteries need charging overnight while some charge in two to four hours. If you are going out on a shooting assignment, give yourself enough time ahead of your departure to charge a few batteries.

- **Turn numbering on.** Ensures your images are numbered sequentially from memory card to memory card. Leaving this turned off restarts numbering after every download. Make sure this is turned on before you start shooting with your new camera.

- **Image size.** Usually you have many choices from raw to fine JPEG to low resolution JPEG. As a general rule, shoot at the highest resolution available. If you are shooting images for the Web only, you can reduce the image quality down.

- **ISO.** This is the equivalent to the film speed setting on a film camera. For best image quality, always shoot at the lowest ISO setting allowed. If you're shooting action, sports, or in low light situations, bump up the ISO. Never use auto-ISO.

- **Auto focus mode.** Most digital cameras have modes to set Auto focus to stationary or moving subjects. For landscape or portraits, stick to the AF-S or stationary setting. For action, sports, or wildlife use the AF-C for continuous focus.

- **White balance.** Some digital cameras have a special button that lets you toggle between white balance settings. Never set your camera to Auto White Balance. Always review white balance in test shots on your LCD. Cloudy settings often add warmth to the photographs.

- **Date/time.** When you first purchase your digital camera, make sure date and time are set correctly. Check the date/time settings frequently. Date/Time stamps are important for managing your images later on your computer.

- **Exposure compensation.** Usually in 1/3 stop increments. This feature is advanced. On some cameras, most photos are slightly underexposed, on some cameras slightly overexposed. Use this feature only after you experiment with your camera.

- **Flash compensation.** Like exposure compensation, you can make adjustments 1/3 stop higher or lower than the metered flash exposure. Experiment with these settings until you get desired results.

- **Format.** Formats the memory card for use and erases all images still on the card. Make sure any images on your memory cards are loaded to your computer and backed up twice before formatting.

I've gotten in the habit of mentally going through my camera setup checklist before taking any picture or heading out on a photo shoot. Using different cameras, I also carry a copy of the manual in my camera bag for each camera, just in case. You never know when you need to figure out how to work a particular adjustment, as seen in Figure 5-5.

Photo courtesy of Sony Electronics, Inc.

Figure 5-5: Make sure you set up your camera to maximize your shot.

This Isn't Your Father's Darkroom

Actually, my father didn't have a darkroom, I did, but he helped me build mine in the basement. I spent a lot of time down there until my parents started to worry about what the heck I was doing all that time in that little room. I spent hours developing photographs and inhaling toxic fumes in a darkroom with that reddish orange safelight. Yes, I was indeed a teenage geek. This section speaks of the digital darkroom. No more toxic chemicals and sickening fumes. No more dark orange and red lights. No more film or print washers. No more little dark room in the basement. It's all zeros and ones from here on out.

The computer

Central to your digital darkroom is the computer. Rules for buying computers haven't changed in 20 years: I recommend that you buy the most powerful you can afford. Heck, you're going to replace it in three years anyway, so you may as well enjoy the speed while you have it. Figure that the computer you just purchased this year will be replaced with another with two or three times the capacity and speed in about three years. If you are using a laptop, figure two years. Figure 5-6 shows you how laptop computers get carried around a lot and take a lot of abuse.

Figure 5-6: Laptops take a lot of abuse due to their portability.

Optimizing equipment

I'm not one of those that have a tendency toward a PC or a Mac. Both are great and both do their jobs very well. Just make sure when you purchase one that it's the fastest you can get.

Make sure you have tons of disk space, a CD and DVD writer, a rockin' graphics card with at least 128MB of onboard memory, and you have got yourself some serious hardware.

The list that follows provides an explanation of the parts of the computer that should be optimized for digital imaging:

- **System memory.** Also known as RAM (random access memory). The memory space where your programs and working files are loaded on a temporary basis. One gigabyte of memory is recommended for Photoshop. Stretch it to one-and-a-half or two gigabytes if possible.

- **Hard disk space.** This permanent storage part of your computer holds programs and data files. Go with the largest hard disk you can. Pay attention to speed. A 7,200 RPM (revolutions per minute) disk spins almost twice as fast as a 4,200 RPM disk. That makes a huge difference when you work with large image files.

- **Graphics card.** This internal component controls the color graphics displayed on your monitor. Make sure your graphics card contains at least 128MB of onboard memory.

- **Display.** Your computer monitor is one of the most important components of your computer system. Displays 17" and larger are best for digital photographers. Pay attention to the dot pitch spec: .21 dot pitch is sharper than the normal .27 dot pitch.

- **Optical drives.** Your CD and/or DVD burners. Some of these drives are combined CD-RW and DVD +/–R. The combo drives often accompany laptops. If you are using a desktop computer, go with separate CD and DVD burners.

- **USB ports.** Standard universal port to plug in peripherals. You can't have enough of these. This is where you plug in your printer, scanner, card reader, camera, calibration device, other printer, and so on. Make sure your computer has at least four of these. Don't worry if you have fewer than four: additional USB splitters are cheap and easy to add later.

- **FireWire port.** Faster data transmission made possible by FireWire. This is becoming a standard interface to have, mainly because of digital video. FireWire comes in handy with directly connecting or "tethering" digital cameras to the computer.

Buy Me More Toys!

Without a doubt, photography can be a resource-challenging endeavor. In other words, there are always more toys to buy. Card readers, gray cards, lenses, paper, ink, flashes, batteries, chargers, flash cords, and so on. I list what I think are the top five toys you may want to ask for for your next birthday.

- **Card readers:** Plugging that little cable into your digital camera and then into the USB port of your computer is a real pain. For the cost of a couple inkjet cartridges, you can purchase a multi-format card reader. These small devices accept Memory Stick, CompactFlash, Secure Digital, and other memory card formats. Transferring your images is easier and faster than plugging in your camera directly to your computer.

- **Tablets:** These devices until recently were primarily used by professional graphic artists and photo retouchers. As with any technology, the price point is now within reach of any digital photography enthusiast. A tablet is used for fine editing of your photographs, giving much more accurate control of all those goodies located in the Photoshop Toolbox. Instead of using a mouse to paint, the Wacom tablet shown in Figure 5-7 provides the fine control you need with over 20 Photoshop pressure-sensitive tools.

Figure 5-7: A tablet offers more editing control than a mouse.

- **Monitor calibration:** Of all the toys, the monitor calibration tool is the one I suggest the most. I cover this in detail in Chapter 9. Calibrating your monitor is the most important step in the color management workflow. The price for one of these devices pays for itself in wasted paper and ink.

- **Portable storage:** If you are taking a trip and plan on taking a lot of photos, you may not have enough memory cards. One of the ways to get around having to lug a laptop with you is to bring along a portable storage device. These devices are basically portable hard disk drives with beautiful LCD displays so that you can browse your images. They are small, too: about the size of an iPod. It's a lot easier than a laptop and cooler to bring one of these along.

✔ **Optical drives:** A few years ago computers didn't come standard with CD-R or rewritable CD drives. Today's computers come standard with CD *and* DVD writable drives. Either is vital to backing up your data and especially to archiving your images. If your computer is a couple years old and you do not have a CD or DVD writer, look into getting an inexpensive internal or external drive.

If You Have the Hardware, I've Got the Software

How many software programmers does it take to screw in a light bulb? Answer: none, that's a hardware problem. Sorry, I was looking for the right spot to put in one of my oldest jokes. Wrapping up this expensive chapter is this section about even more items to add to your digital photography arsenal, software add-ins.

Utilities to make your life easier

Just as Windows and Mac OS are the operating systems of your computer and software programs, Photoshop is your digital photography operating system. To enhance that setup, you always have a few other programs to use in conjunction with Photoshop to make your life easier. As time goes on and Photoshop keeps getting better, more utilities are built right in, such as file organization with Bridge. Noise reduction is improving in Photoshop as well. Here are a few other utilities you can use to enhance your digital photography:

✔ **Scanning software:** Dedicated film and flatbed scanners usually come bundled with software you use to scan and save your scanned images. Serious enthusiasts and professionals often lean toward dedicated software utilities to use with these scanners. One of the most popular of these scanning utilities is the LaserSoft Imaging SilverFast AI. For information on the latest version, visit their Web site at `www.silverfast.com`.

✔ **Noise reduction software:** One of the inherent problems with digital images is the red, blue, and green speckles you find in shadow areas, especially when cropping photos to eliminate unwanted areas of the photo (but retaining the image size) or when printing photos on a large format printer. Typically you find increased noise in images that are shot at high ISOs. To help combat noise and improve image quality, software utilities are available on the market and for download on the Web. An example of one of these utilities is Noise Ninja. Their Web site address is `www.picturecode.com`. To research these further, head to one of the Web digital photography sites, such as the Digital Photography Review software forums at `www.dpreview.com`.

✏ **Image stacking utilities:** Literally thousands of astrophotographers (including me) love taking pictures of the night sky. One of the techniques used to capture digital images of the planets, stars, comets, and nebula is stacking. Stacking is the process of combining many short-exposure images of the sky and then combining all these images into one, thus increasing the quality of astronomical object pictured. Stacking reduces image noise that is inherent in long exposures, as shown in Figure 5-8.

Digital sensors typically do not do well with long exposures. The longer the exposure, the more image noise is produced. Short exposures reduce image noise. The more exposures, the more image detail. Stack many exposures together and you get some breathtaking images of the sky. Head out to your local bookstore and check out the Astronomy magazines or the Web for examples. You'll get hooked just like I did.

Plug it in

Out of the package, Photoshop includes a number of filters that allow you to add dozens of effects to your photos. Photoshop has the inherent capability of plugging in software utilities to increase its already rich feature set. These utilities are called Photoshop plug-ins. For most, installing these plug-ins is as easy as copying the plug-in file right into the Photoshop Plug-In folder.

Auto FX offers a series of suites that are considered among the coolest Photoshop plug-ins available. You can download demos of these plug-ins right from their Web site at www.autofx.com.

nik Multimedia offers suites of their Photoshop plug-in. The nik Color Efex Pro collection offers one of the most popular collections of plug-in among professionals and serious photographers. The nik collection augments the already capable Photoshop with some very good image adjustment filters. The nik Sharpener Pro is a popular image sharpening collection. View and download demos of these at www.nikmultimedia.com.

LizardTech provides the popular Genuine Ractals PrintPro plug-in, which allows you to enlarge images 200 to 400 percent without noticeable image degradation. This is a great tool to print smaller digital images on 8×10 or larger format printers. You can view download information at www.genuinefractals.com.

Figure 5-8: Image noise noticeable in the sky area of this long exposure of the northern lights can benefit from some noise reduction software techniques.

Digital Shui: The Ergonomic Workstation

Believe it or not, computer workstation ergonomics and working environment become even more important for digital photographers. Digital photographers primarily work with light and color. Your working environment must be set up to maximize what your eyes are supposed to see, as well as what your neck and wrists are most comfortable with images like Figure 5-9.

Most people park their desks in corners of the house with poor lighting, seating, and color. If your digital darkroom is in the workplace, chances are you have those dreaded fluorescent lights, the wrong desk height, and a cheap office catalog chair. Neither situation lends itself to a good working digital darkroom. The following list offers some suggestions for improving your working environment.

1. **Use full spectrum lighting.**

   One of the most overlooked areas of the digital darkroom is the lighting used to illuminate the room and computer workstation. The lighting you use to view prints and proofs is critical, too. You need to be in an environment that optimizes the conditions in which photographs will be displayed: Consider the use of full spectrum lighting.

   Full spectrum lighting reduces eye fatigue, increases visual acuity, reduces glare, and provides photographic working areas with a pleasing and stimulating atmosphere. Consult with your local lighting dealer to find the best full spectrum lighting for your situation.

Figure 5-9: Proper workstation ergonomics help you enjoy producing beautiful photographs even more.

2. **Use neutral colored workstations.**

   Working with prints and spending hours viewing images on your monitor require that your eyes remain adjusted in a neutral lighting condition. If your computer sits on a desk that is dark brown or black and the wall is bright white, your eyes are going to have to continuously adjust to the colors of your computer monitor.

You can improve your working conditions by using a neutral gray colored desk. Think about painting the walls of your workspace a more neutral color.

3. **Avoid windows.**

Windows are the most important part of any home or office, but the inconsistent lighting that windows provide make for inconsistent lighting decisions you make. I've worked in offices where I had sunshine pouring in and producing horrible glare on my computer screen for literally half of the day. Drove me crazy. Make sure your working environment has a good set of blinds on your windows.

4. **Reduce neck and wrist strain.**

You can spend hours upon hours in front of your computer workstation editing and organizing images. Make sure your monitor is at proper height and your back, elbows, and wrists are at comfortable levels and supported. Take frequent breaks to reduce the chance of eyestrain, and think about purchasing a digital tablet.

Part II
Shooting for Quality Images

The 5th Wave   By Rich Tennant

CAMERAS

"I want a lens that's heavy enough to counterbalance the weight on my back."

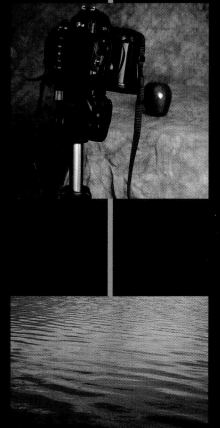

*B*etter photographs start in the camera. Knowing the techniques for using image editing programs like Photoshop can make a blah photo a little better, but properly exposed, composed, and focused images make for much better prints. Get it right the first time out of the camera. Don't rely on salvaging images on the computer later. From setting up your digital camera to shooting sharp photos, this part explains some of the best practices for taking images with your digital camera.

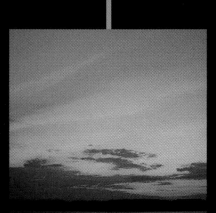

When shooting photos, you need to ask yourself several questions before setting up your camera for a shot. For what medium are you shooting these pictures? What are my choices for file types, and what do they mean? This part helps you understand how to make the right decisions before you begin shooting.

Chapter 6

Getting the Most from Your Digital Camera

I recently went on a photography trip up north. I had five days scheduled to take photographs, and it rained and sleeted for four of those days. On day five, I had my chance to shoot some areas I had scoped out earlier. It took me an hour to get to my location and on the way, I nearly got stuck driving up a steep mountain with narrow muddy roads, but I did eventually get to where I could shoot my vista. It was sunny out later in the day, so I wasn't worried about the dreaded afternoon sun washing out my fall colors.

Upon returning to my campsite, I downloaded all my images to my laptop. Made a cup of coffee and proceeded to review my catch in Photoshop (that's my personal Java workflow). To my dismay, most of my shots were just plain washed out. Even though I shot later in the day, the sun was *so* bright that most of my shots just didn't cut it. Nothing in Photoshop would have helped the shots I took that day.

The lesson to learn here is no matter what plans and opportunities you have, you still have to start out with good images in Photoshop.

Determine Your Output

Shooting digital provides the photographer with many choices of size and format of images, choices photographers didn't have using film cameras. For fine art photographers who want to output large prints, the highest quality file settings should be used. Photojournalists and sports photographers are interested in speed and don't need huge files that choke up their memory cards, as shown in Figure 6-1. Sports photographers often turn down the file size, shoot JPEG instead of raw, and maximize the speed in which their cameras write to the card.

I once asked a photojournalist if he ever shot in raw format. Without thinking, he said "Never." He likes to get it right in JPEG and was not interested in high quality printing. The photojournalist went on to tell me "I don't need to shoot in raw. My pictures are perfect the first time I shoot them." Okay, he had a little ego. He then proceeded to tell me "I'm shooting for black and white newsprint, which looks lousy anyway." I guess I see his point.

Figure 6-1: Photojournalist sacrifice a little size for speed.

I personally shoot landscapes, portraits, still lifes, action shots, and anything I deem interesting. No matter what I'm shooting for, I always set my camera to the highest file quality setting and largest size. My reason is that I'm shooting for fine quality *prints*. I can always downsize for the Web or smaller size printing later.

The sports photographer always shoots for speed and a lower file size, but always for quality for the intended output. I've seen some incredible sports shots photographed at a lower resolution that enlarged in print just fine. The photojournalist I met, well, he really doesn't care, and according to him, his photos look lousy in newsprint anyway.

By the way, he took my picture, and it wound up in the newspaper. He was right: My picture looked lousy.

Figuring Out File Types and Sizes

Firing up your digital camera and trying to figure out all those techie things can be intimidating to most. Most people don't know the difference between a JPEG and a TIFF, and that's okay. It's like when you bought your first VCR and tried getting it hooked up to the TV, at least for those of us (like me) who remember the days before VCRs! The point is, making all those settings in the camera can be, well, a little complicated.

In order to make things simpler when it comes to file types and file sizes to choose, I first explain what each file type means and some tips on its usage.

The JPEG advantage

The most commonly-used file format for digital cameras is JPEG (pronounced *jay-peg*). JPEG is a file format that is most compatible across multiple uses, such as the Web, digital cameras, photo viewers, and photo editing software, such as Photoshop or Photoshop Elements.

The advantage of shooting JPEG files is the image compression. Image compression is simply defined as reducing the size of the file, hopefully with little or no noticeable loss of quality, as illustrated in Figure 6-2. The advantage to using JPEG as your chosen image format is the reduced image size without noticeable loss of quality. You can fit many more images on a memory card in JPEG format than TIFF or raw format.

Figure 6-2: A 2MB JPEG provides great detail and color for this landscape photo.

Digital cameras allow you to make different JPEG quality settings. Most cameras have setting for Fine, Normal, and Basic. For most of your shooting, set your camera to Fine, the highest available JPEG quality setting.

A tale of two compressions

For digital camera file formats, there are basically two different types of compression, *lossless* compression and *lossy* compression. Both have their place in the technical world of file compression and are used everyday by photographers.

The definition of lossless compression is file compression without the loss of data or quality. If you are an avid computer user, WinZip is a utility used to collect and "smush" data files into one. It compresses the data for easier transmission and storage. When you un-zip your files, they remain intact. No loss of quality whatsoever. TIFF

is an example of a file format that can be compressed using lossless compression.

Lossy compression reduces the size of images by throwing away data, which may not be a bad thing if you use it correctly. Usually JPEG images shot at the highest resolution or fine setting can't be distinguished from the same image shot using TIFF or raw formats, unless you re-save the images a few more times. Every time you open a JPEG file and edit it in Photoshop, you lose more data when you save it, because it is recompressed with each save.

TIFF for tat

TIFF (Tagged Image Format) files offer a few advantages over shooting with JPEG, but with a big tradeoff. TIFF images shot out of the camera are among the largest when it comes to file sizes. An image shot in JPEG fine mode may be 2MB in size compared to the same image shot in TIFF at 12MB in size.

The advantages to using TIFF as your shooting file type include the fact that TIFF images can be compressed in a lossless way. TIFF images, like JPEG, are compatible with most image editing software programs. In the printing industry, TIFF format is considered the final format used for printing. In Photoshop, the advantage to TIFF images is that they can be edited in 16 bit mode as opposed to 8 bit mode, which is all that JPEG can offer.

The bottom line for photographers is that you would be hard pressed to find image quality out of camera much different between TIFF and JPEG for most output situations. The only photographers that shoot in TIFF are ones whose cameras do not offer a Raw shooting format and want the absolute best quality they can capture.

Most higher end digital cameras today offer the option to shoot images in Raw format as an alternative to the standard JPEG, thus eliminating the need to shoot using TIFF. In Photoshop, you can always convert your image to TIFF for final printing or distribution media printing.

Monday night Raw

New to the digital camera in the past few years is the offering of a Raw file format. Yes, I know, this sounds like another one of those techie type acronyms to remember, but actually Raw actually means raw! Quite simply, it's described as an unprocessed or *raw* image file.

The Raw image is one where the camera performs no adjustment to the image when the photo is taken, as seen in Figure 6-3. The camera stores all the information its sensor captured. All adjustments normally made by the camera, such as sharpness, contrast, brightness, and color saturation have to be performed in Raw conversion software, such as Photoshop Camera Raw.

Figure 6-3: A Raw image out of camera and the same image adjusted and converted.

The advantage for shooting Raw for digital photographers is simple. The Raw file provides a true digital "negative." Think of shooting an entire memory card full of images, which, compared to the film world, is the equivalent to a roll of film. With Raw images, the photographer can choose to develop these negatives any way he or she chooses.

Compared to TIFF files, Raw files take up about half the storage space due to the fact that Raw files are made up of one 12-bit channel file. TIFF files, on the other hand, are made up of three 8-bit channels. Like TIFF, JPEG is made up of three 8-bit channels but saves storage space through the use of compression.

Adobe has recently announced a standard format for camera and software manufacturers for the Raw format. The Adobe Digital Negative format, called DNG, is an attempt to standardize the Raw image format across platforms. Currently all camera manufacturers offer their own version of Raw. No one knows where the new standard will go in the next few years.

Image size does matter

Simple logic states that if you shoot at the highest image size or *resolution* possible, you can always downsize images to fit a smaller format, say for the Web. If you shoot at a smaller resolution, upsizing an image is more difficult for, say, an 11×14 print or for cropping certain portions of an image. This subject is a no-brainer; shoot at the highest resolution possible. You cover any situation you need for output of your images when you get to that point of the digital workflow.

The rule of thumb while shooting photographs is to always set your digital camera at the highest image size available. Unless all you shoot are images for the Web and nothing else, choose the largest resolution available for your camera. Figure 6-4 illustrates the difference between shooting in low resolution versus high resolution.

Digital SLR file sizes are larger than consumer or prosumer (higher end digital cameras meant for the serious consumer or professional) digital cameras with the same sensor megapixel size. The reason? Digital SLRs contain larger sensors, meaning images actually contain more information. Not only that, digital SLRs have bigger pixels.

Digital camera sensor size does make a difference in quality given the fact that an 8-megapixel Digital SLR produces better quality images for an 8×10 print than an 8-megapixel consumer grade digital camera. That doesn't mean that your 8-megapixel camera can't produce stunning 8×10s. The difference comes when you want to do a lot of cropping in Photoshop or enlarge a print to 11×14 or 16×20. The digital SLR wins out every time, as shown in Figure 6-4.

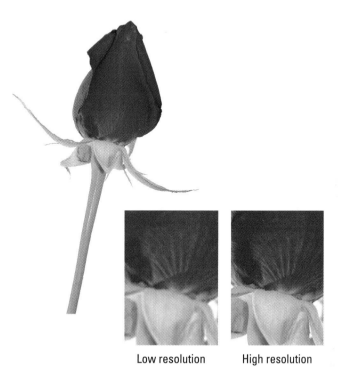

Low resolution   High resolution

Figure 6-4: Shooting in high resolution provides a much crisper image than low resolution.

Typically, image sizes for an 8-megapixel digital SLR sensor comes in three flavors in your camera's menu setup, as shown in Table 6-1:

Table 6-1	Eight Megapixel Digital SLR Image Quality Settings		
Size	*Number of Pixels*	*Size Setting*	*Tips on Usage*
3,456×2,304	8 megapixel setting	Large	Large prints of 13×19, 16×20 or larger. Great image detail for complex landscapes and portraits.
2,496×1,664	4 megapixel setting	Medium	5×7 or 8×10 prints. Typically matches the top quality of a consumer digital camera.
1,728×1,152	2 megapixel setting	Small	Good for the Web.

Though consumer or prosumer can have the same megapixel rating as a digital SLR, manufacturers have to cram the same amount of pixels into a smaller image sensor. This results in a difference in quality from an 8-megapixel prosumer camera and a professional 8-megapixel digital SLR. Now don't go throwing out your spanking new 7- or 8-megapixel camera! The images you are capturing with that camera still rock and are of a quality that you never need to exceed.

Many professionals use these cameras as backups and for everyday shooting. I just purchased one that I use as an everyday carry around camera and a backup to my professional equipment. These cameras are now sporting VR (vibration reduction) and some big lenses that reach from 37mm all the way past 400mm in focal length. Many of these cameras boost some great macro capability as well.

Beating the value in the latest high-end prosumer digital camera offerings is really hard. These cameras provide you with high megapixel sizes, professional quality lenses, and focal lengths from wide angle to super telephoto. These cameras, such as the one shown in Figure 6-5, offer a great alternative to a much more expensive digital SLR system with interchangeable lenses.

Photo courtesy of Sony Electronics, Inc.

Figure 6-5: High-end prosumer digital cameras, such as this Sony, produce professional results.

Setting the Proper ISO

Back before photographers were using digital cameras, they purchased film in different sensitivities. The lower the sensitivity rating (ISO), the finer the grain. My landscapes were always shot at the lowest ISO rated transparency (slide) film I could get, usually at 50 ISO. If I wanted to shoot indoors with low light and action, I'd purchase film at ISO ratings of 200, 400, or even 800, but had to live with increased grain in my shots.

As in film cameras, digital cameras inherited the ISO ratings that indicate their sensitivity to light and subjectivity to image noise, as shown in Figure 6-6. A digital camera set to an ISO level of 100 is comparable to a film camera loaded up with ISO 100 film. Most digital cameras today have a standard ISO setting of 100. Some digital cameras even offer the lowest ISO at 50, and others have the lowest available ISO at 200.

When you increase the ISO of a digital camera, the sensor output is increased or amplified to allow for less light. The amplification that occurs when you increase the ISO setting has a side effect, image noise. Higher image noise is illustrated in Figure 6-6. The good news is that manufacturers are improving the noise levels for high ISOs with every new release.

ISO 200   ISO 800

Figure 6-6: Low ISO versus high ISO. Image noise increases at higher ISO settings.

Wherever possible, set your camera to the lowest ISO you can for the best possible image quality. If you are shooting in low light situations or fast action, you need to increase the ISO in order to achieve the necessary shutter speeds, but doing so may increase the amount of image noise in your camera.

Setting White Balance

One of the few settings that is actually unique to digital cameras is the white balance setting. Setting white balance is the process of telling your camera which lighting type — cloudy, flash, sunny, shade, and so on — you're working with. White balance would be a lot easier to understand if they'd just call it the lighting type setting. I'm going to check to see if I can patent that idea, but in the mean time, I'll explain the concept.

When you change the white balance setting, you are just telling your camera to compensate for the type of light that is illuminating the subject. Light that illuminates a landscape on a bright sunny day is different from the light on a cloudy day. Indoor lighting produced by incandescent light is different from the light produced by those nasty fluorescent lights. Your eyes adjust really well to these different lighting conditions, and your camera needs to adjust to the lighting type as well, either automatically or by manually setting the white balance setting, as illustrated in Figure 6-7. Like I said, they should call it the lighting type setting. I'll let you know how the patent idea goes.

Daylight   Cloudy   Shade

Tungsten   Fluorescent   Custom

Figure 6-7: The white balance setting greatly affects the color temperature of your photos.

Did I mention that they should have called it the lighting type setting? To illustrate my revolutionary concept, the list that follows explains the different white balance settings on your digital camera and gives tips on using each.

- **Auto.** The camera automatically calculates the white balance. Automatic white balance may provide inconsistent results based on the subject matter. Setting the white balance manually dependent on the lighting situation is best.

- **Daylight.** Typical outdoor lighting. Use this setting to shoot outdoors on sunny days. Try the cloudy white balance setting: It adds warmth to your image.

- **Incandescent.** Indoor lighting. Typical household lighting using regular light bulbs.

- **Fluorescent.** Indoor lighting using fluorescent bulbs. Use this while photographing indoors in office and commercial buildings.

- **Cloudy.** Outdoors on cloudy or partly cloudy conditions. This setting works well in many different lighting conditions. Can provide extra warmth to photographs. Experiment using this setting.

- **Flash.** Set white balance to the flash setting when using your onboard flash or external flash. Some digital cameras automatically set the white balance to flash when you attach an external flash or use the built-in flash for your camera.

- **Shade.** Outdoors in shaded light. Experiment viewing the image on your LCD in outdoor situations.

When it comes to white balance, leave nothing to chance. Unless you're shooting in automatic mode, manually set your white balance. If it's cloudy outside and you're shooting landscapes, set the white balance to cloudy. If you are indoors shooting in an office building, set the white balance to fluorescent. If shooting with a flash, make sure you set the white balance to flash.

Use your LCD to review your images to make sure you are setting the white balance correctly. Experiment by shooting the same subject at different white balance settings.

Painting with Light

The word photography is actually Greek or Latin or something for *writing with light*. Regardless of what language, you get the point. The word *photo* literally means light. The word *graph* literally means write. If you really think about it, when you photograph a subject, you are actually capturing the light that is reflected off the subject. How you meter and balance your lighting is vital to photographing exceptional images.

One of the hardest things to do in photography is to get the lighting just right for a particular subject. Controlling or using light is an art upon itself, and I know of many professional photographers that have mastered the craft. You see their work every day in magazines, books, galleries, billboards, and CD covers. Next time you come across an interesting photograph, think about the lighting the photographer used to paint his subject.

Taking advantage of outdoor lighting

Have you ever grabbed your camera for that great shot of your friends or family at that perfect moment when they are doing something considered classic? You fire up the camera, point, and shoot. After reviewing the photograph, you find that the surroundings looked good but that their faces were all dark. Next time, switch spots so that *your* back is to the sun.

Another example would be a situation of driving through the country and pulling over to the side of the road to photograph a really neat vista. After loading the image into Photoshop, you find that it was too bright outside and the colors are washed out, as shown in Figure 6-8.

Figure 6-8: High noon on a sunny day could mean flat images with washed out colors and lack of shadows.

Outdoor photographers prefer to do their shooting early in the day, late afternoon, or early evening. At those times, the bright sun is not directly overhead, washing out shadows. If you shoot early or late in the day, the sun is illuminating your subjects from lower angles, casting interesting colors and shadows that make for great landscape photos.

No matter how many strobes, flashes, hot lights, reflectors, and softboxes you add to your arsenal, nothing compares to the light Mother Nature provides. Outdoor photographers learn to master outdoor lighting for their landscapes. Portrait photographers can tell you the best lighting for portraits is outdoor lighting on a cloudy day.

Figure 6-9 shows you an example of how the best lighting for shooting fall foliage is just after a long downpour. The trees are soaked so they look dark; the lighting is softened by heavy cloud-cover. Perfect to capture rich color contrasted against dark trees.

Figure 6-9: The best time to photograph trees and fall foliage is right after it rains.

Capturing that magic light

Many nature photographers strive to record the magic light nature provides. Nature photographers refer to magic light as the dramatic lighting that appears just before sunrise or just after sunset. The image shown here illustrates how the sun can accentuate color and shadows just before it rises above the horizon. The window of opportunity can be only 5 or 10 minutes. Yep, it means getting up early or staying up late, especially during the summer months. If you are one of those that like to sleep in, you are missing some of the most dramatic light and photo opportunities nature provides. Grab a tripod and check it out one morning or evening. You won't be disappointed. Remember, you can always sleep during the day!

Foolproof outdoor digital photography

Outdoor photography is all about mastering the lighting situations you are faced with. Mother Nature provides enough surprises to make it impossible to plan ahead most of the time. The best rule of thumb for outdoor photography is *plan* on doing the *unplanned*.

The last time I ventured out on a fall color-shooting trip, I wound up with most of my days in torrential rains and 50 miles per hour sustained winds. So much for my plan on capturing those killer colorful forest shots. Instead of wasting those precious stormy few days in the camper watching the Weather Channel, I threw my gear in the van and decided to shoot the weather itself. Figure 6-10 shows you that you can always adjust to the weather conditions and still come home with some interesting photographs.

Figure 6-10: Photograph the wind and motion if you are stuck with a windy day.

Beating the weather and taking advantage of the lighting conditions thrown at you is half the challenge and half the fun of outdoor photography. I offer some other outdoor strategies to keep in mind when trying to take advantage of unique lighting and weather conditions:

- **If it's raining, get the polarizing filter and shoot the forest.** My best forest shots in spring, summer, or fall came on rainy days. I slap a polarizing filter on my digital camera to reduce glare and enhance color saturation.

- **Use your feet.** Get out of the car and walk the trails. You never know where you can wind up and what photographs are available around the bend. Look for rocks, water reflections, mossy areas, and caves.

- **Always shoot with a tripod**. You're going to hear this a lot in this book, but even if your digital camera has VR (vibration reduction), use a tripod anyway.

- **If it's too sunny out, shoot in the shadows.** No sense in wasting the middle of the day napping. You can still get some great shots, such as the one shown in Figure 6-11, on a sunny day. Try shooting in the shadows this time. Napping is overrated anyway.

- **Keep plenty of Twinkies on hand.** Hiking and outdoor photography can be tiring. Keep those Twinkies and bottles of water handy. If you are into healthy foods, maybe some trail mix or health bars would be nice.

✓ **Photograph subjects other than the trees.** While you are hiking and looking for vistas, look around for other subjects, such as colorful reflections, flowers, or mushrooms. Most digital cameras have a macro mode: Take advantage of it!

✓ **Photograph the local architecture.** On your outdoor travels, make sure to capture some of the local man-made scenery; you can add these interesting structures to your portfolio.

✓ **Follow the water.** If you are fortunate enough to come across a river or stream, such as in Figure 6-12, follow it for a while. You can discover some interesting photographs you didn't see at first.

Figure 6-11: Shoot in the shadows during the sunny part of the day.

Using natural light

Ever been in a situation when you had to spend an hour with a friend, family member, or co-worker poring over the photographs of their latest vacation or holiday at their house? I'm sure you were polite and tried to at least look interested, but if you look through all the piles of photographs they are boring you with, chances are they all have one thing in common. Most of the shots were probably taken indoors with flash. I bet the last time you had seen so many red-eyes was when you were cramming for finals!

A simple technique to add impact and artistic qualities to your photographs is by using natural light. Natural light comes from a source that you don't have to have batteries or an electrical outlet for, and it's all-natural. Using and controlling natural light for your subjects greatly improves your photographs, making them more artistic, more interesting, and sets your photos apart from the rest. Remember though; be polite when viewing the pictures taken by others!

One technique to use for capturing still lifes is the use of existing light. For some photographs, it sure beats all those wires and strobes. Natural light often provides some of the best lighting for many subjects that just can't be duplicated with the use of strobes or flashes. Natural and existing light sources provide more accurate color rendition and reduces shadows and harsh lighting in still life shots, as shown in Figure 6-13.

Figure 6-12: Follow streams and rivers to discover scenes you may have normally missed.

Figure 6-13: Natural light used for still life photographs provide soft wrap-around lighting.

Using natural lighting for portraits

For portraits, nothing renders natural soft skin tones better than setting your subject in front of a window. To reduce contrast, try moving your subject a few feet away from the window to let the light wrap around more evenly.

For best results, always shoot your subjects with your camera mounted on a tripod. Unless you're dealing with very bright light, your light is more subdued, resulting in slower shutter speeds.

The portrait shown in Figure 6-14 shows a very natural photograph with simple lighting through a window on a cloudy day. I positioned my model about four feet away from the window, thus reducing the light to her back, allowing for dramatic contrast around her to bring just enough light to illuminate her face.

Figure 6-14: To avoid harsh contrast, try moving your subject a few feet away from the window.

Digital flash

In the old days of using film cameras, you needed to spend a lot of time trying to figure out flash settings due to the fact almost all flash usage was manual. Today's digital cameras with their built-in lenses and awesome metering almost always come equipped with a built-in flash.

Most think of flash photography as something to use indoors when it's dark, or at night when there isn't any light at all. The fact is that you can use flash photography to improve the quality of many photographs in many situations. Technology has come a long way, to the point where flash is now an integral part of the digital camera as opposed to just an add-on.

Using built-in flash

Most compact digital cameras that do have built-in flash usually have similar capabilities in common. These digital cameras at a minimum offer the basic on or off modes and often offer these flash capabilities:

✔ **Default Mode:** Used in all around low-light photography, this is your camera's automatic setting when you turn the flash on. Digital cameras often calculate exposures when flash is turned on, often resulting in correct exposures.

To avoid washing out your subjects with light, using flash at distances greater than a few feet is best.

✔ **Red-eye Reduction Mode:** Most digital cameras come with the capability of emitting a series of pre-flashes that triggers the eyes' pupils to get smaller, reducing the red-eye effect.

✔ **Slow Sync:** This mode is used for shooting in dark situations, usually outdoors at night. The camera sets a slow shutter speed and fires the flash. The flash lights up close subjects and allows the background to be exposed, as shown in Figure 6-15.

Figure 6-15: Use slow sync mode outdoors at night for some great photos.

- ✔ **Fill Flash:** Fill flash is actually a technique and may not even be labeled as a mode on your camera. Fill flash is used in brightly lit, often outdoor situations where you want your subject to stand out. Fill flash eliminates shadows on a person's face and brighten eyes that are dark due to strong overhead lighting. Fill flash is best used to provide light, to even out the lighting between the subject and the background. To use fill flash, set your camera to flash on, which is usually a manual setting.

- ✔ **Flash Compensation:** Many digital cameras let you manually adjust the amount of strength of the flash by allowing you to dial the flash up or down, usually by a button represented by +/–. Experiment with tuning your flash upwards or down to achieve the best results.

Most digital cameras today do a great job metering scenes with the use of flash. Read your user's manual to learn how to use each of the different flash modes that your camera has. Experiment to find which modes work best for you.

Auxiliary flash units

One of the most important accessories you can buy for your digital camera is an auxiliary flash. Using an auxiliary flash (see Figure 6-16) enables you to improve the overall quality of your photographs greatly by providing greater lighting options for you that your built-in flash just cannot provide.

Figure 6-16: Auxiliary flash units offer zoom heads that tilt for using bounce flash.

More advanced cameras allow you to attach external flash to your camera. These flashes are known as *auxiliary* flash units. Auxiliary flash units are more powerful than built-in flashes and emit light greater distances. These external flashes come with the advanced capability of being used wirelessly with other multiple flash units if teamed up with a particular manufacturer's system, such as the Nikon iTTL or the Canon eTTL advanced lighting systems.

In addition to providing more light for your subjects, auxiliary flash units may have the capability to rotate the flash heads, as shown in Figure 6-16, provide for better coverage at wide-angle, and have more advanced modes, such as high-speed sync and balanced fill flash.

Advanced flash units contain a zoom head that automatically matches the focal length of the camera's lens. Consult your camera's owner's manual for a list of compatible auxiliary flash units.

All about red-eye

Whether you are using film or digital cameras, one of the effects of using built-in flash is that horrible red-eye that appears in your photos. Red-eye is caused by electronic flashes lighting up the blood vessels in the back of the eye. The problem of red-eye is more common when the flash is closest to the lens, using a longer focal length lens setting, or when shooting in a dark area, as shown here.

Though most red-eye problems can be cured in Photoshop by using the new Red Eye tool, getting the picture correct out of the camera is still best. The best method is to turn on red-eye reduction in the camera. When red-eye reduction is turned on, the camera emits a series of pre-flashes that cause your subject's pupils to close, thus reducing the amount of red-eye on your pictures.

Another method to reduce red-eye in your photos is to use an external flash. By nature, these flashes are usually attached to the camera's hot shoe and are far away enough from the lens to make a difference. With external flash, you can adjust the flash head to bounce the light off the ceiling, thus eliminating red-eye and casting a soft pleasing light on your subjects.

Many advanced models include a pop-up flash that is also an improvement over a typical built-in flash in reducing red-eye. These pop-up flashes place the flash farther away from the lens thus reducing the red-eye effect.

Pointing your flash head toward the ceiling or wall to bounce the light onto your subject as opposed to directly aiming the flash produces a softer light that's less harsh. Bounce flash is a great technique to use especially when shooting portraits, as shown in Figure 6-17.

Figure 6-17: Bounce flash produces softer, more pleasing portraits.

Flash TTL

Today's advanced flash systems, such as the Nikon iTTL, offer an integration into the camera's overall exposure system. Through-the-lens metering (TTL) is the basic process by which the camera achieves accurate flash exposures. In basic TTL, light produced by the flash is reflected through the camera lens and metered by the camera. Today's advanced systems combine this metering with the camera's autofocus lens and zoom flash head on the auxiliary flash to produce more accurate exposure. Both Canon and Nikon's latest flash systems add the capability to use multiple flashes *wirelessly* as used in the photo shown here. The best part about these new advanced flash system features is that all you really need to do to use it is to just attach your auxiliary flash and turn it on. Everything else is automatic.

Choosing Shooting Modes

Ah yes, you have come across a subject you want to photograph. Being a good photographer who follows a basic shooting workflow, you understand what file types and sizes are best for you and you have set up your digital camera accordingly. You have set the ISO and even adjusted the white balance to where your subject looks pretty accurate on your digital camera's LCD. You have decided how you are going to take advantage of the light you have to work with or flash setup to use. With all these decisions worked out, there is one more little detail to consider: Which mode to shoot in?

If you have a question as to what mode you want to use, determine your objective for the image. If you are shooting an action shot, consider using shutter priority mode set to a higher shutter speed to freeze the action. Shooting a photo where you want the entire frame in focus? Shoot in aperture priority and use a high setting, such as f/6 or f/8, to increase your depth of field, as shown in Figure 6-18.

Figure 6-18: Setting your aperture to a smaller setting of f/6 or f/8 brings more of your image in focus.

If your subject is a portrait or still life, which you want to blur the background as shown in Figure 6-19, shoot in aperture priority mode and set your aperture to a low setting, such as f4 to reduce your depth of field. If your subject is wildlife and you are using a long focal length (such as 200 to 300mm on your zoom lens), consider shooting in shutter priority at a high shutter speed. The high shutter speed reduces the "shake" that increases when you zoom in on objects.

Figure 6-19: Large apertures such as f/2 result in blurred foregrounds and backgrounds.

Explaining aperture settings

One of the most confusing concepts to understand in photography is aperture setting. These terms were probably invented by a politician: They say one thing and mean another! When a term is used, such as "stopping down" the lens to increase depth of field, what's really meant is turning *up* the aperture setting! The terms are all backwards. When you stop *down* the lens to a setting of f/11 or f/16, the aperture diaphragm closes down, letting less light to the sensor but increasing focus from foreground to background. In aperture settings, "opening up" means using a lower f/stop setting and "closing down" means using a higher f/stop setting.

To further explain, the term "opening up" a lens actually means using a *lower* aperture setting of F/5.6 or F/4 to let *more* light onto the image sensor. The portion of the image you focus on is sharp where other areas are less sharp.

Remember that *up* means lower setting and less focus of the foreground and background. *Down* means a higher setting and more focus of foreground and background. Just like politics.

I've listed the advantages and disadvantages of each shooting mode in the text that follows. As you shoot more photographs, you will improve greatly in your ability to use these shooting modes to your advantage, helping you obtain the images you visualize.

- **Aperture Priority.** Adjust the aperture setting to increase or decrease the depth of field of your photo. Smaller numbers, such as f/2, open the aperture diaphragm up and let more light into the sensor while reducing depth of field. Larger aperture settings reduce the diaphragm size and let less light in. The digital camera automatically sets shutter speed. For shots where you want a blurred background, reduce your aperture to f/2 or F/4. To increase depth of field and increase the focus of both foreground and background, increase the aperture setting to f/8 or higher.

- **Shutter Priority.** Adjust the shutter speed and the camera automatically sets the aperture. For action shots where you want to freeze action, use a higher shutter speed, such as 1/500 of a second. To get a blurred effect of moving subjects such as a waterfall, reduce the shutter speed to 1/10 of a second.

- **Manual.** The photographer manually sets both shutter speed *and* aperture. Use this mode when experimenting with special effects type shots or when shooting in odd circumstances, such as long exposures at night.

- **Automatic.** The digital camera calculates the optimal combination of aperture, shutter speed, and ISO sensitivity based on the exposure value determined by the camera's metering system. Automatic mode may be okay to use for most snapshots and even portraits.

- **Creative.** Some digital cameras come with pre-programmed modes, such as sports, portrait, and landscape modes. Use these modes until you're ready to experiment with aperture or shutter priority modes: Most results are sufficient.

Exposure compensation

Exposure compensation, also known as EV (exposure value) compensation is a feature common on prosumer or professional digital camera models. Most of these cameras adjust to a –2.0 EV to +2.0 EV. Exposure compensation is a good tool to use when your camera is producing images that are under or over exposed.

Sometimes the camera meters the light incorrectly and adjusts the shutter and/or aperture (depending if you are using aperture or shutter priority) according to your ISO setting. The combination of aperture, shutter speed, and ISO setting = EV (Exposure Value). Exposure compensation allows for an adjustment to the camera's overall metering per your choosing by subtracting or increasing exposure value to each metered scene.

If you are out taking photos of the family or friends during an outdoor outing and your photos appear overexposed, you may want to reduce the amount of light hitting your sensor. In this case, you can set your exposure compensation to a –1 in order to tone down the metered exposure a bit. If your shots are coming out underexposed, try turning exposure compensation up to +1. These images illustrate the results of using exposure compensation to adjust the final metering of your subject. After you become more familiar with your digital camera's metering system, you will become more proficient in estimating the + or – EV settings to make in order to come out with correct exposures.

Chapter 7

Shooting Sharper Images

*T*here is one thing in the quest for inner peace and tranquility that is the pursuit of the art of photography that makes the creative soul explode in a fury: an unfocused, fuzzy picture. Photo enthusiasts like you and me tote these high-tech digital cameras around their necks (it looks cool). You study subjects, try different angles, get on your knees, and stand on your head to frame the killer photo. After exhaustive photo sessions, the images look good on a 1.8" LCD.

Upon review of your images on your computer, you discover they lack the sharpness needed to print or mount and frame the photo to hang on the wall. You lost the ability to go any further with those shots. If the photos are fuzzy out of the camera, there is nothing you can do in Photoshop to rescue an out of focus photograph.

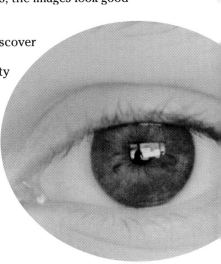

If the fuzzy photo horror story sounds familiar, don't worry! This chapter provides you with the essential steps to achieve sharper images directly out of your digital camera.

Three-Legged Wonders

Tripod is a word meaning three pods. Though the origin of the word is unclear, it is known that *pod* means *leg*. If the word tripod was an English word, I guess it would be called *three legs and a camera attachment thingy on top*. In any case, the number one cure for the common fuzzy photo is the tripod.

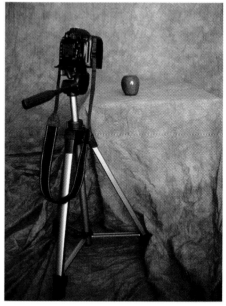

Figure 7-1: Use a tripod whenever possible.

The second best investment you can make after your digital camera is the best tripod you can afford. Equally as important as the tripod is the tripod head. Higher-end models include just the legs; with these, you need to purchase the tripod head separately.

Consider using a tripod for *all* of your photographs, with the exception of situations where you absolutely can't use one, like when you're shooting action shots at a sporting event or taking photos at a party. I use a tripod for all my landscape, still life, and portrait sessions, as shown in Figure 7-1. To make sure I'm covered in all situations, I even carry one in my car at all times. A tripod should be part of your everyday digital camera arsenal.

Tripods provide stable platforms for your digital camera and are essential in consistently achieving sharp photos. Ask any pro the question of how to achieve sharp photos, and I bet he tells you to use a tripod. Tripods do make a difference, especially when enlarging prints, as illustrated in Figure 7-2. Tripods may not be convenient to lug around, but you can get used to it after you see the quality of your images improve greatly.

Without tripod   With tripod

Figure 7-2: Photo taken using a tripod and the same subject without a tripod.

You will absolutely notice the difference in your photographs if you use a tripod whenever possible. The difference made in the sharpness of your photos is visible. When viewing your photographs on a 1.8" LCD, you may not be able to see the sharpness, but when you print your images at 8×10 or larger sizes, you can really tell the difference.

Tips for using a tripod include:

Figure 7-3: Attaching your camera to a tripod using a quick-release plate.

- **Make sure your tripod includes a quick-release plate.** With many of the newer tripods and tripod heads, you can attach a plate to your camera by screwing the plate into the tripod socket. The plate should stay attached to your camera at all times. When you are ready to take some photos, attach the camera to the tripod by sliding the plate into its receptacle on the tripod head and tightening the camera down with the plate attachment lever. This allows for quick connection and de-connection of your camera to the tripod. To remove the camera from the tripod, just open the quick-release lever, as shown in Figure 7-3.

- **Use a tripod that's strong enough to handle your camera.** If you are using a digital SLR and some big lenses with it, make sure your tripod is heavy-duty enough to handle the weight. Manufacturers rate their tripods by how many pounds they can handle. Make sure you have some pounds to spare when it comes to your tripod.

- **Consider a lightweight carbon-fiber model.** Higher end tripods are now made in the extra strong but lightweight carbon fiber material. These tripods are a blessing to landscape photographers who often hike miles to get to their destination and welcome the reduced weight of a tripod to schlep around. These models are a bit more expensive but well worth it if you are an avid shooter.

- **Maintain your tripod.** Like any other piece of valued equipment, you must care for your tripod. After every outdoor photo adventure, make sure your tripod legs are cleaned of dirt and sand. Ignoring your tripod shortens its useful life. If you maintain your equipment, you will get years of use out of it.

Show of Hands?

Even if you have hands as steady as a surgeon's, a case of the shakes can affect your photos. If you are shooting photos without the use of a tripod, you will need to take some simple steps to minimize any movement that will blur your photo. The way you handle your camera makes a huge difference in the sharpness of your photos.

 The best method to stabilize your camera is by holding the bottom of your camera with your left hand while gripping the right side of the camera with your right hand, as shown in Figure 7-4. This goes for both right-handers and left-handers.

Figure 7-4: The proper method for handholding your digital camera.

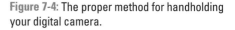

A few other tips to have up your sleeve for handheld shots (no pun intended) include:

- Practice controlled breathing while clicking the shutter. Practice the art of slowly *exhaling* while taking your shot.

- Use your body to create a stable platform. Holding the camera with your right hand while supporting it on the bottom with your left hand, press your elbows against your body and raise the camera to the level where you're comfortable to get the shot. Though you are using an LCD, get in the practice of holding the camera as close to your body as you can.

- Gently press the shutter button half way to focus and then carefully press the shutter the rest of the way to take the photo.

Shooting Secrets for Sharp Photos

In addition to using a tripod or best practices for handheld shooting, your digital camera presents you with options to further make sure your photos are as sharp as you can make them. I often combine the use of a tripod and use in-camera techniques to ensure my photos are sharp. You can say that I use a sharpness workflow.

Use shutter speeds to your advantage

The faster your shutter speed, the greater the chances are that your photo will be sharper. Shutter speed used with or without a tripod plays a critical role in your image sharpness. If you are shooting at slow shutter speeds, your image "picks up" the vibration your camera's shutter makes when you take the picture.

You have a couple of ways to tweak your camera settings to allow for faster shutter speeds. One method is to increase your ISO setting. If the lighting of your subject allows, increase your ISO to the next setting, for example increasing ISO 100 to 200. This 100 percent increase allows you to double the speed your shutter's going to fire at, which can make a difference in the sharpness of your photo, as shown in Figure 7-5.

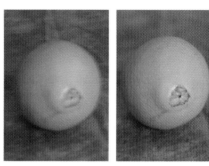

Handheld at slow shutter speed   Handheld at faster shutter speed

Figure 7-5: Faster shutters speeds result in sharper photos.

Be careful with increasing your ISO settings for everyday shooting. It may allow for faster shutter speeds; however, there is a cost: increased image noise. Unless you are using a digital SLR, ISO settings above 200 may result in unacceptable image noise in many digital cameras.

Mirror up!

As if camera folks didn't have enough to deal with when it comes to sharpness, digital and film SLR owners have an additional nagging problem. The problem stems from vibration caused by the internal mirror flipping up when taking the photo. This occurs around $\frac{1}{60}$th of a second and can result in a somewhat blurred photo, even when shot on a tripod.

Some digital SLR cameras come equipped with a function to lock the mirror up in position. This function is called *mirror up*. When you set your camera to mirror up, the first click of the shutter flips the internal mirror to the up position. The second click of the shutter button fires the shutter to take the photo. Mirror up eliminates any vibration caused by the mirror flipping when shooting photographs.

Do not confuse the mirror up function with the function that some cameras have that locks the mirror in the up position so that you can clean the sensor. Same name; different purposes. An example of this is the Nikon D70 digital SLR's mirror up function: Its purpose is to clean the sensor, not to reduce vibration during shooting.

Continuous shooting mode

I'm sure you are used to shooting wild leopards and gazelles running 50 miles per hour over the great African plains. Like the good world traveling photographer that you are, you put your digital camera into continuous shooting mode to make sure you capture focused frames while you pan the animal running across the open vista. Little did you know that continuous shooting mode can be used to produce sharper photos as well, even if you never do go on safari.

Continuous shooting, also known as *burst* mode, is used to fire off a series of frames with one push of the shutter. The first of these frames may be blurry from the vibration caused by pressing the shutter, but subsequent

Figure 7-6: A series of continuous rapid shots. Sharpness varies shot by shot.

frames in the burst may turn out sharper than the first, as shown in Figure 7-6. Try this on your own for both moving and still subjects, and you will discover some images will be sharper than others.

Get rid of the shakes

Vibration reduction, also referred to as image stabilization, is becoming increasingly popular on prosumer digital camera models. The technology is incorporated in one of two ways: The camera itself has built-in capability to reduce vibration, or the lens contains the capability to reduce vibration.

Digital cameras with large focal length lenses, say 35mm to over 400mm, can really use the built-in vibration reduction technology, especially when you use these cameras at the longer end of their lenses focal length. Digital SLR manufacturers are now building the technology into their SLR lenses. Canon markets lenses with their IS (Image Stabilization) version, while Nikon makes lenses with their VR (Vibration Reduction) version.

Whether the technology to reduce vibration is built-in to the camera or the lenses, camera manufacturers are now offering the ability to shoot sharper photos handheld at slow shutter speeds. For example, a shot taken at 200mm requiring a shutters speed of over 1/200 of a second to be sharp would require a shutter speed of only 1/60th of a second with vibration reduction technology.

Your Sweet Spot

Shot at wide open

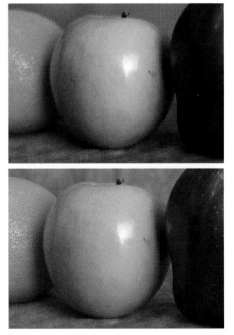

One of the best-kept secrets of the Secret Society of Really Good Digital Photographers (SSORGDP) is to shoot many photos using your lens' *sweet spot*. Every lens made has a sweet spot. The sweet spot is the particular aperture setting of the lens that produces the sharpest image.

On many lenses, the sweet spot would typically be two stops from the maximum aperture of the lens (the lowest f/stop number). On a lens with the maximum aperture of 1.8, move two stops up and the sweet spot is f5.6, as shown in Figure 7-7.

If your lens has a maximum aperture of 2.8 and a minimum of F/22, not using either of those two settings to shoot with is best. Even on procaliber lenses, it's still a good idea to shoot a few stops from the extreme ends of the aperture range.

Shot with lens sweet spot

Figure 7-7: Compare these two photos, one at the max aperture and one in the sweet spot.

By the way, there really isn't a Secret Society of Really Good Photographers or anything else called SSORGDP having to do with digital photography. (I looked it up on the Internet just to be sure.) I made it all up just to make a point. Upon further thought though, maybe someone should start one.

Part III
Setting Up a Photoshop Workflow

The 5th Wave By Rich Tennant

©RICHTENNANT.COM

Jeez—that's impressive! Let's see that airbrush effect again.

To become a better digital photographer, you need to get a new best friend. I don't mean for you to blow off your buddies. I mean get a new best friend in the sense of setting up a Photoshop workflow. Get in the habit of following a system to set up the Photoshop environment, to calibrate your monitor, to correct color settings, and to manage your images.

Knowing your way around Photoshop and setting it up for working with images is half the battle. When you get everything set up, you'll find yourself enjoying the experience of developing your own pictures using Photoshop as your digital darkroom. Fun is what it's all about!

Chapter 8

The Photoshop Working Environment

*W*e live in a world of instant gratification. Our lives are enriched by fast food at our desks, fast Internet connections on our computers, and simple but entertaining Web pages. We expect our e-mails to come up on the screen instantly and hope our inbox is full of funny jokes and links from our friends. At least I do! During a busy day, time is money and our Web surfing and personal e-mail needs to be quick so the boss doesn't notice what we are doing at his expense. I hope my boss isn't reading this!

Photoshop is not one of those software programs that you quickly load up on your computer and rip right into it. It is not a word processor or a spreadsheet that's ready to go the minute you load the program CD onto your computer. Like all professional tools, Photoshop has a few elements that need attention before you begin creating your works of art.

If you are new to Photoshop, have just started, or about to load up CS2 on your computer, much of this chapter will be valuable to you. This chapter is dedicated to showing you how to properly set up image modes, change default settings, get comfortable with the Toolbox, and a little bit more about some Photoshop features you will use on a regular basis.

Un-Defaulting Photoshop

Before you do any serious editing to your photographs, tweaking some of the Photoshop default settings to your particular needs is important. Photoshop comes out of the box "generic." It's not exactly set up for press and layout work, and it's not exactly set up for photographers either.

For basic settings to customize your work environment, Photoshop Preferences can be modified to better suit your needs. You can modify Photoshop Preferences by changing settings in a series of nine windows that you can access separately or by clicking Next in each Preferences window, as shown in Figure 8-1.

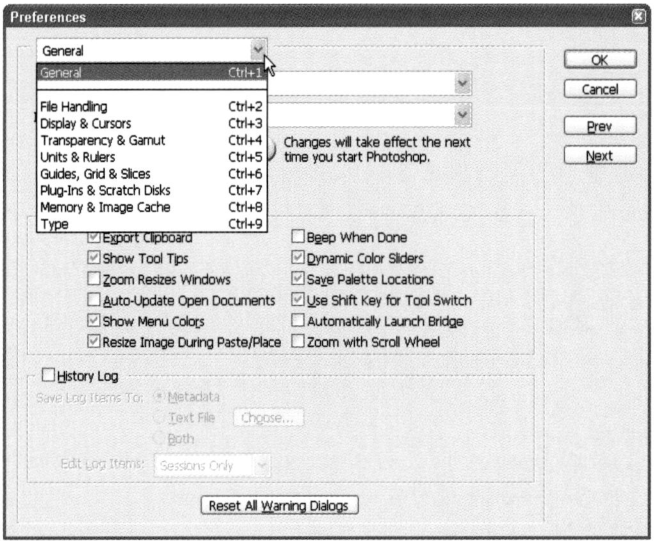

Figure 8-1: The Photoshop Preferences General window links to eight other Preferences windows.

Most of the settings in the nine Preferences windows can be left as is. For digital photographers there are a few settings that may come in handy for you in each of the Preferences windows:

  ✔ **General (Ctrl+1/⌘+1).** This window contains general settings that you can modify, such as starting Bridge with Photoshop, font sizes, and default interpolation methods.

If you want to have Bridge automatically appear when you start Photoshop, check the Automatically Launch Bridge check box in the Options section, as shown in Figure 8-2. I always keep this box checked, because I do want to view my images through Bridge. I also check Zoom with Scroll Wheel, because I want to use this feature with my mouse.

Figure 8-2: The Options section of the Preferences General window.

🖙 **File Handling (Ctrl+2/⌘+2).** File saving and file compatibility settings are in this window.

I usually leave these settings as defaults except for the number of files I want to view when I click the File menu. The default for this setting is 10. I prefer to view the last 20 images I worked on. Just type in the number of images you want to view in the Recent File List Contains field.

🖙 **Display and Cursor (Ctrl+3/⌘+3).** These settings allow you to specify defaults for brush tips and cursors.

Especially when using layer masks, you use different brushes for painting in effects with your images. Consider changing the default brush tips you use in the Painting Cursors section shown in Figure 8-3.

🖙 **Transparency and Gamut (Ctrl+4/⌘+4).** Settings for transparency (transparent background), grids, and colors are here.

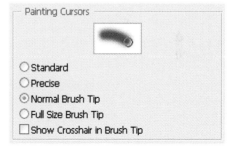

Figure 8-3: The Painting Cursors section of the Display and Cursor Settings window.

I prefer to leave these settings as their Photoshop defaults.

🖙 **Units and Rulers (Ctrl+5/⌘+5).** You can find the default settings for new document resolution and units of measure here.

The most important setting in this window for photographers is located in the New Document Preset Resolutions section shown in Figure 8-4. When you create a new document, this setting sets its default resolution. Photographers usually prefer their output resolution to either be set at 300dpi or 360dpi.

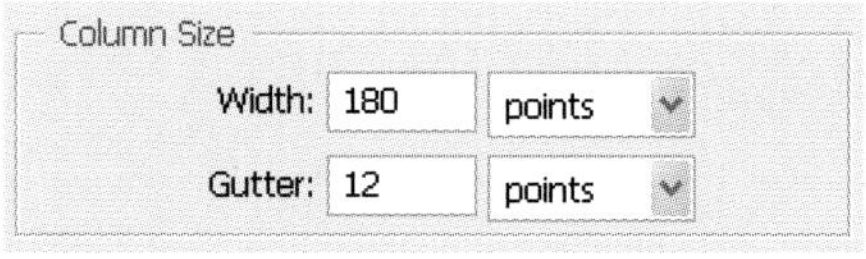

Figure 8-4: The New Documents Preset Resolutions section of the Units and Rulers window.

There is much debate as to the optimum resolution to print at. Truth of the matter is that it depends on the image. For most photo quality printers, 300dpi suffices. For professional grade printers, some photographers prefer to print at 360dpi. Chapter 18 covers more details on printing.

✒ **Guides, Grid, and Slices (Ctrl+6/⌘+6).** This window includes the default colors for guides and grids.

As a digital photographer, I really do not need to adjust any of these settings. Colors and styles for Guides, Grids, and Slices is a personal choice, so please feel free to express yourself!

✒ **Plug-Ins and Scratch Disks (Ctrl+7/⌘+7).** These settings establish where scratch disks are to be stored and indicate where additional plug-in folders can be located on your computer.

Many advanced users of Photoshop use third-party plug-ins as part of their Photoshop arsenal. Instead of loading these plug-ins into the same default Photoshop plug-in folder, they load these in a separate folder. Indicate where these third party plug-ins are located by clicking the Additional Plug-Ins Folder check box and then selecting the folder, as shown in Figure 8-5.

Older plug-ins may require a Photoshop serial number to operate. If you are using these plug-ins, you can type your old Photoshop serial number in the Legacy Photoshop serial number field.

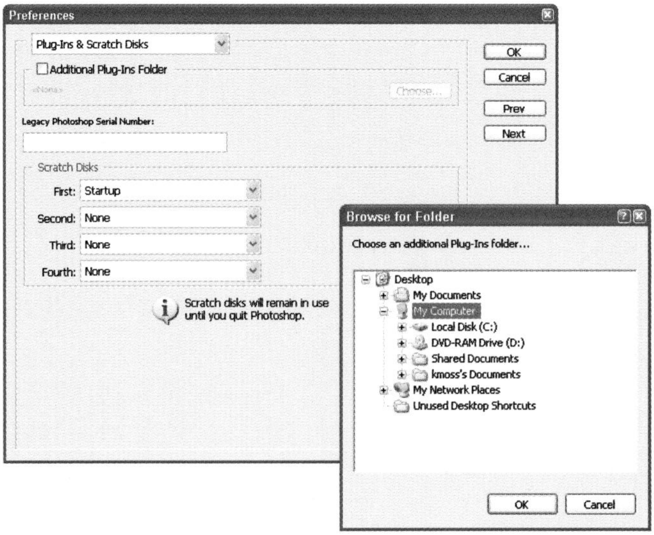

Figure 8-5: The Plug-Ins and Scratch Disk window with the Browse for Folder dialog box.

Some computers do not have enough internal memory for Photoshop to run some operations. Photoshop uses a special technology that allows it to use a part of your hard disk to simulate system memory. Photoshop proceeds to the first, second, third, or fourth scratch disk as these disks run out of space.

Scratch disks only provide temporary resources to Photoshop. Any disk space used during Photoshop operations is not saved permanently to the disk and is deleted when you exit Photoshop.

✔ **Memory and Image Cache (Ctrl+8/⌘+8).** Use this window to determine how much computer memory you can dedicate toward Photoshop operations.

Photoshop is one of those programs that uses as much memory as you can spare. Even though it runs with 256MB of RAM, it's recommended that you at least have 512MB available. Indicate the amount of *available* RAM you would like to dedicate toward Photoshop in the Memory and Image Cache window. The default is 70 percent, but I usually bump this setting up to 80 percent in the Maximum Used by Photoshop field shown in Figure 8-6.

> **Memory Usage**
> Available RAM: 379MB
> Maximum Used by Photoshop: 70 ▸ % = 265MB

Figure 8-6: The Memory Usage section of the Memory and Image Cache window.

✔ **Type (Ctrl+9/⌘+9).** These settings indicate font preview size and language preference for font display.

Nothing really to report here, unless you want to view your font previews in different sizes other than the default setting, Medium. You can change the size of font previews by changing the Font Preview Size.

Selecting Photo Editing Modes

Before you begin the grand adventure of editing your photographs in Photoshop, one important step in your image editing workflow needs to be considered before you begin work on your image: Setting up the type of color and bit modes you will work in while editing your image. You select these choices by choosing the Edit ➪ Mode menu.

Explaining color modes

Before you begin work on a photo, knowing what the image is going to be used for is a pretty good idea. Is the image to be printed on your inkjet photo printer? Displayed on the Web? Used for prepress? The answers to these questions determine which color mode you choose.

The color mode simply lets you determine which color method Photoshop is to use to first display your image while editing and then to output (print) your image. Color modes represent particular numerical color describing methods, also called *color models*.

Choices for color modes used for digital photographers in Photoshop include

- **Bitmap:** Not used for digital photographs. Uses black or white color values to represent pixels in an image.

- **Grayscale:** This mode is used if the original image opened in Photoshop is already a black-and-white image. Most of your photographs captured with a digital camera or acquired using a film scanner are color.

  To produce black-and-white photos in Photoshop, stick with editing the image in your normal color mode and convert to black-and-white later, as described in more detail in Chapter 14.

- **Duotone:** Not used for digital photographs. Duotone is a mode used for specific printing purposes related to two-color print jobs.

- **RGB (Red, Green, Blue):** For digital photographers, RGB is the standard color mode used for editing photographs in Photoshop. RGB is the default color mode and is automatically set up for you when you install Photoshop.

  Unless you are preparing images for prepress or other special purposes, leave RGB as your standard color mode for editing your images in Photoshop.

- **CMYK (Cyan, Magenta, Yellow, Black):** Another standard color mode used in Photoshop, CMYK mode is used mostly for preparing images where color separation is needed for printing press processes.

  Use the Proof Setup command by choosing View ➪ Proof Colors or by pressing Ctrl+Y (⌘+Y on the Mac). You can use this command to soft proof a conversion from RGB without making any actual changes to the file in RGB mode. The Proof Colors command shows you the differences between RGB and CMYK as well as ensuring that your colors are within the gamut of your output device. (Choose View ➪ Proof Setup to select your output device.)

  When it's necessary to submit images for commercial printing, edit your images in RGB mode, and then convert your image to CMYK for your final submission.

✔ **Lab:** Used to edit some Photo CD images, Lab color mode is the interme-
diate model used by Photoshop to convert from one color mode to
another. For digital photographers, Lab color mode is rarely used.

✔ **Multichannel:** Not normally used for digital photographs. Multichannel
mode is used only for specialized printing applications.

The bits have it

The final choice for image modes to set up for working with your images in
Photoshop is to choose either 8- or 16-bit mode to work in. Whether you edit
your image in 8- or 16-bit mode may also depend on your original image. If
you capture JPEG images in your digital camera, the only choice you have is
8-bit mode. If you have your digital camera set to capture Raw or TIFF images,
the wonderful world of 16-bit color awaits you.

RGB images are made up of either three 8-bit or 16-bit grayscale channels.
Each of the three channels represents shades of red, green, or blue (hence
the acronym RGB). RGB represents the combination of the primary colors of
light we see. 8-bit images contain up to 16.7 million unique color definitions
of RGB. 16-bit images contain up to 35 *trillion* unique color definitions of RGB.

Okay, this technical stuff is interesting, but how does it affect editing your
digital photos in Photoshop? The answer is simple. Every time you make an
edit to an image, you throw away image information. The more extensive
your edits are, for example changing exposure, color saturation or contrast,
the more data you throw into the trash. You want to make sure you have
plenty of information to work with to guarantee your image edits do not
degrade the color quality of an image.

New to CS2 is the ability to edit images in High Dynamic Range (HDR) mode, a
32-bit image. Though new to digital photographers, 32-bit editing is used primarily for the motion picture industry and some *very* high-end photography.
Using multiple photos, each captured at a different exposure, creates HDR
images.

The bottom line with which mode you use to edit images in Photoshop is to
choose 16-bit mode to guarantee you are editing images with as much information available as possible.

Not all Photoshop features are available to you in 16-bit mode; however, with
each new version of Photoshop, more functions become available. If you are
shooting JPEG images with your digital camera, you are only given the option
to edit your images in 8-bit mode.

Features available for use in 16-bit mode include

- All tools in the Toolbox except the Art History Brush tool.
- All color and tonal adjustment commands (except Variations).
- Layers and adjustment layers.
- An assortment of filters.
- Crop, rotate, and image size adjustments.
- Support for PSD and TIFF files.

If you need to use a Photoshop tool or filter that is not compatible with 16-bit mode, save a copy of the file to retain its 16-bit mode status, and then convert the image to 8-bit mode to use the tool or filter.

Reaching into the Toolbox

The Photoshop Toolbox (see Figure 8-7) includes over 60 tools used for a variety of reasons in your everyday photo and image editing work. Just imagine that you're an artist and you carry an assortment of artist's pencils, brushes, erasers, and a few other tools in your artist's toolbox. Photoshop includes all these tools plus a slew of others not commonly found in an artist's toolbox, such as a Magic Wand or a Healing Brush. Those are tools you can find in a magician's toolbox!

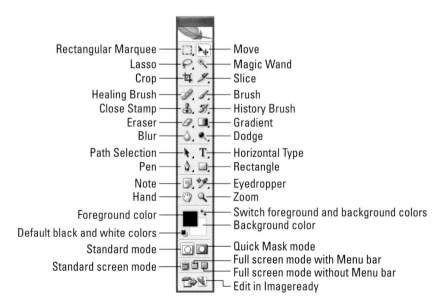

Figure 8-7: The Photoshop Toolbox.

Like a magician, photographers need to know what they have in their bag of tricks and how the commonly used tools work.

The Rectangular Marquee tool

Use the Rectangular Marquee tool to draw rectangles, ellipses, horizontal columns, or vertical columns in an image. Right-clicking the Rectangular Marquee tool brings up the flyout menu that includes other Marquee tools, as shown in Figure 8-8. Using the Rectangular Marquee tool is a quick way to draw a rectangle in your image that you want to crop to.

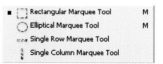

Figure 8-8: The Marquee tools give you four methods of drawing marquees.

The Lasso tool

Use the Lasso tool to corral parts of your image in order to edit the selected portion of the image. The Lasso tool is one of the main methods of making selections within images. The Lasso tool flyout menu, shown in Figure 8-9, offers three methods of creating selections, the Lasso tool, Polygonal Lasso tool, and the Magnetic Lasso tool.

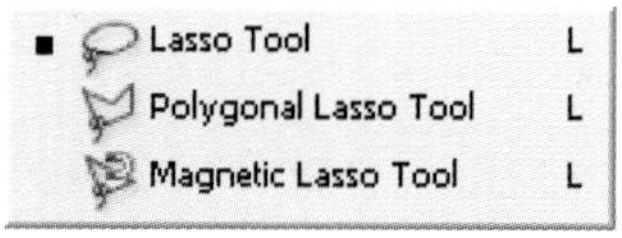

Figure 8-9: Lasso tool flyout menu.

The Lasso tool is commonly used to make selections within your photo that can be easily traced, similar to using tracing paper over a picture to trace an outline. Select the Lasso tool and while holding down the left mouse button, trace over the part of the image you want to select. For more information on the Lasso tool, see Chapter 14.

Cropping with the Crop tool

The crop tool is a simple tool that allows you to draw in parts of your image in which you want to crop, as shown in Figure 8-10. You can specify the width and height of your crop as well as the resolution you want to make the cropped image.

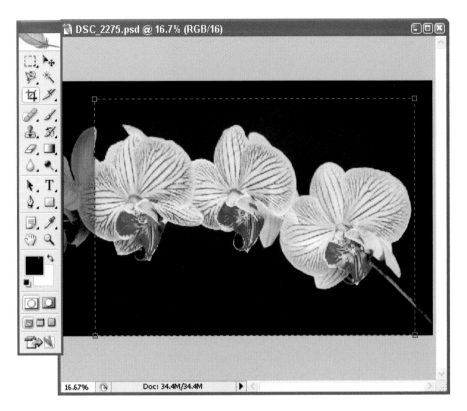

Figure 8-10: Cropping a photo.

Fixing up using the Healing Brush

Among the most powerful tools that Photoshop offers are the Healing Brush tools shown in Figure 8-11. The flyout menu includes four healing brush tools that enable you to correct minor details such as pimples, hair, and dust that appear in places where you usually do not want them. Chapter 14 provides more information on the Healing Brush.

Figure 8-11: Healing Brush flyout menu.

New to CS2 is the Red Eye tool. This tool can be used to quickly and easily remove red eye in your cherished photos.

Cloning around with the Clone Stamp tool

The Clone Stamp tool simply takes a sample of a part of an image and applies that sample to another part of the image. All brush tips work with the Clone Stamp tool, making this tool another great retouching alternative in your arsenal.

The Pattern Stamp tool is also available in the Clone Stamp tool flyout menu, as shown in Figure 8-12. The Pattern Stamp tool re-creates patterns from the cloned selection when applied to another part of the image.

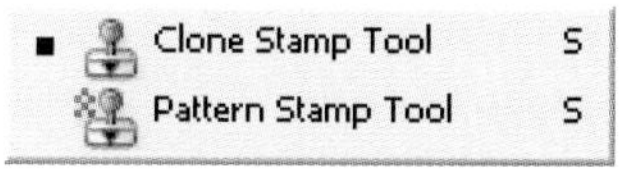

Figure 8-12: The Clone and Pattern Stamp tools.

Removing pixels with the Eraser tool

The Eraser tool is like the eraser you have stashed away in your pencil case. Use the Eraser tool to erase pixels as you move over them with the cursor, changing the pixels according to which eraser you have chosen on the Option bar. Other tools in the flyout menu shown in Figure 8-13 include the Background Eraser and Magic Eraser.

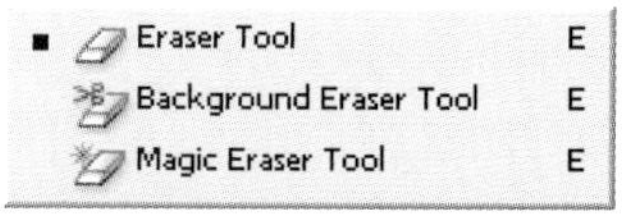

Figure 8-13: The Eraser, Background Eraser, and Magic Eraser tools.

The Eraser tool can do a lot more than just erase pixels. You can use the Eraser tool to remove effects of overall image adjustments made to only certain areas or layers of the image using the Background Eraser tool. To erase all similar pixels within a layer, use the Magic Eraser tool.

Sharpen or blur with the Blur tool

A quick way to blur a portion of your photo or to even sharpen another part is to use the Blur tool, as shown in Figure 8-14. If you are editing a portrait and wanted to get a blurred effect, you can make an overall adjustment to the photo using the Gaussian Blur filter but use the Sharpen tool to selectively sharpen hair and eyes.

Figure 8-14: The Blur, Sharpen, and Smudge tools.

The Smudge tool warps and pushes pixels toward the direction you are dragging the tool, giving you a morphing or *smudge* effect. Like the Liquefy tool, the Smudge tool enables you to achieve some really cool special effects.

Drawing shapes with the Pen tool

The Pen tool actually does more than a pen you use to write letters or checks. The Pen tool in Photoshop creates Beziér, or vector lines, curves, and shapes used for a variety of editing and drawing purposes. The Pen tool flyout menu shown in Figure 8-15 shows different options for the Pen tool, such as the Freeform Pen tool and a variety of anchor-point Pen tools.

Figure 8-15: The Pen tool and flyout menu.

Load up an image and experiment using the Pen and Freeform Pen tools. The Pen tool is a valuable tool in your special effects toolbox when you want to make complex selections.

Leave yourself messages with the Notes tool

A nifty feature to use especially when collaborating with others on the same photograph is the Notes tool, shown in Figure 8-16. When working with others or to remind yourself of specific actions taken on an image, this tool comes in handy.

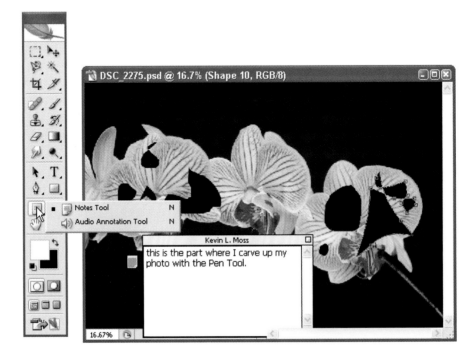

Figure 8-16: Attaching a note to the Photoshop canvas with the Notes tool.

In addition to leaving typed notes within the image, you can also record audio notes if you have a microphone attached to your computer using the Audio Annotation tool.

Abracadabra, the Magic Wand tool

One of the most used tools in the Toolbox is the Magic Wand tool. The Magic Wand is used to make selections, one of the most widely used processes in editing images. The Magic Wand lets you select similar-colored areas of your photo. You can specify the color range and tolerance for the area by indicating these settings on the Option bar.

Figure 8-17 shows the Magic Wand tool selected in the Toolbox and the black background areas selected with the tool. More detailed information on making selections is available in Chapter 14.

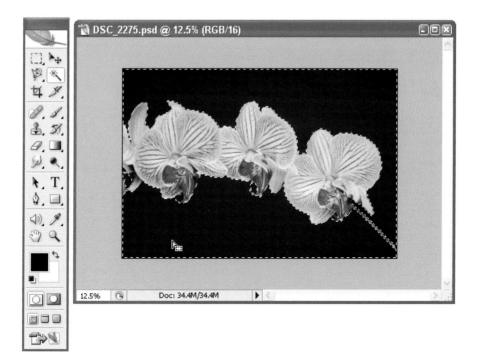

Figure 8-17: Using the Magic Wand to select similarly colored areas of an image.

The Slice tool

The Slice tool is used primarily for Web graphics to create slices, or a rectangular area of an image that you can use to create links, rollovers, and animations. An example of a slice is if you want to carve out a part of an image for a GIF animation while retaining the rest of the image as a high-compression JPEG.

Figure 8-18: The Slice and Slice Select tools.

The Slice tool and Slice Select tools are shown in Figure 8-18.

King of the tools, the Brush tool

The Brush, Pencil, and Color Replacement tools are commonly used elements to brush in changes to your photos. The Brush tool and flyout menu is illustrated in Figure 8-19.

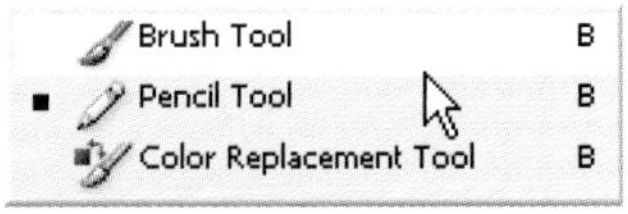

Figure 8-19: The Brush, Pencil, and Color Replacement tools.

Numerous brush sizes, tips, and brush modes are available on the Option bar. They're useful when used in conjunction with many of the Photoshop image editing techniques, which are covered in Chapter 14.

Painting snapshots with the History and Art History Brush tools

You can use the History Brush tool to create special effects by painting a copy of one history or snapshot and applying those changes to an area in the current image window. The History Brush and Art History Brush tools are shown in Figure 8-20.

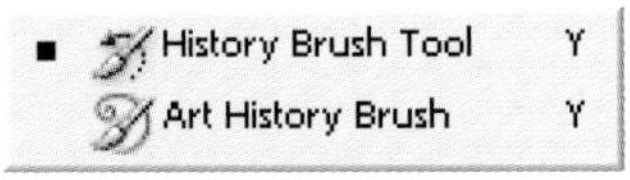

Figure 8-20: The History Brush and Art History Brush tools.

You can use the History Brush tool to selectively apply a change made with a filter, such as a blur effect, and then selectively apply that change only to certain parts of the image.

The History Brush tool copies only from one state or snapshot from a layer to another layer for the *same* location within the image. You can also use the Art History Brush tool to paint in special effects applied to one layer to another layer, giving you the ability to selectively apply artistic effects.

Dodging and burning using Dodge and Burn tools

Back in the day when photographers like me developed photos using enlargers and chemicals, I had a few tricks up my sleeve to touch up my work. Dodging and burning allowed me to darken or lighten certain areas of a print to my liking by either reducing or increasing exposure to certain parts of the print.

Photoshop lets old-timers like me do the same thing with the Dodge and Burn tools shown in Figure 8-21.

Figure 8-21: Dodge, Burn, and Sponge tools.

 The Sponge tool is used to make slight color saturation adjustments to an area. For example, you can decrease the color saturation of a certain area where the color red may be too bright or *blown out,* giving an unnatural look to the photo.

Writing text with the Horizontal Text tools

Used most often by graphic designers, who combine both text and images in their everyday work, the Horizontal and Vertical Text tools shown in Figure 8-22 are methods to insert text into an image. Add text to your photos by:

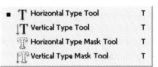

Figure 8-22: Use the Horizontal Text tools to insert text to an image.

1. **Click the Horizontal Text tool in the Toolbox.**

2. **Choose the font you want to use.**

   New in CS2 is the ability to view WYSIWYG samples of each font by clicking the Font menu located on the Option bar, as shown in Figure 8-23.

3. **Click your image and type the text.**

   After typing your text, you can move the text around using the Move tool to place the text exactly where you want it, as shown in Figure 8-24.

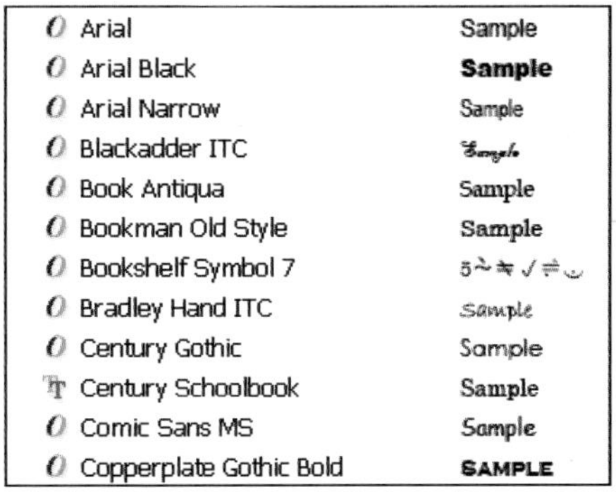

O Arial	Sample
O Arial Black	**Sample**
O Arial Narrow	Sample
O Blackadder ITC	*Sample*
O Book Antiqua	Sample
O Bookman Old Style	Sample
O Bookshelf Symbol 7	5~≈√≠☺
O Bradley Hand ITC	*Sample*
O Century Gothic	Sample
T Century Schoolbook	Sample
O Comic Sans MS	Sample
O Copperplate Gothic Bold	SAMPLE

Figure 8-23: Choosing a font.

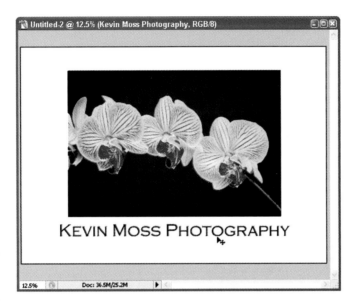

Figure 8-24: Type and move your text to the desired location on your canvas.

Shaping things up with Shape tools

At times you need the ability to draw simple shapes or insert predefined shapes into your photos or canvas. The Photoshop Toolbox offers shape tools to do just that. Figure 8-25 shows all the shape tools available in the Rectangle tool flyout menu.

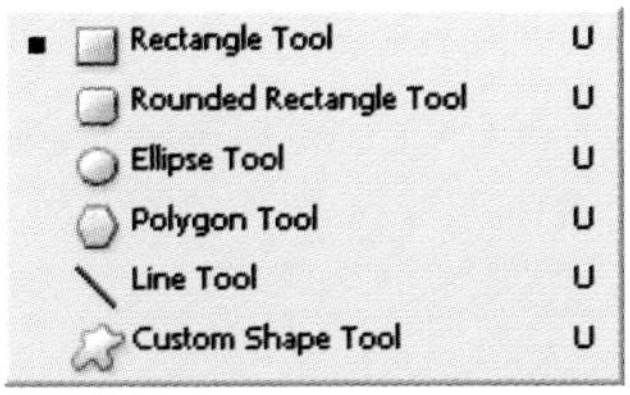

■	Rectangle Tool	U
	Rounded Rectangle Tool	U
	Ellipse Tool	U
	Polygon Tool	U
	Line Tool	U
	Custom Shape Tool	U

Figure 8-25: Shape tools available in the Photoshop Toolbox.

For example, I want to insert a copyright symbol next to my text for the Orchid art poster example I used in the previous section. The process for adding this symbol is as follows:

1. **Right-click the Rectangle tool and choose the Custom Shape tool.**

2. **Choose the copyright symbol from the Option bar Shape selection menu shown in Figure 8-26.**

3. **Drag the Custom Shape tool over the part of your image where you want to insert the symbol.**

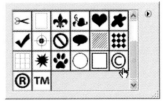

Figure 8-26: Selecting a shape to insert onto the canvas.

Selecting color with the Eyedropper tool

The Eyedropper tool, shown in Figure 8-27, is used to select colors for the foreground or background colors.

I often use the Color Sampler tool to select my black and white points of an image while in my color correction workflow described in Chapter 13. Selecting the black and white points of the image establishes the tonal range of the image, making overall image adjustments more accurate.

Figure 8-27: Eyedropper, Color Sampler, and Measure tools.

 You can use the Measure tool to measure the distance between two points of your image by drawing a non-printable line. The measurement information displays in the Info palette, allowing you to very precisely place images or elements in an image or straighten the image.

Zoom in and out with the Zoom tool

The Zoom tool, provides one of many ways to zoom an image in or out. Click the Zoom tool, place your cursor over your image, and click. You can also right-click your mouse and choose Zoom Out to reverse your zoom, as shown in Figure 8-28.

 Other methods for zooming in and out of an image are the use of the Navigator palette or pressing Ctrl+/- or ⌘+/- on the Mac.

Figure 8-28: Right-click in the image to view zoom tool options.

Presetting Commonly Used Tools

One of the time-saving features of Photoshop is that you can set up your tools the way you like them. You work with these everyday so it's nice to have some of these tools set up with your own customized settings. The method to save settings for commonly used tools in Photoshop is called *tool presets*.

One of the presets I use on a regular basis is crop settings for both my Web site and for printing. I create crop presets including 4×5 inches at 360dpi for prints and 4×5 inches at 72dpi for Web. I save these crop settings as presets so I do not have to go in and manually specify a crop setting every time I crop an image.

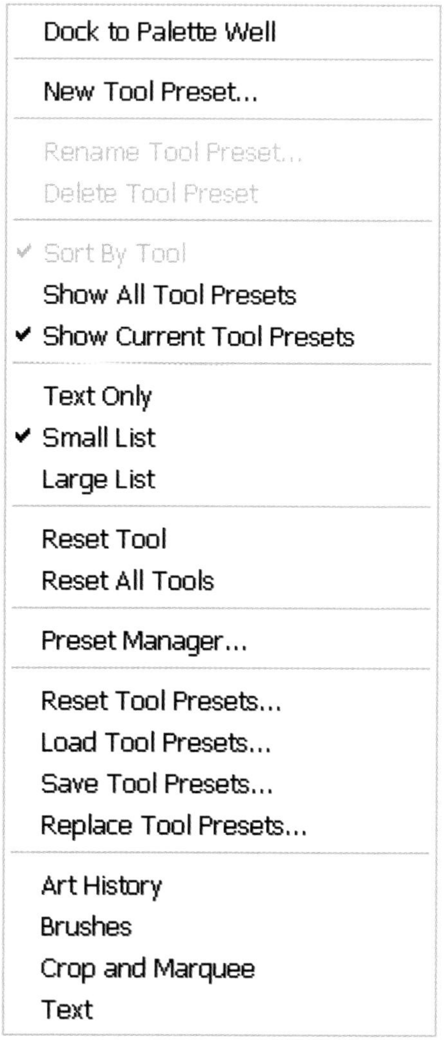

Other common presets to consider are for brush sizes, frequently-used fonts and font sizes, or particular selection settings — see the Tool Presets palette flyout menu, shown in Figure 8-29. As you become more familiar with Photoshop and really nail down your everyday image editing workflow, try setting up your common tools using the Tool Presets palette.

The Tool Presets palette offers some useful features while creating presets:

- You can drag the Tool Presets palette from the Palette well to your image window.

- If you need to view all presets instead of the presets for the tool selected, uncheck the Current Tool Only check box. Re-check the Current Tool Only check box to view only the presets for the selected tool.

- To organize presets by tool type, delete presets, or change the way presets are displayed, use the Preset Manager located in the Tool Presets flyout menu.

Dock to Palette Well
New Tool Preset...
Rename Tool Preset...
Delete Tool Preset
✔ Sort By Tool
Show All Tool Presets
✔ Show Current Tool Presets
Text Only
✔ Small List
Large List
Reset Tool
Reset All Tools
Preset Manager...
Reset Tool Presets...
Load Tool Presets...
Save Tool Presets...
Replace Tool Presets...
Art History
Brushes
Crop and Marquee
Text

Figure 8-29: The Tool Presets Palette and flyout menu.

To setup a Tool Preset:

1. **Click the tool in the Toolbox that you want to create a preset for, such as the Crop tool.**

2. **Make the adjustments to the tool that you want to save.**

   For the Crop tool preset I created a crop size of 19×13 inches at 360dpi in the Crop tool options on the Option bar, as shown in Figure 8-30.

| 🔲 ▼ | Width: | 19 in | ⇄ | Height: | 13 in | Resolution: | 360 | pixels/inch | ∨ | Front Image | Clear |

Figure 8-30: Crop settings made for the preset.

3. **Click the Tool Presets palette in the Palette well, as shown in Figure 8-31, and click to save the tool settings made in Step 2.**

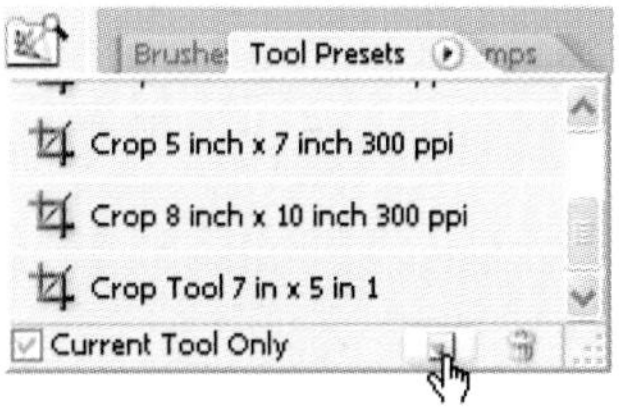

   You can also access the tool presets by clicking the tool button on the far-left of the Option bar or by choosing Window ➪ Tool.

Figure 8-31: Clicking the Create New Tool Preset in the Tool Presets palette well.

4. **Type a name for the tool that you are saving.**

   Photoshop creates a default name for your preset that you can customize to your liking. Click OK to save your Tool Preset, as shown in Figure 8-32.

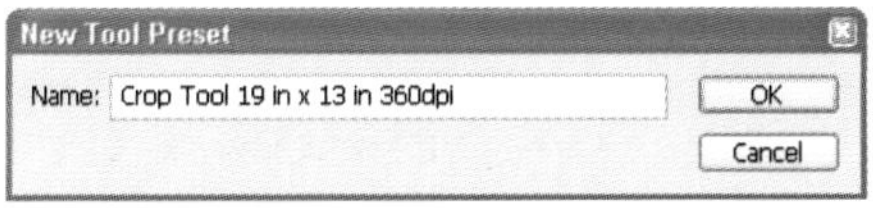

Figure 8-32: Naming and saving your Tool Preset.

As you can see, there are a number of ways to open the Tool Preset palette and to create tool presets that can save you time while editing images.

Rulers, Grids, and Guides

Photoshop offers the capability to precisely position elements of your images. Rulers, grids, and guides are used to map out your photos, allowing you to make adjustments in a measured environment. The combination of these precision tools with the Snap-To feature lets you navigate precisely with your mouse.

You can apply rulers to your image window, providing measurements along the left and top of your image window. Applying grids to an image adds horizontal and vertical lines in your image window to better help you navigate. Guides provide horizontal and vertical lines to your specification in the image window.

Using rulers

I use rulers to help me make precision crops to images where the Crop tool just doesn't cut it, no pun intended! To bring up rulers in your image window choose View ⇨ Rulers or press Ctrl+R (⌘+R on the Mac). You can change the actual units of measure on the ruler from inches to centimeters or other units by right-clicking the ruler (⌘+clicking on the Mac), as shown in Figure 8-33.

Grids and guides

Using grids in your image window allows you to make more precise edits to your image. Grids are non-printable lines you can add to your image by choosing View ⇨ Show ⇨ Grid. Figure 8-34 shows the image window with grids turned on.

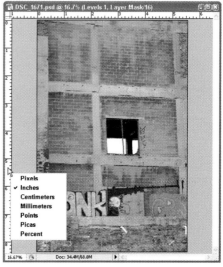

Figure 8-33: Changing the units of measure on the ruler.

Figure 8-34: Grids shown at ¼-inch intervals.

Guides are non-printable lines you pull vertically or horizontally from the ruler into your image by holding down the mouse button while dragging. Pulling a guide from the top ruler is illustrated in Figure 8-35.

Guides are best used to help you align crooked images vertically or horizontally when used in conjunction with the Measure tool or Rotate Canvas command.

Figure 8-35: Dragging a guide from the top ruler.

Chapter 9

Applying Color Management

*I*magine a scenario of just getting home from photographing an event that results in a CompactFlash full of once-in-a-lifetime images. Photographs worthy to be placed upon the pristine white walls of the Metropolitan Museum of Art. Okay, maybe just some pictures of your loved ones that you would know to look great behind the glass of an 8×10 frame on your desk at work. The point is, you have just captured images that you know will blow your hair back as soon as they are printed.

After loading your images to your computer, you gleefully view what looks to be your favorite image of the bunch. After a few tweaks, you send the image to the printer. To your dismay, your photograph comes out of the printer with a reddish cast and is too dark. Not exactly what you edited in Photoshop. You tweak and print the same image a few more times and same result. The print does not match the image viewed on the monitor.

This chapter shows you that by applying a few color management methods, you can make sure the image you are viewing on your computer monitor matches the printed photograph as closely as possible. You first discover how to use Gamma and other methods to calibrate your monitor. I also show you how to correctly apply Photoshop color settings. By applying a few steps to your overall digital imaging workflow, you can save a bundle in printing costs and a bunch of frustration-caused emotional breakdowns, too. Consider color management workflow the Prozac of digital photography.

Caught in the Act of Calibration

The most important step of implementing color management into your workflow is to calibrate your monitor. Calibrating on a regular basis is important because the colors, brightness, and contrast of your monitor change over time. Whether you use one of those big clunky computer monitors (called CRTs), one of those sleek new LCD monitors, or a laptop computer, the rule remains the same: Calibrate on a regular basis.

Most laptop and some LCD monitors do not offer the ability to adjust color balance and contrast. With some of them, only brightness can be adjusted. If you have an LCD monitor, you should still calibrate to ensure optimal brightness settings. Additionally, calibrating is important to ensure colors are completely accurate.

When you calibrate your monitor, you make adjustments to the brightness, contrast, and color balance to match what your calibration software uses as its standard. These adjustments are actual physical changes to the operation of the monitor (but not to the image files you are viewing) and are necessary to produce an accurate profile that your computer uses.

As seen on the monitor   Actual print

By calibrating your monitor, you have effectively set yourself up for a successful color managed workflow. If you skip this step, you are making adjustments to digital files based on *false* information. The results are prints that don't match what you see on you monitor, such as the portrait shown in Figure 9-1.

Figure 9-1: Calibrate your monitor to avoid problems such as this when you print.

Quick and cheap: monitor calibration with Gamma

If you are fairly new to digital photography or Photoshop, one nifty tool you can use to calibrate your monitor and to create a profile is Gamma. Gamma is a Control Panel utility in Windows that is shipped with Photoshop CS2. The Mac version of Gamma was available with previous versions of Photoshop and no longer ships with Photoshop CS2. It is assumed that Mac users will instead use the Apple Display Calibrator Assistant found within System Preferences.

For best results, let your monitor warm up for 30 minutes before starting any calibration procedure.

To calibrate your monitor using Gamma:

1. **Open the Windows Control Panel by clicking Start ⇨ Control Panel.**

2. **Open the Adobe Gamma Wizard.**

   Double-click the Adobe Gamma icon located in the Windows Control Panel (see Figure 9-2) to start Gamma.

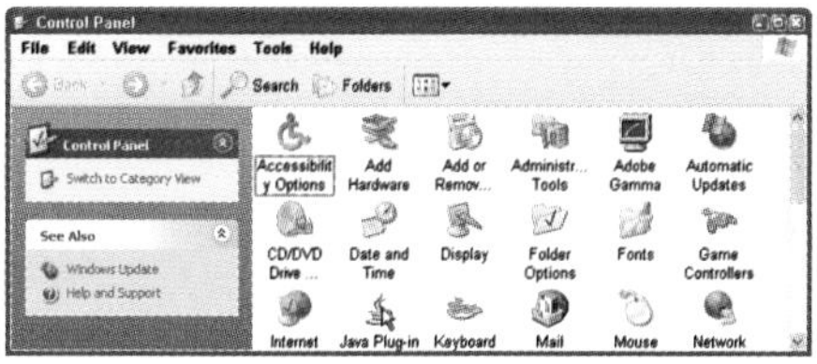

3. **Choose the Step-by-Step (Wizard) version.**

   You are asked to choose either the Step-by-Step (Wizard) method or the Control Panel method. Choose the Step-by-Step method, as shown in Figure 9-3, because it's a lot easier, and then click Next. By the way, the woman in the photo is smiling because she is happy you are using Gamma to calibrate your monitor.

4. **Click Load (see Figure 9-4) to choose your monitor type and then click Next.**

   You are presented with the Open Monitor Profile window.

5. **Choose a profile that matches your monitor or choose one that is similar to it (see Figure 9-5).**

   This selection is used only as a starting point for the process. Click your selection and then click Open. You are then sent back to the Adobe Gamma window shown in Figure 9-4.

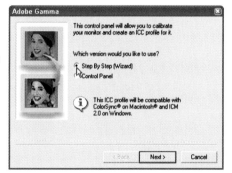

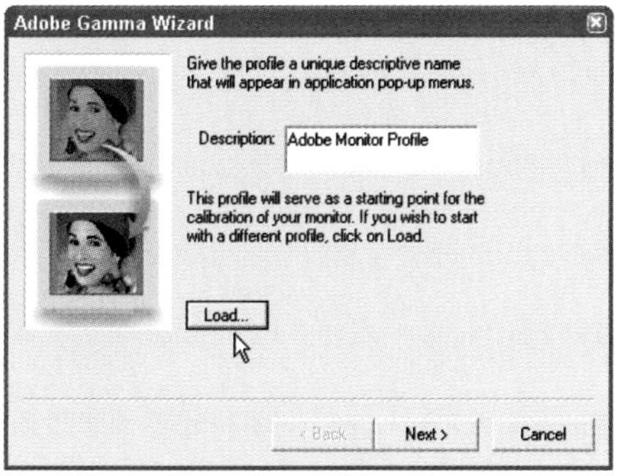

Figure 9-2: The Windows Control Panel and Adobe Gamma icon.

Figure 9-3: Choose the Step-by-Step (Wizard) version.

Figure 9-4: Click Load to choose your display type instead of the default.

TIP

Select a profile that best matches the monitor you are using on your computer by clicking the display type name in the list of profiles shown in Figure 9-5. If your computer monitor is not listed in the profile list, you can always choose the default setting provided in the list of profiles. After your selection, click the Open button and you are sent back to the Adobe Gamma window shown in Figure 9-4.

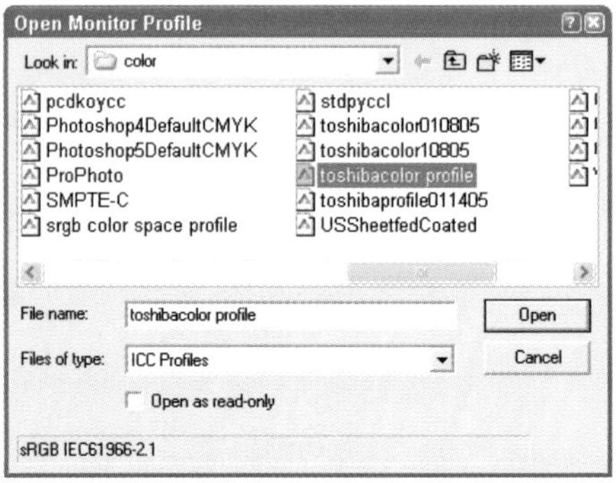

6. **Type a unique description with a date.**

   The profile you chose in Step 5 doesn't appear in the Description field. Don't worry: The monitor you chose in Step 5 is still associated with the process. Just type a unique name with a date, like the name shown in Figure 9-6. Click Next to proceed to the next window.

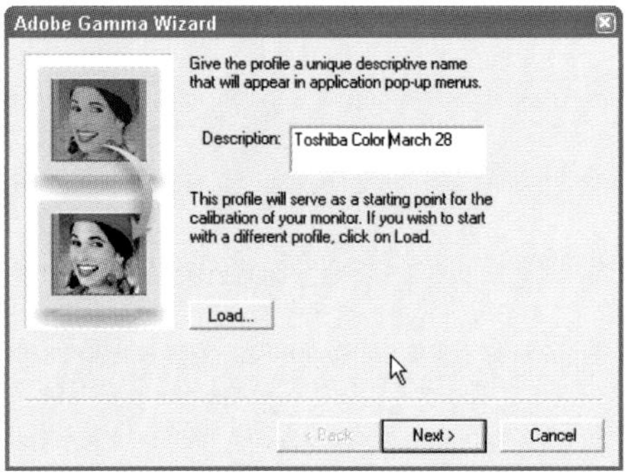

7. **Adjust brightness and contrast.**

   The Adobe Gamma window in Figure 9-7 instructs you to use the contrast adjustment on your monitor and set the contrast to maximum.

   Next, adjust the brightness control until the inside gray square is barely visible against the black surround. Keep the lighting in the room as dark as possible. Click Next to continue.

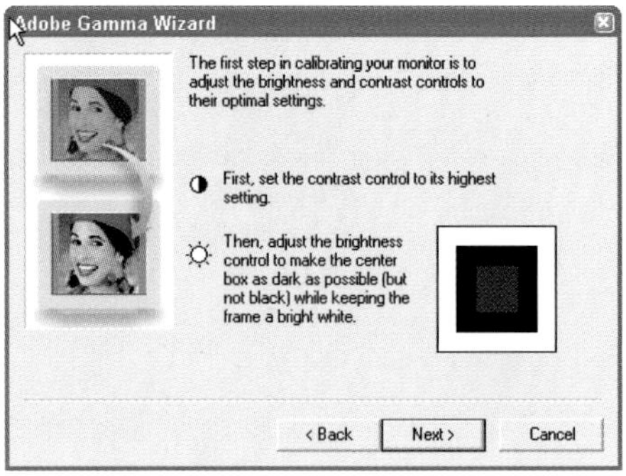

Figure 9-5: Select a Monitor Profile that matches your display or is a close match.

Figure 9-6: Include a date reference for your description.

Figure 9-7: Adjust the contrast of your display.

8. Choose the phosphor type for your monitor.

If you previously chose the type of monitor you are using in Step 5, leave this setting as it appears. If you chose the default setting in Step 5, you can choose Trinitron, as shown in Figure 9-8. If you actually know the phosphor values of your monitor, choose Custom and enter the values. You can look up these values in your monitor manual. Click Next to proceed.

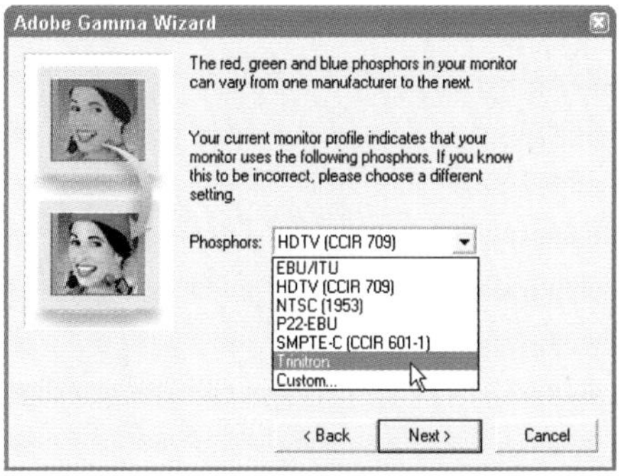

Figure 9-8: Most users can accept the monitor profiles default that appear in this step.

9. Adjust gamma settings.

Keeping View Single Gamma selected as shown in Figure 9-9, move the adjustment slider to the right or left until the center gray box begins fading into the outer box. This adjustment sets the relative brightness of your monitor. Make sure to choose Macintosh Default or Windows Default in the Gamma field. When you are done, deselect the View Single Gamma Only check box, and then click Next.

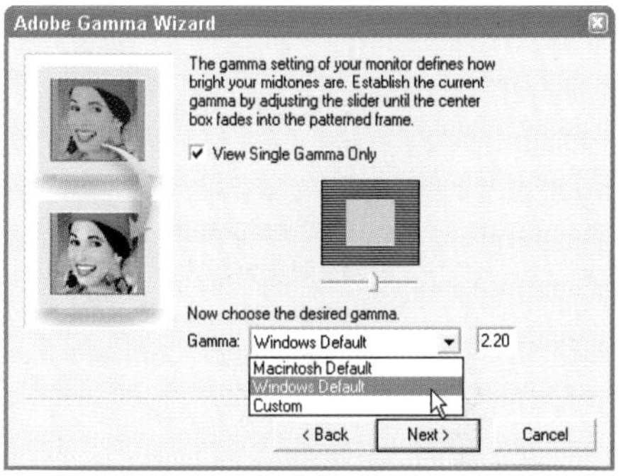

Figure 9-9: Making single gamma settings.

10. Adjust red, green, and blue gamma.

In this step, eliminate color imbalances by adjusting each RGB (red, blue, and green) slider, shown in Figure 9-10, until the color box in the middle blends in with the outer box Deselect the View Single Gamma Only option, and then click Next to continue.

Figure 9-10: Adjust relative brightness.

11. **Set the hardware white point to 6500K.**

    Most monitors are set with a native white point of 9300K. For photographers, 6500K provides the cleanest and brightest white point that matches daylight the closest.

    After making your selection, such as the one in Figure 9-11, click Next to continue.

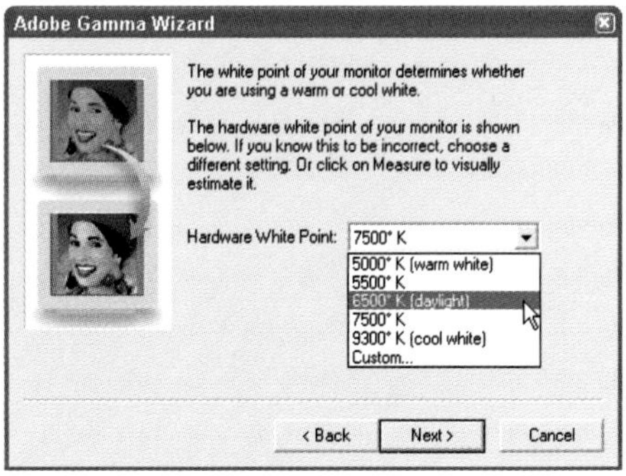

Figure 9-11: Setting the desired white point of your monitor to 6500K.

12. **Set the adjusted white point the same as the hardware white point.**

    It is recommended that you set the adjusted white point to match the hardware white point. Choosing another setting can result in unpredictable results. For most applications, leave this setting as Same as Hardware, as shown in Figure 9-12. Click Next to continue.

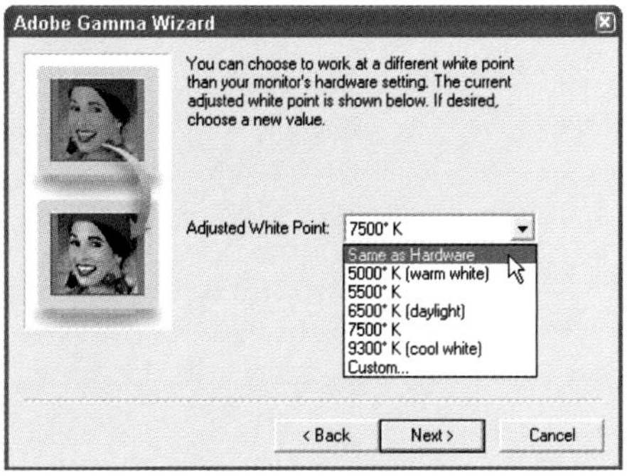

13. **View your changes and click Finish.**

    You have adjusted the brightness, contrast, and color settings of your monitor to the optimum values. You can view how these changes look by clicking the Before and After options shown in Figure 9-13 to see the difference. Click Finish.

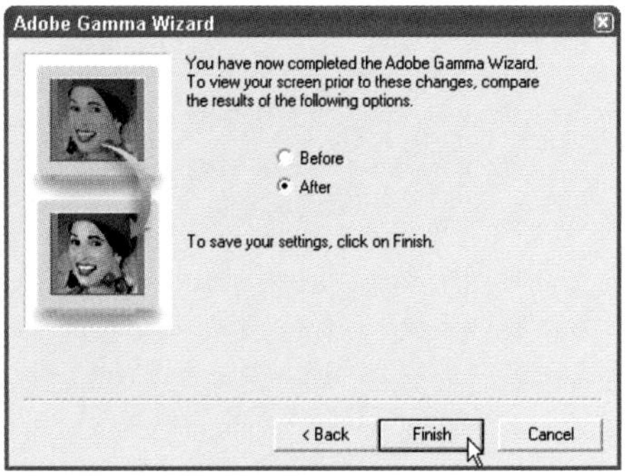

Figure 9-12: Setting the adjusted white point to Same as Hardware.

14. **Save your new profile.**

    Now that you have calibrated your monitor with Gamma, it's time to save this information into a new monitor profile that your computer and Photoshop CS2 can use by typing a new profile name in the Save As window File name field shown in Figure 9-14.

Figure 9-13: Use these options to view how the new adjustments look on your monitor.

15. Make sure the file type is left as ICC Profiles and click Save to complete the calibration.

Keep the existing profiles intact by using a unique profile name you can easily identify. Make sure you include the date of the profile in the filename, as shown in Figure 9-14. This identifies your unique profile with a date so you know the last time you calibrated your monitor.

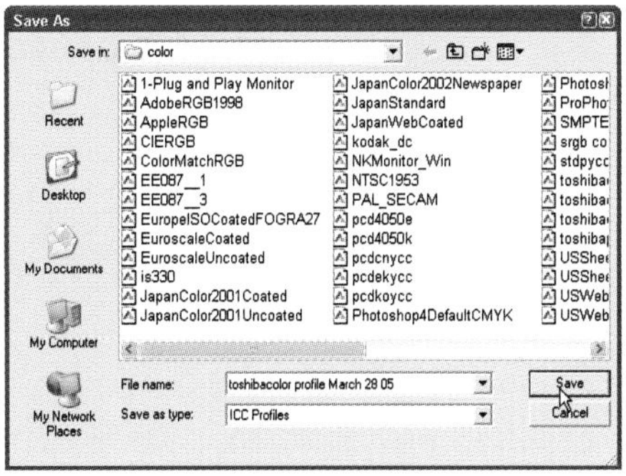

Figure 9-14: Saving the new monitor profile.

Gamma is a decent tool to calibrate your monitor if you're a casual Photoshop user and don't print a lot of photographs. If you're more serious about digital photography and regularly produce prints on a photo-quality printer, you should strongly consider purchasing a more advanced colorimeter (a device that measures the color displayed on your computer monitor) and software. The results with this equipment will be very noticeable. The money will be well spent just in the saving of time, paper, and ink cartridges. The next section covers colorimeters and advanced calibration tools.

Better calibrating using colorimeters

The best solution for calibrating your monitor is specialized software used in conjunction with a colorimeter that reads the actual values produced by your monitor. Today's top products include the ColorVision Spyder2, the ColorVision Color Plus, Monaco Systems MonacoOPTIX, and Gretag Macbeth Eye-One Display.

Prices for these products vary, but if you are on a budget consider the ColorVision Color Plus. This software and colorimeter are considered a good value for the money for most home systems, and Color Plus provides much more accurate calibration than Gamma or Colorsync for the Mac. Professional or serious photographers may opt for the more high-end ColorVision (shown in Figure 9-15), Gretag Macbeth, or Manoco products.

Figure 9-15: A colorimeter reading color values from a LCD display.

Important facts concerning using a monitor calibration package to calibrate your monitor include

- ✔ Colorimeters read color from your monitor much more accurately than you can when you look at your monitor, thus providing a much more accurate color profile.

- ✔ All the monitor calibration products mentioned include colorimeters that attach to an LCD monitor as well as a CRT.

- ✔ The software programs are easy to use and provide step-by-step instructions while performing the calibration of your monitor. Usually the steps to calibrating your monitor with any of these products aren't any more difficult than using Gamma or Colorsync on the Mac.

- ✔ Most of the monitor calibration solutions automatically remind you to calibrate your monitor every few weeks. This is important because monitor characteristics change over time, thus making calibration on a regular basis important.

- ✔ Calibrating you monitor every two to four weeks is recommended.

- ✔ Make sure the lights in the room you're working in are dimmed and the blinds are closed when performing monitor calibration. Lighting candles and incense is cool though.

Gamma automatically is added to your startup folder when you first load Photoshop. Make sure you remove Gamma from the startup folder if you calibrate with another product. You want to be careful to make sure your computer uses the correct monitor profile.

Implementing Photoshop Color Settings

In addition to making monitor calibration part of your color management workflow, it's equally as important to make sure the Photoshop color settings are correct for the type images you normally process. If you work with photographs that are meant for a variety of different output methods, you need custom color settings in Photoshop.

You don't want to expend a lot of energy shooting photos only to find that they turn out wrong when you output your images to print or screen. Using a proper color management workflow can help you get your colors right. Make color settings the very first stop in your image editing workflow.

Understanding color and working space

Getting confused in technical jargon regarding color and working space is easy. *Color space* is the range of colors available to you for editing of your images. It's the colors you used in your old paint-by-numbers set, only instead of 12 colors, you have millions!

CMYK (working space for press type printing) and *grayscale* (used for editing black-and-white images) are working spaces targeted toward specific purposes, which I describe in the list that follows.

For photographers, the most important color space you use is RGB. Most of the photographer's work is geared toward printing first, press and the Web second. Digital photographers incorporating a color management workflow opt to use Adobe RGB (1998) first to edit images, and then convert to different color spaces if a particular output requires it.

Adobe RGB (1998)

sRGB

The list that follows explains the differences and different uses of the color spaces available in Photoshop. Figure 9-16 shows how using different color and working spaces for a photo affect how they look.

- **Adobe RGB (1998).** A color space designed to match the color gamut of inkjet printers. Highly recommended for use with images to be printed on inkjet printers.

- **sRGB.** A color space designed for displaying photos on computer monitors, such as Web graphics and Web photos.

Colormatch RGB

- **Colormatch RGB.** A color space designed for a color gamut between sRGB and Adobe RGB (1998). Use for images with multiple purposes and output.

- **CMYK Working Space.** Designed for a number of various output processes. For each output process there are particular CMYK standards to use. Recommended when you are editing images in another color space and then converting to CMYK per particular output destination.

CMYK

- **Grayscale Working Space.** Default color space for grayscale images (black-and-white). Not recommended for use by photographers. It is recommended to always edit images in a color space and then convert images for black-and-white printing.

Grayscale

Figure 9-16: Different color spaces affect how color is rendered.

Digital camera color space

In addition to color spaces used in Photoshop, your digital camera also uses different color spaces. The color space used in your digital camera determines the range of colors that are available in the image files it produces. It makes sense to use a color space in your camera that's going to match the final output of your images, giving you the broadest range of colors possible.

Most digital camera's default in-camera color space is sRGB. sRGB is a great color space for images viewed on monitors, specifically the World Wide Web, but doesn't lend itself as the best color space for printing. If your camera has the option to have its color space set to Adobe RGB (1998), use that setting for optimal

results. It's a good practice to shoot in the same color space as you use when editing your photos in Photoshop.

As part of your overall color management workflow, I recommend always editing your photographs in Adobe RGB (1998) and saving the image as a master file. Adobe RGB (1998) provides the widest color gamut available to edit your images. For output destined for the Web or special printing, you can always convert your master to sRGB or CMYK for output later. Even while outputting your images in black-and-white, I recommend using an RGB working space for your master image.

Applying Photoshop color settings

In this section, I explain how to set up each setting in the Photoshop Color Settings window. This is one of the most overlooked color management workflow steps and makes a *huge* difference when used properly. Additionally, I explain when and how to assign a color profile to an image.

If most of your work is preparing images for the Web, printing, or publishing, the first step after calibrating your monitor is to set up your default color settings in Photoshop. To set up color settings:

1. **Choose Edit ➪ Color Settings or Ctrl+Shift+K (⌘+Shift+K on the Mac) to bring up the Color Settings window.**

2. **Click the More Options button.**

   This expands the Color Settings window so you can see all the options, as shown in Figure 9-17.

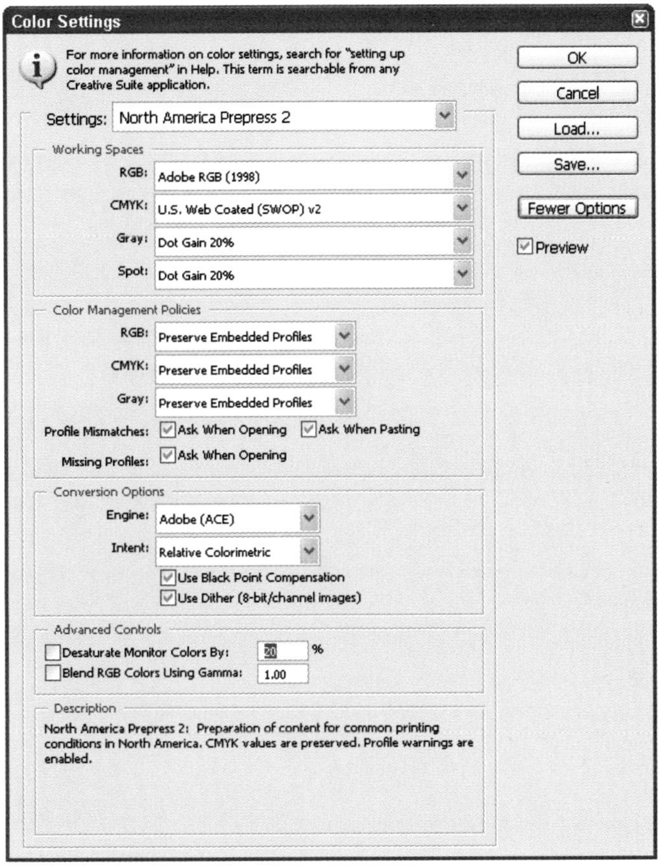

Figure 9-17: Photoshop color settings.

3. Set color Settings to North American Prepress 2.

The default for Setting is the North American General Purpose 2, which is not very good for photographers. Select US Prepress Defaults, as shown in Figure 9-17. This setting works best for photographers.

4. Set Working Spaces.

Change the Photoshop default for the RGB working space to Adobe RGB (1998) as shown in Figure 9-17. Adobe RGB (1998) is the best working space for photographers, providing the widest color gamut for color saturation.

For most of your image editing, use Adobe RGB (1998) to edit your master images. If needed, convert to the sRGB working space for final output for Web images.

5. Set Color Management Polices.

Make sure to leave RGB, CMYK, and Gray set to Preserve Embedded Profiles. This ensures that color settings are maintained in images that you open in Photoshop.

Leave the Profile Mismatches and Missing Profiles check boxes selected. These settings ensure that you are prompted to choose which color space to apply when you open an image in Photoshop that does not match your default working space.

6. Set Conversion Options Settings.

I recommend leaving the defaults for these settings to Adobe (Ace) for the Engine and Relative Colorimetric for the Intent.

The Engine setting controls Photoshop methods used for converting colors from one profile to another. The Intent setting specifies the rendering intent used for conversions from one profile to another. The bottom line? Adobe (ACE) and Relative Colorimetric are optimal conversion settings for photographs.

For best results for editing photographs in Photoshop, leave the default Use Black Point Compensation selected. This option ensures the black point of your image matches the black point of your print (or output).

7. Click OK to save Color Settings.

Assigning color profiles

The final step to ensuring a proper color workflow is to make sure that images you open in Photoshop contain the correct color profile you have set up in the Color Settings window. When you open an image that doesn't match the default color space you set up in Photoshop, you're prompted with the window shown in Figure 9-18.

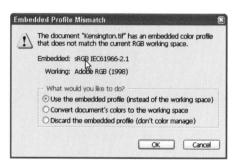

Figure 9-18: Setting the RGB Working space to Adobe RGB (1998).

✔ Select the Use the Embedded Profile option if you want to leave the image's working space as is.

Remember that if you leave this option selected, you won't be working in the default color space you indicated in the Color Settings window.

✔ Select the Convert Document's Colors to the Working Space option if you want to use your default color space. This is recommended for most images.

✔ Select the Discard the Embedded Profile if you don't want to use a color profile for the image.

There are times when you're working on an image in Photoshop where you need to convert the image to another working space. I've suggested the best color workflow is to edit your images in Adobe RGB (1998) and then covert later for specific output needs. The combination of using *monitor* profiles explained earlier in this chapter and assigning *color* profiles will ensure you are using a proper color management workflow.

The process to assign color profiles to an image is as follows:

1. **Choose Edit ⇨ Assign Profile.**

   The Assign Profile window appears.

2. **Select either the Don't Color Mange This Document or the Working RGB option.**

   Figure 9-19 shows the Working RGB set to Adobe RGB 1998.

Figure 9-19: Assigning a color profile to a photograph.

3. **Select another profile from the dropdown list in the third option (see Figure 9-20) if you desire.**

   This choice is rare for most photographers, however, you can use this option to assign a specific profile. For example, a printing company for press services may have supplied a profile to you.

   For most photographs, you want to select the Working RGB option, the same option you indicated in the Color Settings window as your default working space.

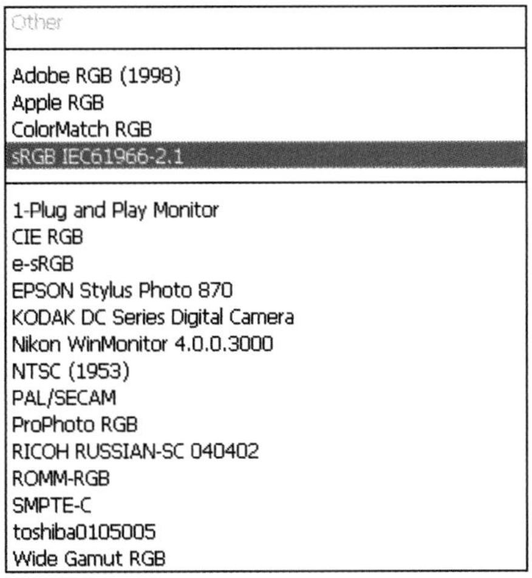

Figure 9-20: Selecting another profile.

Reviewing Color Management Workflow

Best practices for processing images in Photoshop includes a series of workflows that make up your overall image editing process. Color management is a workflow that is vital to your overall efforts.

A review of the elements of your color management workflow covered in this chapter includes:

1. **Set your digital camera to the color space that most resembles the color space you are using in Photoshop.**

   If your digital camera has the option to be set to Adobe RGB (1998) or something close to it, set it.

2. **Calibrate your monitor.**

   If possible, purchase a calibration product such as the ColorVision Spyder 2, ColorVision Color Plus, Monaco Systems MonacoOPTIX, or Gretag Macbeth Eye-One Display. If you don't want to purchase a solution, use Gamma or the Apple Display Calibrator Assistant.

3. **Apply Photoshop Color Settings.**

   Choose Edit ⇨ Color Settings or Ctrl+Shift+K (⌘+Shift+K on the Mac) to bring up the Color Settings window.

4. **Apply correct color settings to images that do not match your default color space.**

   Your digital camera may not produce image files with your desired color space embedded. Photoshop prompts you to use your color settings you made in Step 3. Indicate that you want to use your default color settings by selecting the Convert Document's Colors to the Working Space option in the Embedded Profile Mismatch window.

Chapter 10

Using Bridge

igital cameras are great because you can take as many photos as you want without having to worry about envelopes full of negatives. You don't have the hassle of buying film and taking it up to the corner pharmacy for processing. Just shoot, fill up your card, and load 'em up to the computer. No more boxes in the closet full of envelopes of pictures and negatives! (Come on, *everyone* all has boxes of pictures and negatives in the closet!)

Digital cameras are still fairly new to many people, but after a few months or even years of building up your digital portfolio, you can wind up with thousands of image files in tens or hundreds of folders on your hard disk. If you are like me, you may even run out of hard disk space in just of few months!

Even though computer hard disk drives are actually efficient for storing your image files, there is a downside: How do you organize thousands of images? It's hard enough keeping up with printing the latest batch, let alone organizing, renaming, adding your index information to your files, and keeping them in order. You can feel like you are no better off than you were when you kept all those piles of negatives, photos, and envelopes in the hallway closet.

Fear not, my digital friends: This chapter introduces you to the Adobe world of image management, Bridge, the Photoshop answer to your image management workflow.

Navigating Around Bridge

Bridge is the Adobe upgrade to the File Browser from previous versions of Photoshop. Adobe built Bridge from the ground up as a stand-alone program for file management across all the applications that make up the Adobe Creative Suite. For Photoshop, Bridge serves as the program you can use to implement your file management workflow.

 More than just a simple file browser for photos, Bridge enables you to view, search, sort, manage, and process Raw image files. You can use Bridge to create new folders, edit metadata, rename, move, and delete files. You can rotate images and run batch commands on entire groups of files. Everything you want to do to manage files can be accomplished with Bridge.

 Bridge keeps Camera Raw and metadata information in a cache. As you continue to use Camera Raw and add metadata to images, the cache becomes very big. If you don't plan on keeping the metadata or Camera Raw settings, clear out the cache by choosing Tools ➪ Cache ➪ Purge Cache. Purging the cache permanently deletes the metadata cache and thumbnails. Be sure you want that data deleted.

Starting Bridge

You can start Bridge a few different ways. As a stand-alone application, you start Bridge by:

- Start Bridge from the Windows Start menu or from the Mac OS desktop.
- In Photoshop, choose File ➪ Browse.
- Press Ctrl+Alt+O or ⌘+Option+O on the Mac.
- Click the Bridge icon in the Photoshop Option bar.

Driving across the Bridge

Consider Bridge a program within a program that has some unique features you'll want to become familiar with. Before diving into the file management workflow, I've listed descriptions of the components that make up the Bridge work area, as shown in Figure 10-1.

- **Menu bar.** Contains Bridge commands within the File, Edit, Tools, Label, View, Window, and Help menus.
- **Option bar.** Contains the Look In Menu, Go Up a Folder, Filtered/Unfiltered Images, New Folder, Rotate Left/Right, Trash, and Switch to Compact Mode buttons.
- **Look In menu.** Displays the folder hierarchy, favorites, and most recently used folders. Use as a fast method of locating folders containing images.

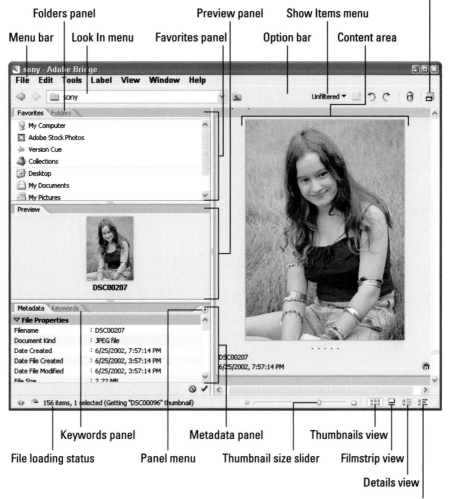

Switch to compact mode

Folders panel   Preview panel   Show Items menu

Menu bar   Look In menu   Favorites panel   Option bar   Content area

Figure 10-1: The Bridge work area.

Keywords panel   Metadata panel   Thumbnails view

File loading status   Panel menu   Thumbnail size slider   Filmstrip view

Details view

Versions and Details view

- **Favorites panel.** Gives you fast access to folders, Version Cue, Stock Photos, and the Bridge Center.

- **Folders panel.** Shows folder hierarchies and lets you navigate folders.

- **Preview panel.** Shows a preview of the selected image.

- **Metadata panel.** Contains metadata information about the selected image. Allows you to add various types of information about the file in multiple areas.

✔ **Keywords panel.** Lets you add keywords to the image information; you can organize images with the keyword, which allows for meaningful file searches.

✔ **File loading status.** Shows the status of loading files from the selected folder.

✔ **Content area.** Displays resizable thumbnails of images and basic file information.

Managing Photos with Bridge

Let me go back to the earlier discussion where I describe that box you have tucked away in the closet that has all those old forgotten envelopes of negatives and photos. It's unorganized and worst of all, it's a box! Photos are meant to be mounted and framed, in a photo album on your coffee table, or displayed on your personal Web site!

If photos are meant to be shown, and photographers like to show off their work, it makes perfect sense to organize your digital negatives with a rock-solid process — the image management workflow.

The image management workflow that you can implement with Bridge is described in these steps:

1. **Navigate image folders.**

   You can view photos that you download directly from your digital camera or card reader. This is a lot better than the old light tables that used to be used to view those little negatives and slides.

   Bridge lets you view images as thumbnails, and you can specify how you want to view these thumbnails on your computer. For example, you can enlarge thumbnails for easier viewing.

2. **Load photos into Photoshop.**

   You can load photos into Photoshop just by double-clicking the thumbnail of the desired photo.

3. **Add information with the Metadata panel.**

   You can view information provided by your digital camera for technical information about each photo.

4. **Apply labels and ratings.**

   You can color code your photos for easier retrieval later. You can also add ratings to your photos on a scale from one to five stars.

5. **Sort and rename photos.**

   By adding keywords, labels, and ratings to your photos, you can easily sort files at a later time. Renaming files is a snap using Bridge: double-click the filename and type a new name.

6. **Organize images.**

   Bridge provides you with all the tools needed to organize your photos for access tailored to your needs.

Navigating folders

If you are familiar with navigating folders using Explorer, My Computer, or on the Mac Finder, navigating folders in Bridge will seem familiar to you. Bridge allows you to view your folders in a number of different ways so that you can find the images you want. Figure 10-2 shows how you can view folders using the Folders panel.

The Folders panel gives you an Explorer-like view of your computer and your storage devices, such as a CD-ROM.

Another method for viewing folders and their contents through Bridge is the Look In menu. The Look In menu is located on the Option bar.

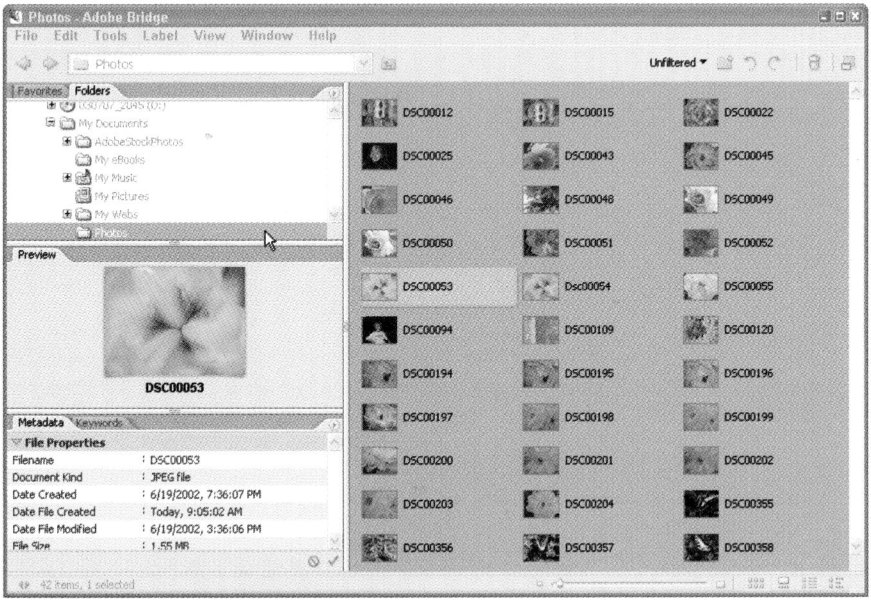

Figure 10-2: Navigating folders using the Folders panel.

The Look In menu (see Figure 10-3) gives you a hierarchical view of the folders contained in your Desktop, Favorites, and most Recent folders. Click a folder in the Look In menu, and the contents of that folder are displayed in the viewing area.

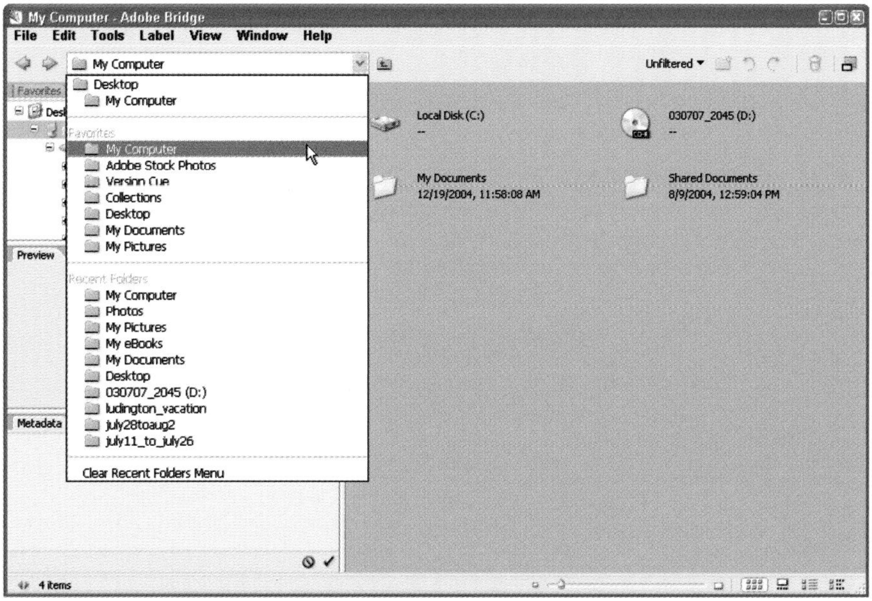

Figure 10-3: Navigating folders using the Look In menu.

Loading up your photos

Some photographers like to load their photos into Photoshop the old-fashioned way by using the File ➪ Open command in Photoshop. Some photographers, including me, prefer the visual displays and the search methods offered in Bridge. Whatever your style, Bridge can accommodate.

There is no steadfast rule as to how to browse and open images in Photoshop. It's totally up to personal preference. Play around with Bridge to find out the best way for you to browse and open images.

Visually looking at images is one of the advantages to using a file management utility such as Bridge. The Folders panel and Look In menu provide great ways of looking for your image folders in a hierarchical view. It's easy to visually navigate your computer's contents to find the photos you want to work on in Photoshop.

To load photos into Photoshop using Bridge:

1. **Find the folder where the desired image files are stored by using the Bridge Folders panel or Look In menu.**

2. **View the images stored in the contents area of Bridge.**

   You can use the scroll bar to view the images that do not appear in the contents area.

3. **Double-click the image you want to load in Photoshop or right-click the image and choose Open, as shown in Figure 10-4.**

The image loads into a Photoshop image window. If you haven't already started Photoshop, it automatically starts with the selected image ready to edit.

Figure 10-4: Choosing a photo to load into Photoshop.

Adding descriptions using metadata

Metadata is information about a file that contains file information from your digital camera and other information you can add, such as author information, copyrights, and keywords. Metadata information isn't stored inside your image file, but in a standard Extensible Metadata Platform (XMP) format. Metadata is stored in a separate file called a *sidecar* file.

You can use metadata information you add to an image sidecar file later to organize, keep track of files and versions, search, and sort images. As your image library grows, this information becomes more valuable to help you manage your image library. This feature is what makes Bridge so powerful.

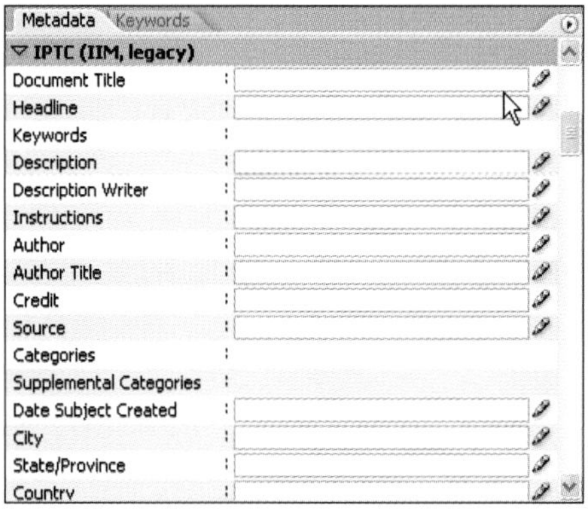

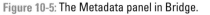

Figure 10-5: The Metadata panel in Bridge.

You add metadata information to image sidecar files by typing the information in the Metadata panel in Bridge, as shown in Figure 10-5.

I find the best method to add metadata information is by choosing File ➪ File Info or by pressing Ctrl+Shift+Alt+I (⌘+Shift+Option+I on the Mac). The File Info window (Pictures–Adobe Bridge window on the Mac) appears, as shown in Figure 10-6.

If you copy images from a CD to your computer's hard drive, the files may inherit the read-only property from the CD. Obviously, you can't add metadata to files residing on a CD-ROM, but after you copy these files to your hard disk, all you need to do is remove the Read-Only properties for these files using Windows Explorer or the Mac Finder. After changing the properties, you can then add metadata.

The first window that you see is the Description window. On the left side, you see a number of pages in which you can view or add additional metadata.

As you click through and add or view data in each page of the File Info window, you can always click OK to save your added information or Cancel to quit. The different File Info metadata pages include

- ✔ **Description.** You can add general information about your image here.
- ✔ **Camera Data 1.** Shows you information provided by your digital camera.
- ✔ **Camera Data 2.** Shows you more information provided by your digital camera.
- ✔ **Categories.** You can enter information based on Associated Press categories.

✔ **History.** Shows you Photoshop history information if the image was previously edited in Photoshop.

✔ **IPTC Information Pages.** You can enter information about the photographer and images per ITPC standards. If you are wondering who the heck the ITPC is, it is a London-based press and telecommunications organization that sets standards for news media data.

✔ **Adobe Stock Photos.** Provides information for images obtained through Adobe Stock Photos.

✔ **Origin.** You can enter additional information for images targeted for news media.

If it seems that many of the File Info pages are meant to be used by the press according to IPTC standards, you're right. Photoshop is a tool used by professional press photographers around the world. Take advantage of the standards IPTC has put forth and increase the manageability of your growing image library. You can visit the IPTC (the International Press Telecommunications Council) site at `www.iptc.org`.

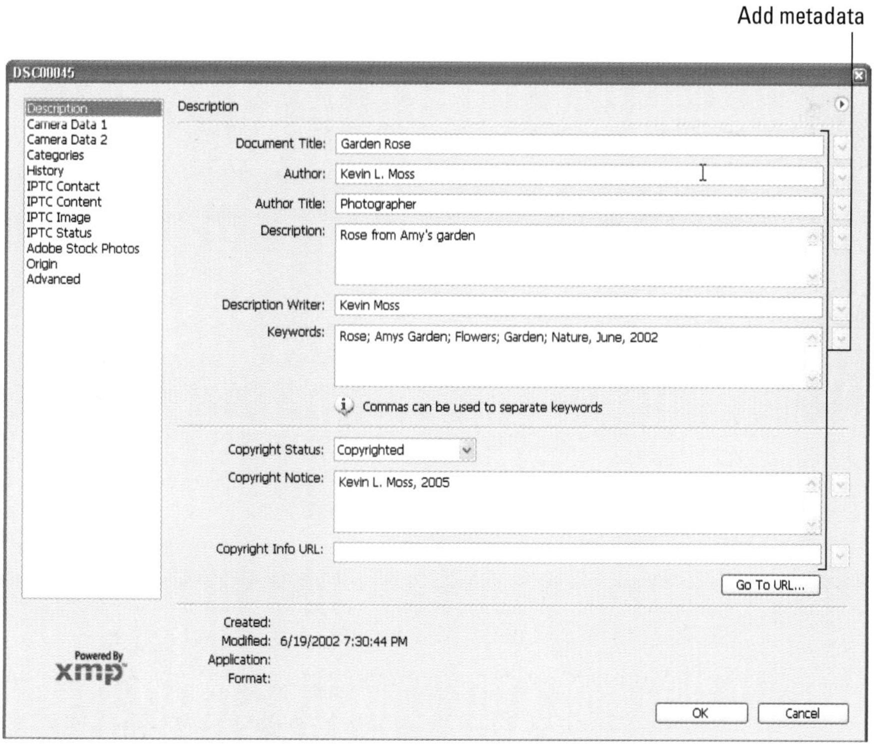

Add metadata

Figure 10-6: The File Info window.

Finding lost treasures

One of the fun parts of writing this chapter on Bridge was that I went back a few years into my image library and viewed some older images. The examples shown here include images from long-forgotten folders. The vast amount of digital images taken over the years makes it easy to forget hidden treasures.

You may find it a worthwhile exercise to go back to your own long-ago-loaded image folders and choose a number of them for editing in Photoshop. You never know what lost treasures you'll find in there!

Organizing Images

Organizing the large number of digital photos can be a daunting task. Fortunately, Bridge offers some simple methods of applying tags to your images that enable you to easily categorize your photos for later viewing.

As part of your image management workflow, make a habit of applying ratings or labels to your photos when you first transfer the images to your computer. View these new images with Bridge and apply your labels and ratings at the same time you apply any metadata information. You'll be thankful in the later months and years that you did.

Applying labels and ratings

Bridge now offers more advanced methods to organize and search images by applying labels and images. In previous versions of Photoshop, flags were available to apply to images. You could flag an image as on or off. CS2 now offers a better way of flagging images — by color!

Figure 10-7 shows where to apply color labels to images in Bridge. For the example shown, I applied color labels to the images in the Bridge content area by right-clicking the images and choosing Labels from the menu. I use green as a "go," (use the image and print it) as a "no-go," (don't use the image), and yellow as a "maybe" (consider using the image at a later time).

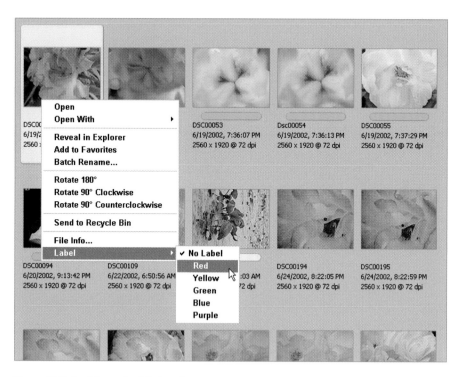

Figure 10-7: Applying color labels to images.

Applying color labels makes viewing and organizing photos later much easier when you want to view only the images in a folder labeled with a color. You can view these images by clicking the Unfiltered button on the Bridge Option bar and choosing a color, as shown in Figure 10-8.

An additional way to organize and view images is to apply a rating to your images. You can apply ratings to your images from one star to five stars, as shown in Figure 10-9. I apply high ratings, four or five stars to images I intend on processing, printing, or posting to the Web. Images that I rate at three or lower may never get processed, though I always reserve the right to change my mind!

To apply ratings to images:

1. **Select images that you want to rate with the same rating.**

   Click the images while holding down the Ctrl key on a PC or the ⌘ key on the Mac.

2. **Choose Label ➪ Rating.**

   You can apply ratings from one star to five stars. You can also choose color labels.

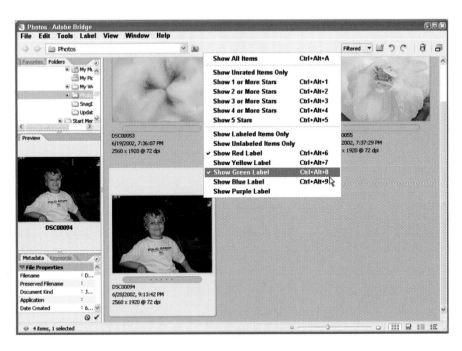

Figure 10-8: Applying a filter to only view images with a certain color label.

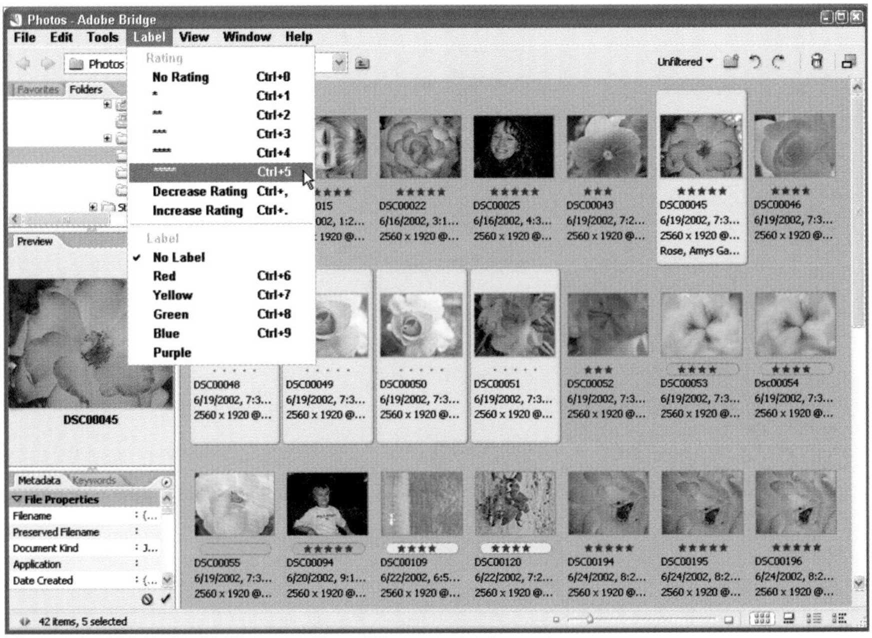

Figure 10-9: Applying ratings to selected images.

Notice that all the photos of the young people in Figures 10-8 and 10-9 are rated at five stars. I want to make sure that those precious treasures are rated high because I like to include those photos in my digital scrapbooks projects.

Sorting and searching photos

Applying labels and ratings to your photos after you load them into your computer and view them in Bridge is a great method to sort and search for photos later. To sort photos in Bridge, choose View ➪ Sort. Select the sort method from the Sort menu: I chose the ratings sort in Figure 10-10.

You can sort images in a folder using a number of sort methods available in the Sort menu including ratings and labels.

Toggle your sorts by selecting and deselecting Ascending Order in the Sort menu. Bridge defaults this setting to Ascending, where your highest rated images appear at the bottom.

![Screenshot of Adobe Bridge window showing the View menu open with the Sort submenu displaying options including Ascending Order, By Filename, By Document Kind, By Date Created, By Date File Modified, By File Size, By Dimensions, By Resolution, By Label, By Rating, By Version Cue Status, and Manually.]

Figure 10-10: Sorting photos by rating.

Reviewing Your Image Management Workflow

Bridge gives you the tools to get control of image management before you wind up with a mess on your hard drive. By applying a few steps in your image management workflow, viewing and retrieving images will be a lot easier down the road when you have hundreds or thousands of images in your collection.

Review the steps to take while using Bridge in your image management workflow:

1. **Navigate image folders.**

   Use Bridge to view photos that you download. Use Bridge as your digital light table.

2. **Load photos into Photoshop.**

   You can load photos into Photoshop just by double-clicking the thumbnails of the photos in Bridge.

3. **Add information with Metadata.**

   View technical information provided by your digital camera, and add additional information for each photo. This is your *cataloging* step in the image management workflow.

4. **Apply labels and ratings.**

   Color code and/or apply ratings to your photos for easy retrieval later.

5. **Sort and rename photos.**

   By adding keywords, labels, and ratings to your photos, you can easily sort files at a later time.

Mastering Camera Raw

*E*ver been in the situation where you've just moved into a new house and the delivery guys put your furniture in all the wrong places? It's like living in a world where someone else is making all the decisions, and it doesn't sit so well. In the real world, you should be in charge: Tell those guys exactly where you want each piece of furniture to go. More importantly, don't serve the pizza and soda until they're done with the work.

When you first open images in Photoshop, many of the settings for color, hue, brightness, contrast, and sharpness were made for you in the digital camera. If your camera only provides TIFF or JPEG file formats, you really don't have a choice in the matter. Somebody has arranged the "furniture" for you. Raw format offers you the advantage of having complete control of overall image data. You can tweak your image the way you want before you even open the image in Photoshop. *You* have control over the processing of the image, instead of the digital camera. You don't have to accept whatever the digital camera *arranges* for you.

What Is Raw and Why Do I Need to Shoot in It?

Shooting and processing Raw images is the first step in your image processing workflow if your digital camera has the option to capture raw images. High-end prosumer and digital SLR models now offer raw format as one of the standard file formats you can choose from. If your digital camera does have the capability to capture images in raw file format, you owe it to yourself to try this format out and process images in Camera Raw. You'll discover how much more control you have over editing your images and producing output to larger sizes. Figure 11-1 shows a raw image without any adjustments and the same image adjusted using Camera Raw.

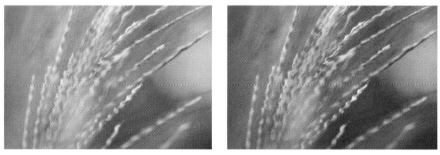

Original raw image   Processed with Camera Raw

Figure 11-1: Raw image processing gives the photographer more control over image data.

Raw files are best compared to film that has not been processed yet. When you make the exposure and shoot an image in the digital camera, the data exists in the file in an unprocessed state that's not yet an image file. It's not a processed image such as a TIFF or JPEG: It's just *raw* data. Using Camera Raw, the photographer can process raw images. *You* have the ability to make decisions on processing that *you* deem to be the best fit. If you shoot in JPEG or TIFF format, the digital camera decides how the image is to be processed.

The final reason to shoot in raw is control. A raw file can be processed a number of times. If you keep the original raw image, in the future you can always go back and process the data in the image anytime. If you shoot in JPEG, the camera processes the image data before it saves it to the memory card. It's done at that point and you can't go back to your camera and adjust anything.

Digital cameras now have the capability to shoot in the same color space as you use to edit images in Photoshop. If your digital camera has the ability to capture images in Adobe RGB format, you can capture your images in the same color space you edit images in. Combine that with capturing images in raw format, and you retain more control over your images.

Advantages to shooting and processing raw images

For many digital camera and Photoshop junkies, shooting JPEG format out of their cameras and processing in Photoshop produces great results. Many of the images in this book were set up just that way: shot in JPEG and processed in Photoshop.

The truth is that there are some photos I've taken over the years in JPEG format that really could have used that extra control that Camera Raw provides. Not that Camera Raw can save lousy images, but that more control to overall image settings would have made some of my shots even better. There are advantages and some disadvantages for both.

Advantages to shooting in raw format and processing the images in Camera Raw before editing include

- **Ability to adjust white balance after the shot.** Occasionally, your digital camera (or you, the photographer) doesn't set the white balance exactly as the light of the scene requires. You wind up with magenta-ish, bluish, or yellowish casts in your photos. It's a bear to correct that in Photoshop, but it can be done easily to raw images using Camera Raw. Camera Raw allows you to adjust the image for the correct white balance using the White Balance preset choices or the Color Temperature slider.

- **Ability to adjust overall exposure.** Digital cameras are great, but sometimes the digital camera light meters don't give you the correct exposure. Some shots come out underexposed or overexposed. Camera Raw allows you to easily adjust exposure, whether over or under, to make the photograph look as though it was correctly exposed. Figure 11-2 shows an image adjusted in Camera Raw where the exposure was increased +1 stop to correct underexposure. The image was then adjusted for brightness, contrast, and saturation, all without sacrificing valuable image data.

Original raw image   Adding +1 stop of exposure

Figure 11-2: Camera Raw can make adjustments to actual image exposure without sacrificing image data.

✔ **Ability to fine-tune shadow details.** Fine adjustments to shadow details can be achieved by making these adjustments to raw images.

✔ **Ability to make overall corrections without losing image data.** Raw image brightness, contrast, and color saturation can be easily adjusted to your personal taste. None of the adjustments made in Camera Raw result in loss of image data.

Overall image adjustments made in Camera Raw do not result in loss of image data. The same adjustments made while editing in Photoshop *do* result in some loss of image data, which can affect image quality as the size of your prints increase.

✔ **Upsizing images while maintaining quality for large format printing.** Camera Raw provides you with the ability to upsize raw images to large sizes for large format printing while maintaining more image data. This results in better quality 11×14 or 13×19 inch prints as opposed to upsizing JPEGs in Photoshop. More data, better quality images is the rule.

✔ **Recover from some shooting mistakes.** If you shot photographs outdoors and had your digital camera's white balance manually set to indoor lighting, the incorrect color cast can easily be fixed while processing your image in Camera Raw before editing your image in Photoshop. Fixing the digital negative is a lot easier than trying to compensate in Photoshop.

Disadvantages to shooting and processing raw images

Like anything in life, there are always some disadvantages to something that's good. Eating ice cream is one of the best things in life, but there is a downside, specifically related to the waistline! Some of the drawbacks to shooting and processing raw images include

✔ **Raw images take up more space.** Where a high resolution JPEG may take up two or three megabytes each, a six megapixel digital camera produces the same image in raw format at five megapixels. If you are using a 512MB CompactFlash card in your camera, you can fit 90 raw images on it, but if shooting JPEG, you can fit 180 images on the same card.

✔ **Shooting can be slower in the digital camera.** Some digital cameras take a few more seconds to process raw images. If you are shooting action, the processing time for raw may cost you some action shots over shooting in JPEG mode. Newer digital SLRs compensate for these problems and offer excellent processing speeds for raw image capture.

✔ **Processing raw images adds another step to your overall workflow.**
With JPEG, you can open images and begin editing immediately in
Photoshop. If you are opening a raw image, you must make adjustments
in Camera Raw first and then open the images in Photoshop.

One of the features of Bridge is the ability to batch process images. If
you have a number of similarly exposed images, you can apply raw
adjustments made to one image to the rest, saving you time and making
up for some of the extra steps required for processing raw images.

✔ **Camera Raw requires some knowledge of color controls and balance.**
If you are relatively new to Photoshop and making adjustments to image
color, white balance, brightness, and saturation, using Camera Raw may
be a little intimidating at first. Practice making adjustments in Camera
Raw and use your best judgment to what makes your photos look best.

✔ **Lack of digital camera industry raw image format standards.** Nikon,
Canon, Sony, Sigma, and other digital camera manufacturers all maintain
different versions of their raw files. Each manufacturer offers a proprietary version of raw image processing software for their camera's raw
format. Camera Raw offers photographers a standard raw processing
software program that most digital camera raw images can be processed
in instead of using one of the many manufacturer supplied raw conversion programs. On the same subject, Adobe has taken the initiative to
come up with an industry standard raw format called DNG (Digital
Negative) format. It is yet to be seen if the manufacturers adopt this
format.

Processing Raw Images

If you shoot raw images in your digital camera, one of the first steps in your
overall image editing workflow is to process your image in Camera Raw. In
this section, I explain in detail each individual step in processing a raw image
so that you can then complete the editing of that image in Photoshop. When
you have finished your Photoshop edits on images that began in the raw
format, you'll realize the power and control you can have over your images.

Getting around Camera Raw

Camera Raw is actually a Photoshop plug-in that automatically starts in
Bridge when you open a raw image file. It's a program within a program
within a program, if you think about Bridge as a standalone program as well.
Best of all, it's a seamless process to users of Photoshop. To open Camera
Raw, all you have to do is open a raw file in Bridge or choose File ➪ Open and
then select a file that is in raw format.

When you open a raw image, the image automatically loads to the Camera Raw window shown in Figure 11-3. Like other Photoshop windows and dialog boxes, Camera Raw allows you to control adjustments to the image using tabs, sliders, and menus.

Zoom tool

Hand tool

White balance tool

Color sampler tool

Crop tool

Image setting options

Straighten tool

Histogram

Rotate tools   Option bar   Image preview   Image settings

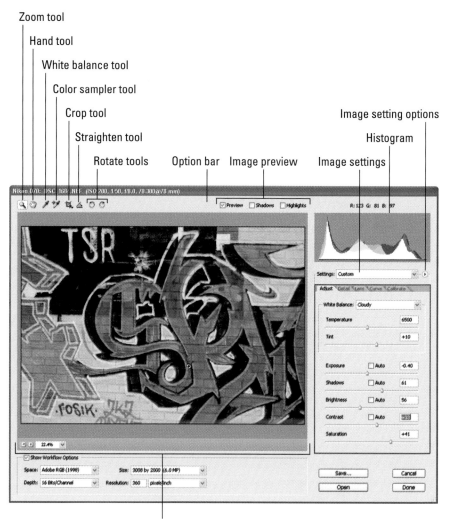

Image window

Figure 11-3: The Camera Raw window.

Step-by-step

Like any other process where you have to make a small number of changes to an image to make it look good, converting images in Camera Raw requires a little organization to make sure you do things in a proper order. Processing raw images is a workflow upon itself, but if you follow these easy steps, you'll be processing your raw images accurately and efficiently in no time flat, step-by-step.

1. **Using Bridge, open a raw image file.**

   Right-click the selected image and choose Open, as shown in Figure 11-4.

2. **View your image and prepare your plan of attack.**

   Does your white balance look correct? Is the image too dark or too light? Do you want to lighten up or darken the shadows in the image? How much color saturation do you want?

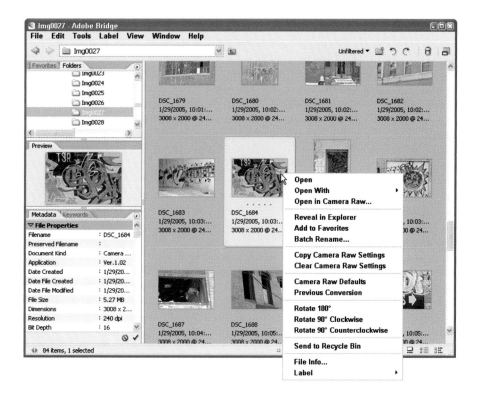

Figure 11-4: Opening a raw image file in Bridge.

Take a minute and evaluate the raw image before diving in and making adjustments in Camera Raw. Planning up front makes for a better image to edit in Photoshop later.

3. **Check the image for sharpness.**

Chances are that this is the first time you have viewed the image this large in size. Use the Zoom tool or press Ctrl+ (⌘+ on the Mac) to enlarge your image even further. Is your image in focus? If you find the image does not cut it when it comes to focus and sharpness, you may want to decide to look for another image to process.

To further check for sharpness of your image, click the Details tab in the Settings panel and move the Sharpness slider all the way to the right, as shown in Figure 11-5. This gives you a view of your image sharpened.

Zoomed image preview

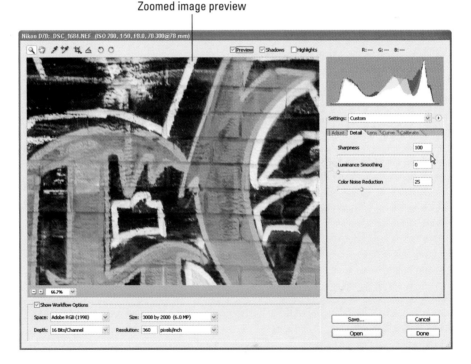

Figure 11-5: Sharpen the image for viewing.

Use the Sharpness slider only for viewing purposes. It is better to sharpen images as the last step of your image editing workflow when working in Photoshop than in Camera Raw. See Chapter 15 for sharpening techniques. Use the Sharpness slider for viewing purposes only, when you evaluate images.

4. **Adjust white balance and tint.**

   After evaluating my image, my first adjustment is to make sure the white balance of the image is correctly set. Camera Raw automatically displays your image with the white balance set as the photograph was captured in your digital camera. You can adjust the white balance two ways: Choose a setting from the White Balance dropdown list shown in Figure 11-6, or use the Temperature slider to adjust the white balance, as shown in Figure 11-7.

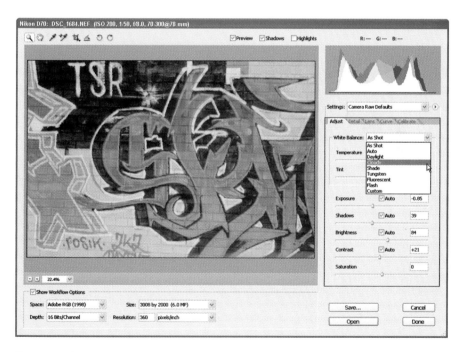

Figure 11-6: Adjusting white balance using the White Balance dropdown list settings.

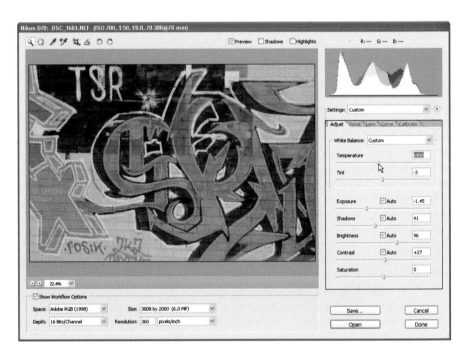

Figure 11-7: Adjusting color temperature using the Temperature slider.

After adjusting the white balance or the color temperature, I use the Tint adjustment slider to fine-tune my image to ensure there isn't any unwanted color cast to the image. I want to make sure the image isn't too bluish, reddish, or purplish.

The goal to adjusting white balance (or color temperature) and tint is to make sure your photo is displayed with a proper tonal range from black to white without a color cast. *Color cast* is when an image has a bluish, reddish, yellowish, or magenta-ish color to it. These color casts can be minimized using the white balance or temperature adjustments in Camera Raw.

After adjusting white balance and tint, select the Preview check box on the Camera Raw Option bar to see what the image looked like before you made any adjustments and then after you made the adjustments.

5. **Adjust image exposure.**

The next step in the Camera Raw workflow is to adjust the overall exposure of the image. Select the Highlights option on the Option bar. Move the Exposure slider to the left just until visible, or *hot,* pixels start to appear in the image preview area, as shown in Figure 11-8. (Hot pixels are areas of the image where pixels begin to turn the color red.)

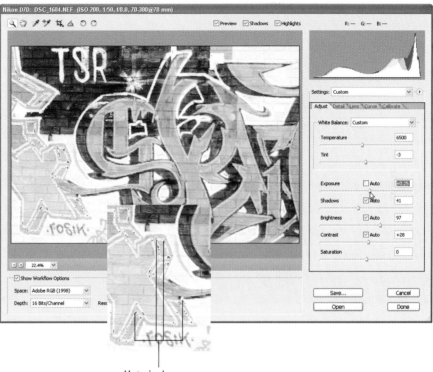

Hot pixel areas

Figure 11-8: Moving the Exposure slider until hot pixels appear.

When you press and hold the Alt key (Option key on the Mac) while you move the Exposure slider to the right, the image will appear black. Slowly move the slider to the right until the red colored pixels start to appear. When pixels start to appear, leave the slider at that spot. Moving the slider further starts to eliminate the image data for those pixels showing in the preview window. Back off the adjustment by moving the slider slightly to the left until the hot pixels disappear.

6. **Adjust for shadow detail.**

The next step in the Camera Raw workflow is to make adjustments to shadow area detail of your image. With Shadows selected in the Option bar, move the Shadows slider to the left until hot pixels (shown in the blue colored areas in Figure 11-9), start to appear.

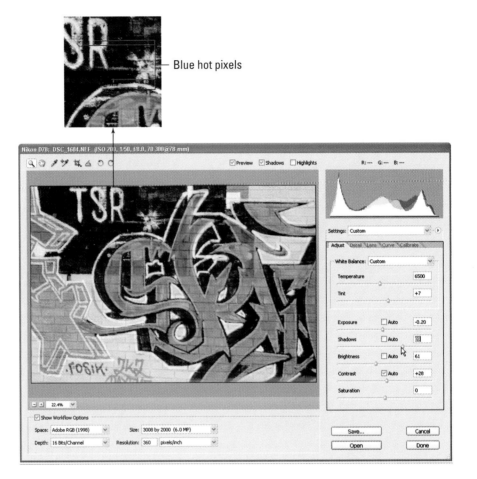

Blue hot pixels

Figure 11-9: Moving the Shadow slider until hot pixels appear.

The term *hot pixels* refers to areas of the image that start to lose detail if adjustments are too extreme. In the example shown in Figure 11-9, shadow detail gets lost in the areas where blue starts to appear.

You may find the shadow adjustment is a matter of your personal taste. I tend to like darkened shadow areas of some of my images, and I may use more adjustment than other photographers would. Make your Camera Raw adjustments to where you are pleased with the results.

7. Adjust brightness.

Using the Brightness slider (see Figure 11-10), move to right or left until you are pleased with the result.

Figure 11-10: Adjusting overall image brightness, contrast, and color saturation.

8. Adjust contrast.

Contrast is the difference between the dark and light areas of your images. Increasing contrast darkens the dark areas of the image, lights up the lighter areas of your image, and punches up the colors.

When adjusting contrast, be careful not to turn it up so high that your photograph appears unnatural. As with all image adjustments, sometimes *less is more*.

9. Adjust saturation.

Moving the Saturation slider to the right increases the amount of color saturation in your image. Most raw images need an increase in color saturation. Move the slider to the right to increase saturation or to the left to reduce saturation.

Adding too much saturation to the image causes certain colors to *blow out,* or become over saturated. This results in *clipping,* which means loss of data in that area. You know when an area of your image is blown out when the color starts to look too bright in that area and the detail of that area starts to decrease.

10. **Double-check that workflow options are correct.**

Before opening the image in Photoshop for further editing, make sure Show Workflow Options (located on the bottom-left of the Camera Raw window) is selected. Figure 11-11 shows the settings I made for this image. I have my color space set to Adobe RGB, bit depth set to 16 bit, image size to 6 megapixel (a good resolution for 8×10 prints), and my resolution set to 360 dpi. If you intend to print your images at a larger size, choose a larger setting from the Size dropdown list.

11. **Click Open to open the image in a Photoshop image window.**

You are now ready to make final overall adjustments and edits to your image in Photoshop. If you click Done, your raw adjustments are saved to the images XMP sidecar file.

If you open a previously adjusted raw file and decide that you want to undo your adjustments, choose Camera Raw Defaults in from the Settings dropdown list.

Figure 11-11: Final workflow settings.

12. **If you want to save the adjusted raw file to another format to edit later, click Save.**

    You can specify a different filename and file format in Camera Raw.

You can choose the new Adobe DNG (Digital Negative) raw format in the Save Options window, as shown in Figure 11-12. DNG allows for a standard raw format that you can convert different proprietary types of raw files to.

In addition to the new DNG raw format, you can save your file in the normal TIFF, JPEG, and Photoshop (PSD) file formats.

Whenever using the Save options, always remember to specify a new filename to prevent copying over the original file.

For many converted raw images, you may find that additional adjustments to levels, brightness/contrast, and hue/saturation aren't even needed. The more you edit images using Camera Raw, the more accurate your overall adjustments become.

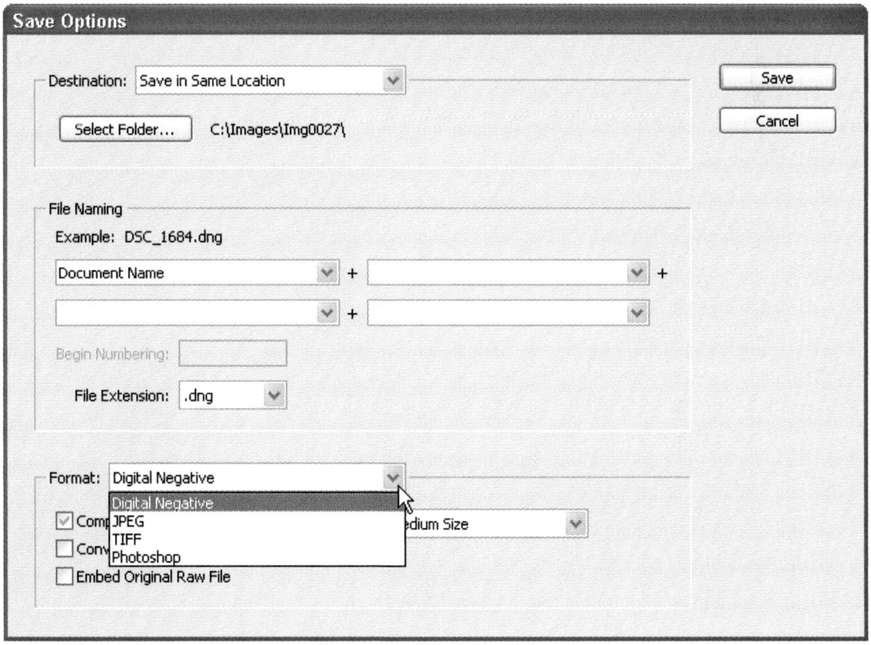

Figure 11-12: Camera Raw Save Options window.

Reducing noise in raw files

Image noise causes those nasty *artifacts,* the colored speckles found in the shadow areas of an image, which you may notice in your image. Digital camera image noise becomes more prevalent in higher ISO settings, especially from consumer digital cameras. Noise becomes more noticeable when enlarging your images on screen or in print. Quite often, image noise is more noticeable in the shadow areas of your image.

The Detail tab in the Camera Raw window, shown here, contains controls to reduce image noise.

Camera Raw offers image noise reduction for luminance (grayscale image noise) and color noise. The Luminance Smoothing slider reduces grayscale noise, or *grain*, in the image, while the Color Noise Reduction slider reduces color artifacts in an image. Moving both sliders to zero turns off noise reduction.

Original raw image   Adjusted raw image

Saving and applying Camera Raw settings

If you shoot a lot of raw photos, you soon realize that opening these one at a time in Camera Raw and processing these one by one can be a chore. Wouldn't it be nice to take a flash card full of similar raw files, load them up on your hard disk drive, adjust one image, and copy the adjustments to the rest? I bet that would save a lot of time, especially if all the images were shot under similar conditions.

Good news! Camera Raw offers you just that:

1. **Save Camera Raw settings in an image you intend to use as a source image.**

   When you are done applying Camera Raw settings to this image, clicking Open, Done, or Save saves settings to the image sidecar file (XMP file).

2. **Copy Camera Raw Settings from the source image in Bridge.**

   Right-click the image, as shown in Figure 11-13 and choose Copy Camera Raw Settings from the flyout menu. You can also choose Edit ⇨ Apply Camera Raw Settings ⇨ Copy Camera Raw Settings or press Ctrl+Alt+C (⌘+Option+C on the Mac).

Figure 11-13: Copying Camera Raw settings from the source image.

3. **Select the images you intend to copy the Camera Raw Settings to.**

   While you press and hold the Ctrl key (the ⌘ key on the Mac), click the images that you want to paste the source image Camera Raw settings to.

4. **Right-click and choose Paste Camera Raw Settings (see Figure 11-14).**

   From the window that appears, choose the individual adjustments you want or leave the defaults selected. Paste Camera Raw Settings is also available in the Edit ⇨ Apply Camera Raw Settings menu or by pressing Ctrl+Alt+V (⌘+Option+V on the Mac).

5. **Click OK to paste the chosen Camera Raw settings to the selected images.**

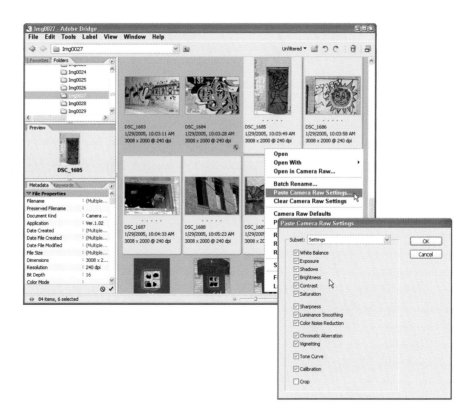

Figure 11-14: Selecting Paste Camera Raw settings.

TIP

If you mistakenly apply Camera Raw settings to one or more images, you can always revert back to their original default settings by right-clicking the selected images in Bridge and choosing Clear Camera Raw Settings.

Correcting lens shortcomings with the Lens Tab controls

Wouldn't it be nice if software could cover up for your digital camera and lens shortcomings? You would never have to worry about exposure, white balance, focus, or composition. Hey, everyone could be a great photographer! Camera Raw gives the photographer some ability to compensate for two problems that occasionally occur, chromatic aberrations and vignetting.

Chromatic aberration happens when the camera lens doesn't focus red, green, and blue light. The result in some photographs is color fringing, or abnormal colors that appear in the high contrast edges of the photograph, as shown in Figure 11-15.

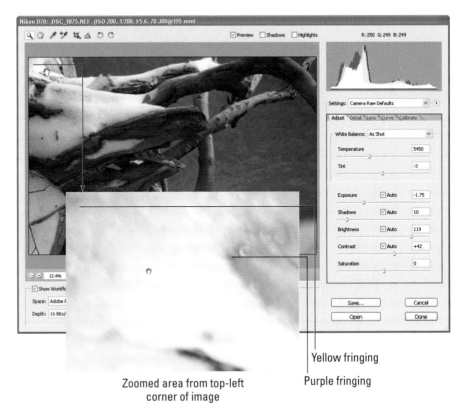

Yellow fringing

Purple fringing

Zoomed area from top-left corner of image

Figure 11-15: Correcting chromatic aberrations.

To correct chromatic aberrations visible in a photograph:

1. **Zoom in on one of the corners of the image to about 300 percent.**

   Pick a corner with a light background and dark foreground if possible.

2. **Click on the Lens Tab.**

3. **Move the Fix Red/Cyan Fringe slider to compensate for the red and cyan fringing shown in Figure 11-16.**

   Make the adjustments to the right or to the left until the fringing is minimized.

4. **Move thc Blue/Yellow Fringe slider to minimize any blue and yellow fringing.**

   Make the adjustments to the right or to the left until the fringing is minimized.

5. **Click Open or Done when finished.**

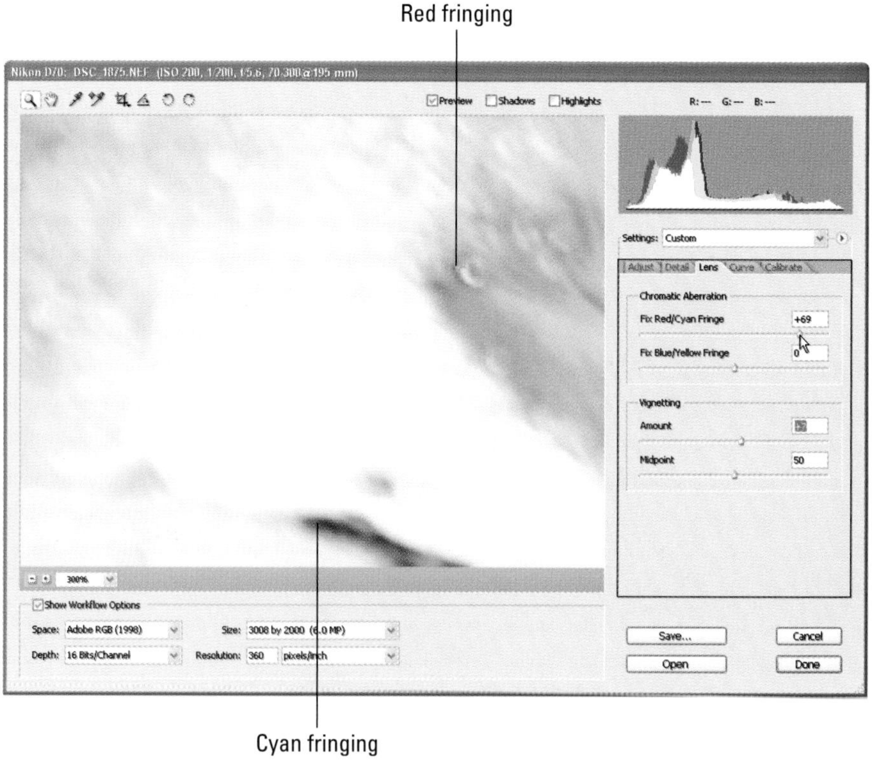

Figure 11-16: Moving the Fix Red/Cyan Fringe slider.

Vignetting is a visible dark border noticeable in the corners and around the image frame, as shown in Figure 11-17. Vignetting occurs when lenses are used to their extreme adjustment limits. Vignetting may occur when a lens is used wide open or at its largest aperture setting while at its widest angle.

To minimize vignetting:

1. **Click the Lens tab in Camera Raw.**
2. **Move the Vignetting Amount slider to the right to lessen the dark corners of the image, as shown in Figure 11-18.**

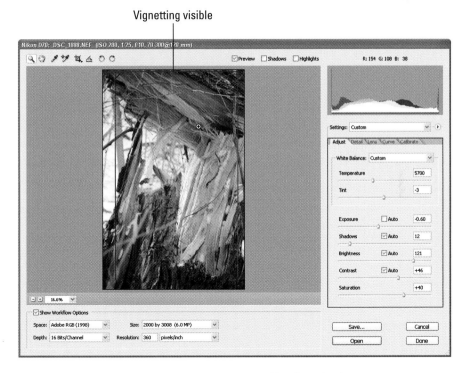

Figure 11-17: Vignetting is noticeable in the corners and borders of an image.

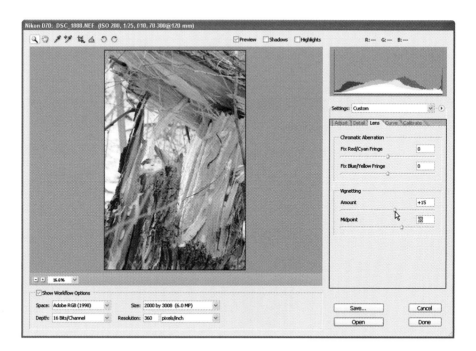

Figure 11-18: Correcting vignetting.

3. **Use the Vignetting Midpoint slider to expand or minimize your adjust-ment to the center area of your image.**

   Moving the slider to the left applies your adjustments to the center, while moving the slider to the right minimizes the changes more toward the edges.

4. **Click Done or Open when finished.**

Reviewing Camera Raw Workflow

If you shoot in raw format with your digital camera, you'll like the control Camera Raw provides you over your images. Having the ability to make adjustments to white balance, exposure, shadows, brightness, contrast, and saturation *before* editing images in Photoshop is a powerful advantage. Adjustments made in Photoshop usually results in loss of information. Now you can make these overall adjustments in Camera Raw without loss of infor-mation, increasing the overall quality of your photographs.

The following is a review of the steps in your raw conversion workflow:

1. **View image thumbnails in Bridge and open the Raw image to convert.**

2. **Review the image.**

   Evaluate the image for white balance, exposure, brightness, contrast, saturation, and lens details. Formulate your plan of attack.

3. **Adjust the image for white balance using the White Balance drop-down list or the Temperature slider.**

4. **Make any necessary adjustments to tint using the Tint adjustment slider.**

   After adjusting the white balance, make any further adjustments to reduce color cast in your image.

5. **Add or subtract from your overall image exposure using the Exposure Adjustment slider.**

   In Camera Raw, you can make adjustments to the image exposure by moving the Exposure slider to the left or right without losing image data. This is a powerful tool: Judging exposures while shooting and viewing on 1½ inch LCD screens can be difficult.

6. **Lighten or darken shadow detail using the Shadows adjustment slider.**

7. **Adjust brightness using the Brightness adjustment slider.**

   Especially after adjusting an image's overall exposure and shadows, you may want to increase or decrease image brightness to your liking.

8. **Increase or decrease image contrast using the Contrast slider**.

   Move the slider to the right to increase contrast in your image, and to the left to decrease.

9. **Increase color saturation with the Saturation slider.**

   Increase color saturation by moving the slider to the right, and decrease by moving it to the left..

10. **Compensate for color fringing or vignetting using the tools in the Lens tab.**

11. **Click Open to open the image in Photoshop**.

    Click Done to return to Bridge with your changes added to the image sidecar file, or click Save to save the image in another image format.

12. **Apply your raw image settings to other images using Bridge.**

    To save time in editing similar images one at a time in Camera Raw, apply one Raw setting to other images.

Chapter 12

Preparing to Correct and Edit

*W*orking on complex projects like painting your house, changing the oil in your car, assembling bookshelves, or processing an image in Photoshop requires some upfront planning. If you are the type that likes to dive into things, that's great, except sometimes things do not go according to plan.

If you do not plan carefully for some projects, you can wind up painting half the house the wrong color before anyone notices and points out the mistake. You can pour the wrong type of oil in your car's engine or assemble some furniture with four or five parts left over. You may have completed the tasks quickly, but you also may have experienced some quality problems along the way.

Processing an image in Photoshop is a complex task that should be planned before you start each image project. Using the practices illustrated in this book helps: Some basic planning for each image goes a long way. Mix in a little bit of file management and proper sizing and you are on your way to efficiently producing consistently high quality images and prints, without any parts left over!

Organize to Maximize

One of the most laborious tasks when working with hundreds or thousands of image files is keeping them organized. Even if you don't take a lot of photos, image files add up over the years. The best way to manage your digital camera files is to maintain a few basic groups of file folders on your computer's hard disk.

✔ **Original image folders.** Original images downloaded from your digital camera should be loaded into a separate folder on your computer's hard disk. Whenever you download a memory card full of new image files from your camera to computer, create a new folder for these images.

After downloading images to your computer from your digital camera or memory card, make sure you immediately make a backup of your new images to CD or DVD. Make two backup copies, one for everyday use and one for the fire safe or safety deposit box.

✔ **Working image folders.** Whenever you open an image in Photoshop or convert raw images in Camera Raw, save your working copies in a separate folder.

Never work on the original image file. You want to make sure your original is always intact for safekeeping and archiving purposes. If an original image is altered, saved, and then closed, there is no way to go back and change it to its original state. If you make a mistake with a file, you always want to be able to go back to a copy of the image before you altered it.

✔ **Final output folders.** When you complete editing an image in your working folder, save a copy of the file to an output folder. I personally maintain many output folders, because this allows me to organize my work into separate projects.

Setting up your image storage process before you begin processing and outputting your images is important. Whatever type of computer you use, the process is the same.

Keep all of your images "in one basket," or folder structure, so that you can more easily perform an organized backup. Back up all your image files on a regular basis to an external hard disk, CD, or DVD. Losing your images is the same as losing original negatives (back in the days of film). An ounce of prevention is better than a pound of cure, and there isn't a cure for losing files when your hard disk crashes!

A Wee Bit of Planning

When you first view an image in Bridge, Camera Raw, or Photoshop, have a game plan on how you'll edit the image in Photoshop. Digital cameras are really good at capturing great images, but most images can use some tweaking. An important practice to include in your overall workflow is to plan your edits, like I've done in Figure 12-1.

Figure 12-1: Planning for edits in Photoshop increases your chances of success the first time.

It may take you a few minutes, or just a few seconds, but take a good look at the image and go through an image evaluation checklist, such as the list that follows.

1. **Is the image in focus and sharp?**

   There is no sense in taking the time to edit an image that's out of focus or doesn't have the right depth of field. Take a close look to make sure your image is sharp.

2. **Is the image properly exposed?**

   If you shoot JPEG images and your exposures are off, making those corrections in Photoshop is more difficult than if you are shooting raw images. Evaluate your image to see if you need to make corrections for underexposure or overexposure.

3. Is the white balance correct? Do I need to correct a color cast?

If your image has a yellow, magenta, blue, purple, or red tint to it, chances are your image was captured with the wrong white balance settings. These adjustments are easier using Camera Raw, but if you shoot JPEG, you have a little more work to do in Photoshop.

4. Do I need to adjust brightness or contrast?

Some of your images can always use adjustment to brightness and contrast. Photographers differ on how much contrast they want in their images. That's usually a personal decision based on individual taste. Check to see if your image needs some tweaking for brightness or a little extra punch with an increase in contrast.

5. Does the image need an increase in saturation?

Most digital camera images can use a little increase in color saturation. However, there are some images that come out of the camera saturated just fine. Carefully evaluate your image for color saturation.

Adding too much color saturation can often blow out certain colors in your image. This often happens with reds in images. Be careful not to add too much color saturation to your images, because over saturated colors look too bright and unnatural.

The best way to know when your colors are too saturated is to turn on Gamut Warning. Gamut Warning shows you areas of an image that are out of gamut — areas where color cannot be reproduced by a specified output device. Turn on Gamut Warning by choosing View ➪ Gamut Warning.

6. Does the image need straightening?

For landscape photos especially, check the horizon. Is it straight? This is often overlooked, so make sure your horizons are level.

7. What is the intended output?

Determine what type of image you're producing. If for print, what is the maximum size? If you don't plan on using the image for the Web, consider producing a version of the finished product for a Web site in the future.

Maintain working image that you can use for printing at the largest size you can produce. You can always downsize an image to print at smaller sizes or to use on the Web.

A little up front planning can go a long way in your overall efficiency using Photoshop. Planning for your image editing can help you reduce errors and get it right the first time. Figure 12-2 shows the final processed image after I went through the image-editing checklist.

Before

After

Figure 12-2: Take time to evaluate your images before editing, and you'll like the end result.

Editing Images in Layers

I love big sandwiches with lots of layers. I start with a fresh slice of wheat bread, the basis of every great sandwich. I then add a layer of lettuce and then some roast beef. Add a little layer of mustard, another layer of cheese, and I'm almost there, at least half way! Add another slice of fresh bread, some more lettuce, a layer of tomato, and then the final slice of bread. There you go, my triple-decker, nine layers in all. (Accompanied with a diet soda: After all those calories I have to cut back somewhere!)

I could have been satisfied just with the first slice of bread, but by stacking eight other layers of goodies, my finished product is much more appealing.

Editing images in Photoshop is based on a premise of performing each individual change to an image in its own layer. Think of each layer as a transparency, and each transparency containing a particular change. When you open an image file in Photoshop, the original image is used as a *background layer*. Add a layer to make an adjustment and that layer is placed on top of the background layer. Each new edit is contained in a new layer, stacked from the bottom on up. Stack the images together and you have a composite image, a finished product just like my hero sandwich!

Getting to know the Layers palette

The Layers palette contains all the layers that make up an image. You use the Layers palette to control all layers; you can create new layers, hide layers, and work with groups of layers. The Layers palette is shown in Figure 12-3: Click the palette menu button to display the Layers flyout menu.

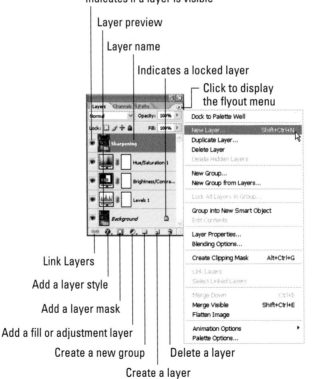

Figure 12-3: The Layers palette with the Layers flyout menu.

By default, the Layers palette is visible in Photoshop. If you inadvertently close the Layers palette while you're working in Photoshop, you can always start it up again by choosing Windows ⇨ Layers or by pressing the F7 key.

Important facts about working in layers include:

- **Background layer:** When opening an image file, Photoshop creates the bottom-most background layer. There are certain changes that cannot be made to the background layer in Photoshop: You cannot delete, reorder, or change the opacity or blending mode of the background layer.

  Before editing your image, make sure you always make a duplicate of the background layer. It is a best practice to not perform edits to the background layer. Reserve that layer as the original to base all your edits on: It's your backup parachute in case anything goes wrong.

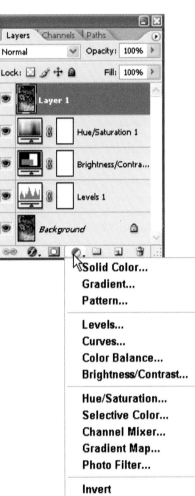

- **To show or hide the contents of a layer, click the eye icon.** If the eye icon is visible, the contents of the layer are visible. If the eye icon is not visible, the contents of the layer are hidden.

- **Rename layers by double-clicking the layer name and typing the new name.**

- **Changing layer order:** To change the order of your layers, click a layer and drag it to the position where you want that layer to appear.

- **Creating new layers:** Click the Create a New Layer button. Choose the layer type in the flyout menu, as shown in Figure 12-4.

You can also create a new layer by dragging an existing layer to the New Layer button, which is located on the bottom of the Layers palette.

Figure 12-4: Creating new layers.

⮡ **Deleting layers:** Click the layer and drag the layer to trashcan icon located on the bottom right of the Layers palette. You can also right-click the layer and choose Delete Layer from the flyout menu, as shown in Figure 12-5.

⮡ **Flattening Layers:** Flattening layers combines all layers into one layer. When you flatten an image, your ability to make changes to individual layers is lost. Flattening layers is usually performed in order to create a version of an image to print or to submit for publishing.

If no layers are selected, the entire image is flattened into one layer with the top layer's name. If two or more layers are selected, only those layers are combined into one layer, again taking the top layer's name.

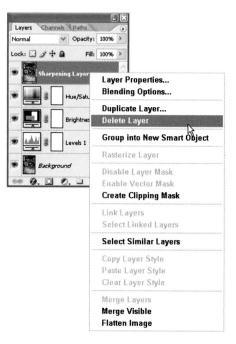

Figure 12-5: Deleting a layer using the Layers flyout menu.

To maintain your image edits, save your image before flattening the image. Make sure to save flattened versions of your image files using another filename.

Adjustment and fill layers

Adjustment layers are layers that allow you to change color or tonal values of an image without affecting the original (background) image. When you create an adjustment layer, changes made in that layer are viewable along with all the adjustments you made in the layers underneath it. You can use adjustment layers to make enhancements to color balance, brightness, contrast, and color saturation.

An adjustment layer affects all the layers beneath it in the Layers palette. The advantage is that a change made to an adjustment layer doesn't need to be repeated in the layers stacked beneath it. For example, if you want to change the brightness of an image, you have to make that change only once to the overall image.

Fill layers allow you to fill the layer with solid colors, gradients, or patterns. A fill layer does not affect the layers beneath it.

The following list describes the types of adjustment and fill layers you can use in your image editing workflow:

- **Solid Color:** A solid color layer is considered a fill layer. Create a solid color layer to fill an image with a color. You can use it to create a colored background for an image.

- **Gradient fill layer:** You can use gradients to apply a color in a transition from light to dark. It's useful for creating a dark-edged vignette for some images or a transitioned color background. Figure 12-6 shows different types of gradients.

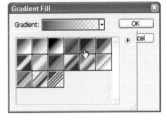

Figure 12-6: Choosing a gradient type.

  Gradients are used to create some cool image special effects. You can experiment with images by adding or reducing the opacity of the fill layer.

- **Pattern fill layer:** Create a layer containing a pattern from the pattern menu shown in Figure 12-7. Adjust the layer's opacity to strengthen or weaken the pattern effect.

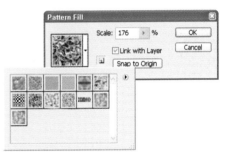

- **Levels adjustment layer:** You can make adjustments to levels of red, green, blue, and midtones in this layer. Chapter 13 covers the procedure for using the Levels adjustment layer to make overall color corrections to an image.

Figure 12-7: Choosing a Pattern Fill.

- **Curves adjustment layer:** The curves adjustment layer lets you make specific changes to tonality and color in an image. You can use it to complement changes made in the Levels adjustment layer. For most photos, only slight changes to the Curves grid are necessary, as shown in Figure 12-8. Chapter 13 covers advanced color correction using the Curves adjustment layer.

- **Color Balance adjustment layer:** The Color Balance adjustment layer makes changes to color hues in an image. For most photos, these corrections are not needed if you adopt a workflow, like the one in Chapter 13 that illustrates how to eliminate color cast in the Levels adjustment layer.

- **Brightness/Contrast adjustment layer:** You can make adjustments to the image's overall brightness and contrast in this layer.

- **Hue/Saturation adjustment layer:** One of the last steps in your image editing workflow is creating a Hue/Saturation layer and punching up the color saturation in your image to make your colors *pop.*

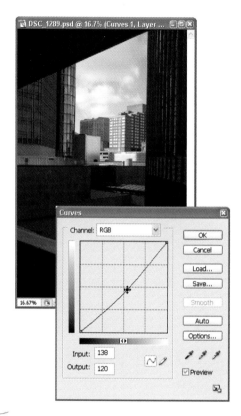

Figure 12-8: Making slight color adjustment to an image in the Curves grid.

Sizing Images

Like any other technical area, digital photography has its share of acronyms. Why engineers, tech writers, and the technology powers-that-be come up with these acronyms is beyond me. When it comes to sizing images, photographers have to deal with such acronyms as DPI (Dots per Inch), PPI (Pixels per Inch), and SES.

Actually, SES isn't an acronym describing anything in digital photography or Photoshop. It means *Squirrel Eating Strawberries,* which occurred outside my window at the moment I was writing this. I grabbed my camera and took a few shots. Check out one of the photographs in Figure 12-9.

Always be ready for action. Good photo opportunities will come to you. Keep a digital camera nearby at all times. You never know what you'll come across during the day.

Digital images are actually made up of tiny square dots called *pixels*. Everything you do in Photoshop has to do with changing these pixels. Obtaining a good understanding of pixels and their relation to quality photographs is what using Photoshop is all about.

To the human eye, it's impossible to view the individual pixels that make up an image. Enlarge an image in Photoshop to 800 percent, and you can see the square pixels appear, as shown in Figure 12-10.

Figure 12-9: Squirrel eating strawberries (SES).

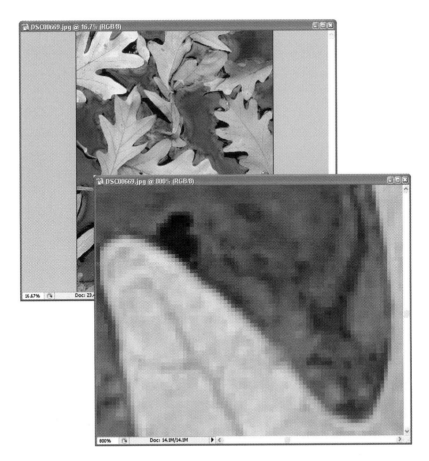

Figure 12-10: Digital images are made up of square pixels.

A resolution of sorts

The subject of print size can be confusing. It's best to think of print size and print resolution as referring to the same measurement. *Printer* resolution is another story — see Chapter 18.

To understand how to size images to your intended output, reviewing the different resolution concepts is important:

- **Resolution:** Described as the size of an image. An image with the resolution of 2,960×1,920 pixels contains 4,915,200 pixels, or roughly five megapixels.

- **Interpolation:** Also called resampling, interpolation is the method to change the number of pixels in an image. An example would be interpolating a two megapixel image file to a five megapixel image file in order to provide enough image data to print a quality 8×10 inch print.

  Interpolating images results in a loss of image quality. This may be noticeable in your prints.

- **DPI:** Referred to as dots per inch, DPI is a measurement used by printer manufacturers to describe the resolution capability of their printers. This setting has *nothing* in common with image resolution: Printer resolution is measured differently.

- **Print Size/Print Resolution:** In Photoshop, print size/print resolution is referred to the output size of an image. For most prints from an inkjet printer, you want to set your resolution at 300 or 360 pixels/ inch, as shown in Figure 12-11. Set your image size by choosing Image ⇨ Image Size or by pressing Ctrl+Alt+I (⌘+Option+I on the Mac).

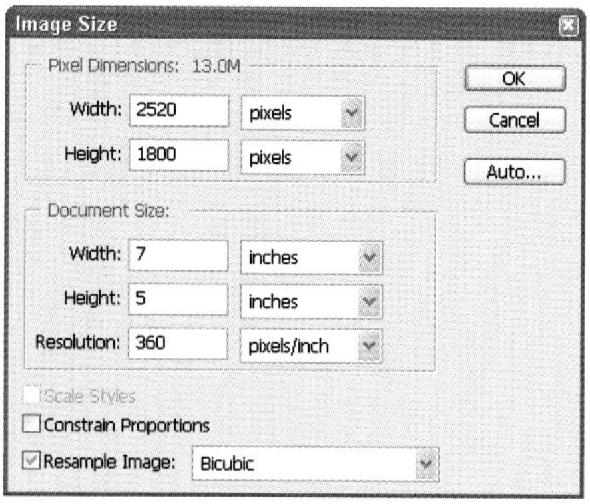

Figure 12-11: Setting image sizes for output using the Image Size dialog box.

Cropping the night away

Cropping an image in Photoshop is an efficient way to specify the exact output size of an image you open in Photoshop. With cropping, you can specify an image's width, height, and output resolution all in one click and drag of the mouse.

The steps to cropping an image in Photoshop are as follows:

1. **Open an image in Photoshop.**

   Choose File ⇨ Open or select an image to open in Bridge.

2. **Determine the image output size and resolution.**

   If you intend to print the image at 8×10 or 5×7, the optimum resolution for your printer is 300 or 360 pixels/inch.

   Newer model photo quality printers print at an optimum setting of 360 ppi (pixels/inch) although most produce great results at 300 ppi. Experiment with your printer to find the best resolution.

3. **Click the Crop tool in the Toolbox.**

4. **Set the width and height in the Option bar, as shown in Figure 12-12.**

5. **Set the resolution to 300 or 360.**

   Use 300 or 360 so that you maintain the same number of pixels in the image, thus keeping the same image size.

6. **Click the image and drag the crop box to the desired cropping area.**

Click to view the image's native size

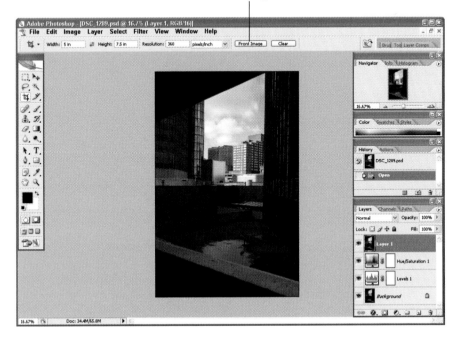

Figure 12-12: Setting up image size using the Crop tool.

7. **Move the crop box to the desired position in the image you want cropped, as shown in Figure 12-13.**

8. **Click the check icon in the Option bar or double-click the cursor within the crop area to complete the crop.**

   To cancel the crop, click the cancel icon next to the check.

If you are processing raw images in Photoshop, take advantage of the Camera Raw image sizing features by setting the maximum image size in Camera Raw before opening the image in Photoshop. More information on upsizing images can be found in Chapter 11.

Sizing and cropping images is usually one of the final steps in my overall image editing workflow. I typically resize my images as a step before sharpening to ensure that the correct amount of sharpening is applied to the correct number of pixels. While working on a typical photo in Photoshop, save cropping and resizing for the end of your image editing workflow, just before sharpening.

Click to cancel

Click and drag to resize crop   Click to complete

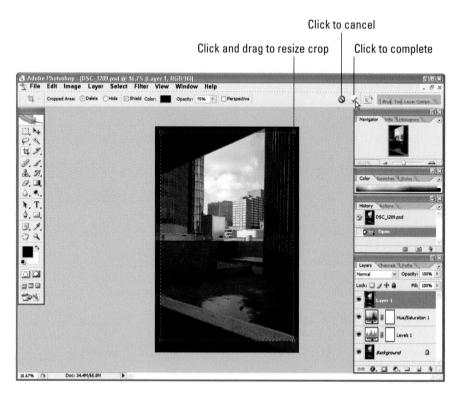

Figure 12-13: Setting up image size using the Crop tool.

Part IV
Working with Images in Photoshop CS2

The 5th Wave   By Rich Tennant

"I'm going to assume that most of you — but not all of you — understand that this session on 'masking' has to do with Photoshop."

Quality photographs produced by artists, professional photographers, or hobbyists are grounded in the discipline they apply to their craft. If you ask 10 professional photographers their secret to producing great photographs with Photoshop, eight or nine will tell you it's sticking to a structured process, an image workflow.

Next in our Photoshop adventures, we dive into the best practices for creating quality, or "fine" images using Photoshop CS2. Performing overall image adjustments, image editing, creating unique special effects with filters, and preparing your images for final output are covered in detail in this part. The sum of these techniques provides you with a workflow you can use to create those stunning photographs with Photoshop.

Chapter 13

Making Image Corrections

*T*echnology never ceases to amaze. Stick a little plastic card into a cash machine, type a few numbers on a keyboard, and it spits money back at you. Hit a few buttons on your remote control and automatically replay the TV show you missed a few hours ago, in slow motion if you want!

Digital cameras have had fully automatic and preprogrammed modes since the beginning, but unbelievably some of the high-end professional cameras have wireless LAN capabilities that allow you to shoot a photo and immediately send it to your computer. With some fancy software setup, you can have these automatically print on your inkjet printer!

Technology is moving fast, but overall image adjustments, such as exposure, correcting for color casts, brightness, contrast, and color saturation still need to be adjusted by the photographer in Photoshop. Technology hasn't replaced the photographer's trained eye, so until then, you can make overall image corrections in Photoshop, and wait for your printer to kick out the perfect photo.

Making Automatic Color Adjustments

The main reason that many photographers use Photoshop is that they can make color and tonal adjustments to photographs with more control than they ever had in the traditional darkroom. If you're new to Photoshop, you can use the automatic adjustments to make overall corrections until you're comfortable making the corrections on your own. To produce fine prints, your best practice is to develop a workflow to consistently make overall corrections to your photographs. I end this chapter with a summary of a typical color correction workflow that you can try.

This chapter provides you with the steps necessary to perform overall color and tonal adjustments to your images. I also provide some quick methods to make automatic, or *auto,* adjustments on images that work well for snapshots or proofs.

As with anything in life, death and taxes are considered the only sure things. Another sure thing is that there usually isn't an easy way to complete a complex task. Of course I'm referring to making easy color, brightness, and contrast adjustments to your photographs.

But then again . . .

Photoshop offers some quick methods of autoadjusting the color and tonal values of your photographs. For snapshots and proofs, there is nothing wrong with taking a shortcut, and Photoshop offers three basic auto adjustments to do just that. Auto Levels, Auto Contrast, and Auto Color are three commands to use if you're in a hurry. Consider this your "quickie" auto adjustment workflow.

Auto Levels

The Auto Levels command automatically adjusts the darkest point and the lightest point of the image in order to provide a correct tonal range between blacks and whites. Adjusting levels and removing color cast is usually the first step in performing overall adjustments to an image.

To make an Auto Levels adjustment to an image:

1. **Choose an image and open it in Photoshop using Bridge.**

2. **Create a duplicate of the background layer.**

   By creating a new layer, you can apply changes but not affect the original image layer. Choose Layers ⇨ Duplicate Layer from the Layer menu or right-click the background layer in the Layers palette and choose Duplicate Layer, as shown in Figure 13-1.

Figure 13-1: Duplicating the background layer and providing an appropriate layer name.

Make a habit of creating a new layer for changes to the image. By properly using layers, you can back out or change any adjustment you make in your color adjustment workflow.

3. Apply the Auto Levels adjustment.

Choose Image ⇨ Adjustment ⇨ Auto Levels or press Ctrl+Shift+L (⌘+Shift+L on the Mac).

Figure 13-2 illustrates the image before and after the Auto Levels adjustment was applied. The adjustment made established the image's tonal values from the blackpoint of the image to the whitepoint.

In some images Auto Levels can actually introduce unwanted color, or color casts. When this occurs, back out of your changes by choosing Edit ⇨ Undo or by pressing Ctrl+Z (⌘+Z on the Mac).

Before   After

Figure 13-2: Applying Auto Levels increases the tonal range from black to white.

Applying Auto Contrast

The next stop in your quickie auto adjustment workflow is applying Auto Contrast. Auto Contrast automatically adds punch to a photograph by making the dark areas darker and the light areas brighter. Applying Auto Contrast to an image doesn't introduce any color cast to an image.

To apply Auto Contrast:

1. **Create a new layer by duplicating the previous layer.**

2. **Apply the Auto Contrast adjustment.**

   Choose Image ➪ Adjustments ➪ Auto Contrast. You can also press Ctrl+Alt+Shift+L (⌘+ Option+Shift+L on the Mac).

Figure 13-3 shows how applying Auto Contrast to the image produces more pronounced dark areas and light areas than seen in Figure 13-2.

Figure 13-3: Auto Contrast makes dark and light areas of the image more pronounced.

Applying Auto Color

Applying Auto Color to an image punches up the colors a bit by adjusting the shadow areas, midtones, and highlights of the image. Colors that are not exposed properly and look unnatural benefit from the Auto Color adjustment. Auto Color is available only when an image is edited in Adobe RGB (1998) or sRGB modes.

To apply Auto Color to the image:

1. **Create a new layer by duplicating the previous layer.**

2. **Apply the Auto Color adjustment.**

   Choose Image ➪ Adjustments ➪ Auto Color or press Ctrl+Shift+B
   (⌘+Shift+B on the Mac).

Auto Color, Auto Contrast, and Auto
Levels can be used independently of
each other. If you apply these adjustments one after another, you may
wind up with an effect different from
the effect you'd get applying just one
at a time. Experiment with auto
adjustments on individual photos to
find the result that you like the most.

Figure 13-4 shows the changes to the
image color from applying the Auto
Color adjustment.

Figure 13-4: Auto Color slightly adjusts color in
shadows, midtones, and highlights.

Making Color and Tonal Adjustments

There are going to be many photos you open in Photoshop where auto
adjustments are not going to provide the exact color and tonal adjustments
you want. Auto adjustments may bring you close, but maybe not close
enough to get the color and tones you want in your images. Changes such as
correcting for color casts or adjusting levels, brightness, contrast, and color
saturation should be made using adjustment layers in a step-by-step process.
For most photos, you can use the overall adjustment workflow that I've suggested here.

Overall adjustment workflow

You can probably tell by now that I use workflows when shooting and processing photos. So far I've presented workflows for shooting in Chapter 6,
file management in Chapter 12, and raw image processing in Chapter 11.
The next series of steps I'll outline includes an overall adjustment workflow.

In the next few sections I'll be showing you the steps to making overall
adjustments to an image, including:

1. **Evaluate the image for needed adjustments**.

   Look at the image and come up with a game plan on how you intend to make overall corrections.

2. **Correct tonality using the Levels adjustment layer.**

3. **Make further adjustment to color using the Curves and Color Balance adjustment layers.**

4. **Adjust brightness and contrast to your image according to your taste.**

5. **Punch up the color in your image using the Hue/Saturation adjustment layer.**

Figure 13-5 demonstrates how going through an overall adjustment workflow steps improves the overall color and tonality of an image.

Keep in mind that not all images need every single adjustment made to them. Many images may need only slight adjustment to levels but may not need any increase in saturation, for example. Likewise, some images may not require an adjustment in contrast. Experiment and make only the adjustments that give you the image you envisioned while shooting.

Before   After

Figure 13-5: Using an overall adjustment workflow improves color and tonal quality of images.

Evaluating your image

The first step in an overall adjustment workflow is to evaluate your image. Did the image look good straight out of the camera? Is it too dark, too light, too flat (lack of contrast and color saturation), or does it have a color cast?

One quick way to evaluate an image is to view the image using variations. Variations offer multiple thumbnails of an image, providing different versions or *variations* of color balance, contrast, and saturation.

To view variations, choose Image ➪ Adjustments ➪ Variations. Figure 13-6 shows the different thumbnail choices offered.

The Variations command is only available for images in 8 bit per channel mode. Though you can choose thumbnails to make adjustments, using adjustment layers to apply actual adjustments is recommended.

Figure 13-6: Using variations to evaluate an image.

Adjusting levels

The second step in my overall adjustment workflow is adjusting levels. Adjusting levels provides a method of making exact corrections to the tonal value of your image by fine-tuning colors contained in the image's highlights, midtones, and shadows.

To adjust colors and tone using the Levels command:

1. **Create a Levels adjustment layer.**

   Click the Create New Adjustment or Fill Layer button from the Layer palette, as shown in Figure 13-7. The Levels dialog box appears.

Figure 13-7: Creating a Levels adjustment layer.

2. **Make sure the Preview box is checked.**

   With Preview selected, you can view the image changes as you move the slider.

   Keep the Channel selection RGB. You'll be correcting levels for the entire image, all three color channels (red, green, and blue) at the same time.

As you become more familiar with adjusting levels in Photoshop, experiment with changing the Channel selection to the red, green, or blue channels and adjusting them individually. If you are a new user of Photoshop, keep the RGB Channel selected.

3. **View the histogram and slide the Shadows input slider to the right, up to the point where the curve of the histogram begins, as shown in Figure 13-8.**

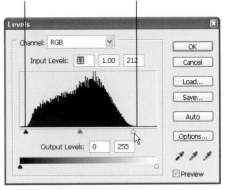

A histogram provides a snapshot of the tonal range of an image. The histogram shows how much detail is in the shadow area on the left, in the midtones in the middle, and in highlights on the right.

Histogram data is different for every image. For many images, the histogram curve begins all the way to the left, where no shadow input slider adjustment is needed.

Figure 13-8: Moving the Levels Shadows and Highlights input sliders.

4. **Slide the Highlights input slider to the left up to the point where the highlights curve begins.**

5. **Move the Midtones input slider to right slightly, checking the image for improved color saturation and contrast in the image.**

In many images, using the Midtone slider to darken the midtones improves the appearance of an image.

6. **Click OK to complete the Levels adjustment.**

If you are not satisfied with the effects of your Levels adjustment, press and hold the Alt key (Option key on the Mac) and click Cancel to reset the settings to the original values. You can then re-create a Levels adjustment layer and attempt to adjust levels again.

You can experiment with adjusting levels in any of the following ways; view the results in your image:

✔ **Set the blackpoint of your image by clicking the Blackpoint Eyedropper and clicking a dark part of the image.** This provides a more accurate blackpoint as a baseline for adjusting levels in your image.

- **Set the whitepoint of the image by clicking the Whitepoint Eyedropper and clicking a lighter part of the image.** This provides a more accurate whitepoint as a baseline for adjusting levels in your image.

- **Darken shadow areas by moving the Shadows input slider to the right.**

- **Adjust the darker midtones by moving the Midtones input slider to the left. Lighten midtones by moving it to the right.**

- **Increase contrast and brighten up highlights by moving the Highlights input slider to the left.**

Figure 13-9 shows the results of the levels adjustments. Moving the Shadow input adjustment slider to the right darkened the shadow areas, moving the Midtones input slider to the right darkened the midtones, and moving the Highlights input slider to the left brightened the highlights.

Before   After

Figure 13-9: The image before levels adjustments and then after levels adjustments are applied.

Ooooh those curves

Making adjustments to the tonal range of an image using levels means making only three adjustments: shadows, midtones (gamma), and highlights. The curves adjustment allows for up to 14 different points of adjustment throughout the tonal range. As with levels, settings made in the Curves layer can be applied to other images.

To adjust an image's tonality using the Curves adjustment layer:

1. **Create a Curves adjustment layer.**

   Click the Create New Adjustment or Fill Layer button from the Layers palette and then choose Curves.

2. **Increase the number of grid lines to provide a more precise grid.**

   Press and hold the Alt key (the Option key on the Mac) while clicking inside the Curves grid to increase the number of grid lines, providing a more precise environment, as shown in Figure 13-10.

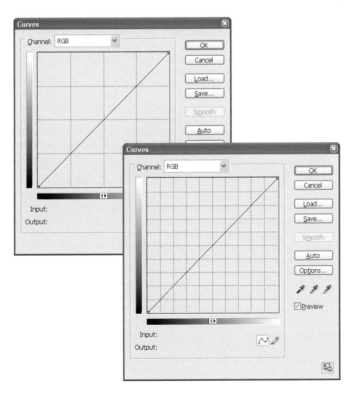

Figure 13-10: Using the Curves adjustment window.

3. **Make tonal adjustments by clicking the curve line and dragging it to the desired grid point or by clicking Auto.**

Drag the curve to the upper-left to brighten and lower-right to darken. Experiment with creating adjustments for shadows, midtones, and highlights.

Figure 13-11 demonstrates how the Auto curves feature can improve color in shadows, midtones, and highlights in this underexposed image.

Before   After

Figure 13-11: Using the Curves adjustment layer to improve this underexposed image.

Adding a Brightness and Contrast adjustment layer

The next step in the overall adjustment workflow is to create a Brightness/Contrast layer. The purpose of creating this layer is to make fine-tuned adjustments that increase or decrease brightness and contrast in the image.

Brightness is simply making the overall image brighter or darker. Adjusting contrast can make the darks darker and the lights lighter or vice versa. Experiment with these adjustments, and you may discover that adjusting levels and curves in the previous steps may have already provided the brightness and contrast you want to the image.

To add a Brightness/Contrast adjustment layer:

1. **Click the Create New Adjustment or Fill Layer button from the Layers palette and then choose Brightness/Contrast.**

2. **Make sure Preview is selected in the Brightness/Contrast dialog box (see Figure 13-12).**

3. **Adjust the amount of brightness and contrast of the image by moving the sliders for each adjustment to the right to increase the amount or to the left to decrease the amount.**

Figure 13-12: Adjusting brightness and contrast while viewing the image

For the image illustrated in Figure 13-13, I added both brightness and contrast to add brightness to the image while maintaining contrast between the light and dark portions of the sky.

> **WARNING!**
>
> Be careful not to overadjust brightness or contrast because doing so can make your photo appear *overprocessed*. Adding too much brightness or contrast can make the light portions of the image too bright and dark portions of the image too black.

4. **Click OK to save the adjustments made in the Brightness/Contrast layer.**

Figure 13-13 illustrates the changes made to the old barn image after the Levels adjustment was completed and then after the Brightness/Contrast adjustment layer was added.

Levels and Curves applied   Brightness/Contrast adjustments layer added

Figure 13-13: Before adjusting brightness and contrast compared to after.

Adding color with the Hue/Saturation adjustment layer

The final step in the overall adjustment workflow is to add color saturation to the image. For many images that you take with your digital camera, a little extra punch to the colors can enhance the "wow" factor of your photos.

With any overall adjustment, sometimes *less is more,* meaning that you may need to make only a slight correction. When adjusting color saturation, sometimes all you have to do is move the saturation slider just slightly to the right until you see the colors pop up a little.

To create a Hue/Saturation layer:

1. **Click the Create New Adjustment or Fill Layer button from the Layers palette and then choose Hue/Saturation.**

2. **Make sure Preview is selected in the Hue/Saturation dialog box.**

3. **Increase image saturation by moving the Saturation slider slightly to the right, as shown in Figure 13-14.**

   As a rule, increase the saturation until you see the colors start to pop.

   Adding too much color saturation can cause certain colors in the image blow out, or become so saturated that detail is lost in those areas. Be careful not to add too much color saturation. If some areas seem to become too saturated, back off your adjustment slightly until you are pleased with the result.

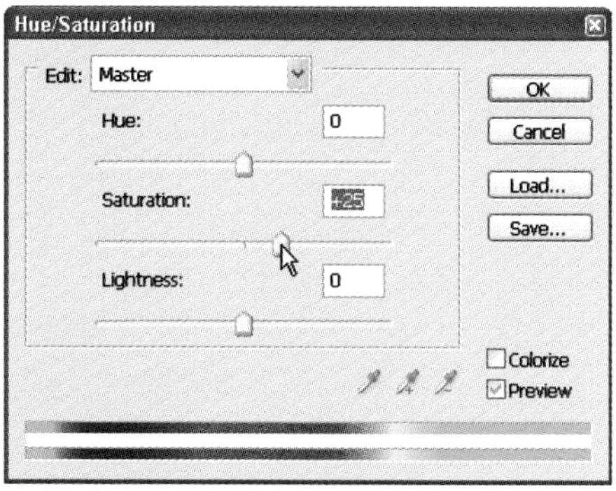

Figure 13-14: Increasing saturation by moving the Saturation slider slightly to the left can make your colors pop.

You can use the Hue/Saturation adjustment layer to adjust individual color hues or saturation amounts. This is an advanced method of color correcting your images. Experiment with changing the hue, and/or saturation of each color to see the result. You may find that just making adjustments to the Master (the default setting) can be just fine for your photos.

4. **Click OK to save your settings.**

Figure 13-15 shows the old barn before and after color saturation was added using the Hue/Saturation adjustment layer. The photo appears to be slightly more vibrant but not over-processed.

Before   After

Figure 13-15: The old barn looks a little more vibrant with a dash of color saturation.

Fixing photos with the Shadow/Highlight command

New in Photoshop CS, the Shadow/Highlight command could be considered an overall adjustment deserving of its own layer in Photoshop. Alas, being new, it first may have to prove itself for a few versions. (Layers are a very closed group and not very friendly to outsiders.) Until then, I'll use the command as introduced in Photoshop CS.

The Shadow/Highlight command lightens or darkens areas based on neighboring pixels. You can adjust photos that have washed out areas (overexposed areas) or dark areas due to backlighting with the Shadow/Highlight command.

The old barn photo used to illustrate adjustment layers is a prime candidate for use with the Shadow/Highlight command:

1. **Use the background layer or create a new layer.**

   If creating a new layer, merge the visible layers into it by choosing Layer ➪ Merge Visible or by pressing Ctrl+Alt+Shift+E (+Option+Shift+E on the Mac).

2. **Start the Shadow Highlight command by choosing Image ➪ Adjustments ➪ Shadow/Highlights.**

3. **Adjust the image using the Shadow/Highlights dialog box shown in Figure 13-16.**

4. **Select Show More Options to show all options available.**

5. **Move the Shadows Amount and Highlights Amount sliders right to increase and left to decrease amounts.**

   Experiment with the Tonal Width to change the range of tones in the shadows or highlights being adjusted. The Radius slider controls the size of the area around each pixel.

Figure 13-17 shows how the dark shadow areas of the old barn photo now show more detail and the sky color and detail are enhanced.

TECHNICAL STUFF

The Shadow/Highlight command also lets you adjust the color, midtone, and brightness of the image in the Adjustments area of the window. Experiment with these sliders to fine-tune the areas changed by the Shadow/Highlight command.

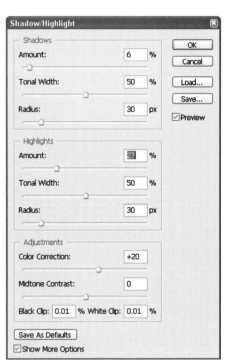

Figure 13-16: The Shadow/Highlight command can help fix backlit and blown-out areas of an image.

Before After

Figure 13-17: The Shadow/Highlight command helped the old barn photo by bringing out detail in the trees and sky.

Making changes to exposure

New to Photoshop CS2 is the Exposure command. Though intended for high definition images (HDR), the Exposure command can be used to adjust images in 8 or 16 bit modes that were underexposed or overexposed in the camera. Normally, this would be the first adjustment in an overall workflow. However, exposure can be compensated for in the raw conversion workflow that I suggest in Chapter 11, or through the levels and curves adjustments covered earlier in this chapter.

If you are shooting and converting raw files using Camera Raw, there is no need to use the Exposure command as this feature is one of the feature adjustments used in Camera Raw.

To change the exposure of an image:

1. **Use the background layer or create a new layer.**

   If creating a new layer, merge the visible layers into it by pressing Ctrl+Alt+Shift+E (+Option+Shift+E on the Mac).

2. **Choose Image ➪ Adjustments ➪ Exposure.**

   The Exposure dialog box is shown in Figure 13-18.

3. **Make sure the Preview option is selected.**

4. **Move the Exposure slider to the right to increase exposure.**

   Move the Exposure slider to the left to decrease exposure in an image.

5. **Click OK to finish.**

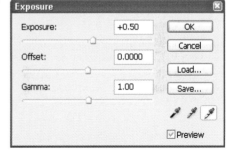

Figure 13-18: Using the Exposure command to increase the exposure of a slightly underexposed image.

Figure 13-19 shows that just by adding a half increment of exposure to the original image's exposure, the overall quality of this portrait improves greatly.

Before   After

Figure 13-19: Small increments of exposure can make a big difference in the quality of a photograph.

Adding just the right amount . . .

Making some overall adjustments to your digital files is almost always necessary. How you have your digital camera set up for in-camera adjustments and how well your images are exposed affect how much adjustment is necessary. Many photographers prefer to do all image adjustments in Photoshop instead of using the camera to adjust settings such as color saturation and sharpening.

When making overall image adjustments, make sure not to overdo it. Changes made to levels, curves, brightness, contrast, and color saturation should be made in necessary increments only.

Adding too much exposure, brightness, contrast, or color saturation can make your photos look overprocessed.

If you shoot photos in raw format and use Camera Raw to process images before you open them in Photoshop, you may need to make fewer corrections in Photoshop. Exposure, white balance, brightness, contrast, and color saturation adjustments can all be made in Camera Raw and may not need any further adjustment in Photoshop. See Chapter 11 for more about Camera Raw.

Reviewing an Overall Color Correction Workflow

Keep in mind that the way to digital photography success is to maintain a certain level of order in your digital workflow universe. Without order, there would be chaos. If it seems this sounds like something straight out of a corny movie, you may be right!

The point I'm making is that when you're doing overall color corrections to your images, follow the step-by-step workflow covered in this chapter, or create your own. Your images will look a lot better and your digital workflow universe will stay chaos-free for another day.

The steps in your overall color correction workflow should include:

1. **Open the image in Photoshop and evaluate the image to determine your plan of attack**.

   Does the image contain a color cast (too blue, magenta, yellow, and so on)? Is the image too light or too dark? Do you want to increase the contrast? Do you want to add color saturation? Take a few moments and visualize how you want your image to appear.

2. **Create a Levels adjustment layer to correct color.**

   If you are just getting used to adjusting levels, make an overall correction in just the RGB channel.

3. **Create a Curves adjustment layer to make finer color levels adjustments.**

   Experiment with making slight adjustments across the tonal range of the image.

4. **Create a Brightness/Contrast adjustment layer.**

   Adjust brightness and contrast to your image according to your taste. If you want your image to appear more dramatic, for example, with darker black areas and lighter white areas, increase the contrast to your liking.

5. **Punch up the color in your image using the Hue/Saturation adjustment layer.**

   Move the Saturation slider to the right to increase the amount of color in your image.

By consistently following the same steps in your overall adjustments workflow with every image you work with in Photoshop, you soon find how efficient using a workflow is. You can experience even more efficiencies working in Photoshop when you realize the advantages to making these corrections in separate layers. When you do that, you can go in and change individual adjustments at a later time instead of having to do everything all over again.

Remember that when making overall adjustments to your image, less is more. For many images, slight adjustments during your overall adjustment workflow do the trick. Overdoing it can make your photos look fake and unrealistic.

Chapter 14

Your Image Editing Workflow

*M*ost people thumb through a stack of 4×6 photos you've taken and get through them as quickly as possible. It's not that they're being rude, but they're just looking for the highlights. Okay, maybe they are being rude and just want to get through the stack without *appearing* rude. I've done it looking at other people's photos; you've done it looking at other people's photos. With snapshots, if you've seen one, you've seen 'em all.

Photographs on the other hand, are a little different. I don't like showing other people my photographs until I've gone through all my image workflows, printed using my best practices, mounted, framed, and signed it in the lower-right corner of the mat with a number 2 pencil. No one thumbs through a stack of prints. I want my photographic work to stand out.

What makes photographs stand apart from snapshots is the work you put into shooting, correcting for color, editing, and then displaying your work. This chapter shows you how to perform little corrections that go a long way in making your photos worthy of being mounted, framed, and hung on your living room wall.

Select to Correct

When editing photos, you often want to makes changes to only a part of the image. Photoshop offers a variety of tools to make selections, which are areas within an image. When selecting only a portion of an image, you then have the ability to make edits to that selection without changing the rest of the image. Having some knowledge of using these tools is necessary in order to make edits to your images. Selections are used mostly in an image editing workflow to selectively make changes to your photos. Figure 14-1 illustrates a selection made in an image.

Figure 14-1: Selecting an area of an image to edit.

By selecting part of your images, you can adjust those selected parts with some of the tools covered in Chapter 13. Additionally, you can replace a dull background with a vibrant color, darken a bright sky, brighten a dark sky, and selectively sharpen or blur a part of your image.

The process for making a selection and then adjusting your selection typically looks like this:

1. **Create a new adjustment layer by choosing Layer ⇨ Duplicate Layer.**

2. **Select the part of image you want to modify using the Magic Wand or Lasso tools.**

   Experiment with changing the Feather setting. The amount of feathering determines how sharp or smooth the edges of the selection are. For the image in Figure 14-2, I applied a feather radius of 2 pixels by choosing Select ⇨ Feather (Ctrl+ Alt+D or ⌘+Option+D on the Mac) and then typing 2 in the Feather Radius field in the Feather Selection window.

Figure 14-2: Making adjustments to selections can quickly change the appearance of your image.

3. **Apply corrections to the image.**

   For the flowers in Figure 14-1, I wanted to change the gray background to white by choosing Image ⇨ Adjustments ⇨ Hue/Saturation and then turning up the Lightness setting to lighten-up the background. Figure 14-2 shows the result of first selecting the background using the Magic Wand and then adjusting the lightness of the selection to achieve my desired effect.

Abracadabra, the Magic Wand tool

I use the Magic Wand tool to select backgrounds in images that I want to change. I can lighten the background, darken the background, replace the background with parts from another image, or blur the background. Whichever adjustment I want to use, I first need to separate the subject from the background to make my edits.

The Magic Wand tool works best when the area you are selecting is one color, or close to one color, and has distinct boundaries from the remaining area.

To make a selection with the Magic Wand tool:

1. **Click the Magic Wand tool in the Photoshop Toolbox.**

   Figure 14-3 shows the selection tools available in the Toolbox.

2. **Click the area you want to select with the Magic Wand.**

   The Magic Wand selects the area that is a similar color to where you clicked, as shown in Figure 14-4. You can add areas that are not selected by holding down the Shift key and clicking the Magic Wand in the unselected area.

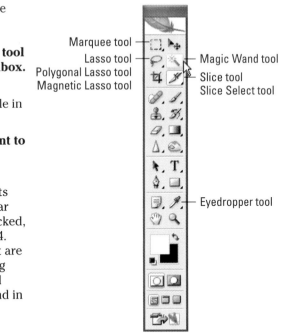

Marquee tool
Lasso tool
Polygonal Lasso tool
Magnetic Lasso tool

Magic Wand tool
Slice tool
Slice Select tool

Eyedropper tool

Figure 14-3: The Toolbox offers a number of selection tools to use to make selections in your images.

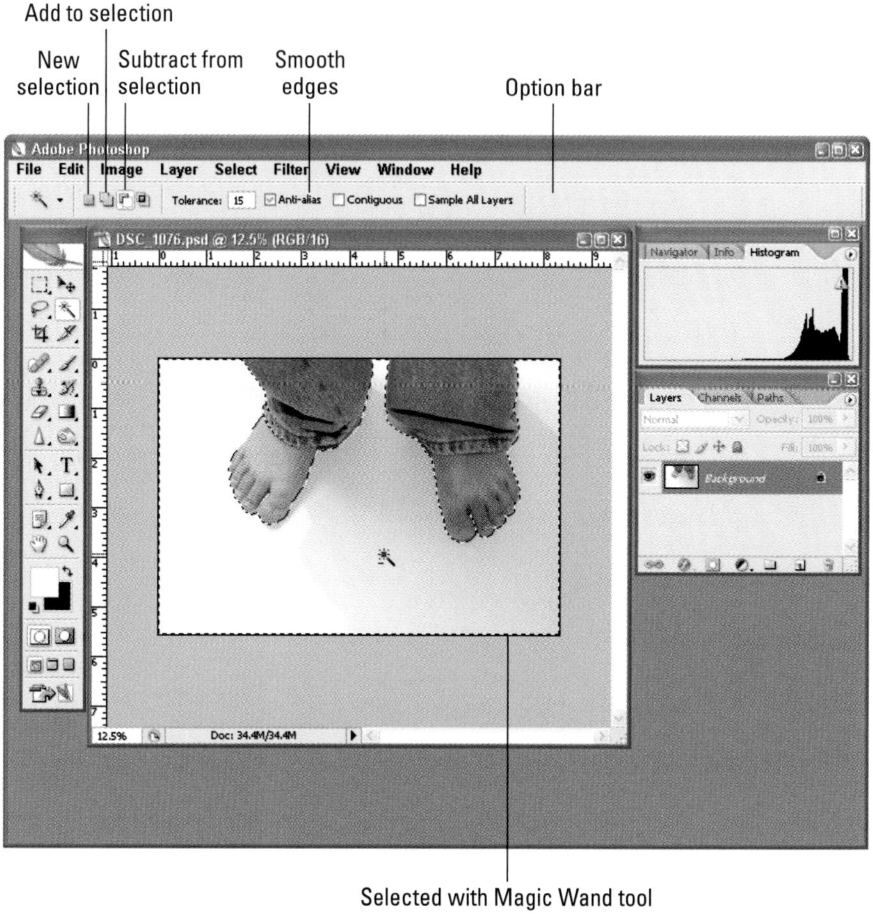

Add to selection

New
selection

Subtract from
selection

Smooth
edges

Option bar

Selected with Magic Wand tool

Figure 14-4: Selecting an area of an image you want to edit separately from the rest of the image.

3. **Remove spots that were selected by clicking the Subtract from Selection button on the Option bar.**

   You can also press the Alt key (Option key on the Mac) while clicking with the Magic Wand.

The Magic Wand tool works just as well to select the subject of an image instead of the background. Select the background and then choose Select ⇨ Inverse to swap the selections for the rest of the image.

Lassoing around

Seeing the Magic Wand tool at work makes you wonder what other selection tools Photoshop has waiting for you. The three lasso tools are used to create finer selections in your image.

- ✐ **Lasso tool:** Used for free-form drawing of selections.

- ✐ **Polygonal Lasso tool:** Used for drawing straight edges of a selection.

- ✐ **Magnetic Lasso tool:** Best used to trace more complex shapes. The selection marquee (the dotted lines surrounding your selection) snaps to the selection like metal to a magnet when using this tool.

To make selections using the Lasso tool:

1. **Click the Lasso tool in the Photoshop Toolbox.**

2. **Draw your selection with the Lasso tool, as shown in Figure 14-5.**

   I chose this selection to reduce the glare in the selected spot of the orange without affecting the rest of the image.

   You can always get rid of your selection if you want to start over by choosing Select ⇨ Deselect or by clicking Ctrl+D (⌘+D on the Mac) to deselect your selection.

Figure 14-5: Selecting an area of an image you want to edit separately from the rest of the image.

3. **Switch to the Magnetic Lasso tool to make selections on hard-to-draw objects.**

To select the entire orange as a selection, using the Magnetic Lasso tool shown in Figure 14-6 provides a much more accurate selection than using other Lasso tools.

4. **Use the Polygonal Lasso tool for selections that include straight lines.**

The Polygonal Lasso tool is great for making selections like the one shown in Figure 14-7, where the areas to select are shapes that have straight lines such as boxes, rectangles, or triangles.

Selection options

When you make selections with any tools, options are available to make your selections more precise. The Select menu provides functionality to help you work with selections. The most commonly used options in the Select menu include:

- ✔ **All:** Use this command to select the entire image. You can also use the shortcut Ctrl+A (⌘+A on the Mac).

- ✔ **Deselect:** Choose Deselect to remove the selection outline you have made. When making selections you often have to deselect in order to start over to make the correct selections. You can also use the keyboard shortcut Ctrl+D (⌘+D on the Mac).

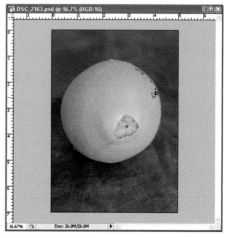

Figure 14-6: The colors and shapes in the image make the Magnetic Lasso tool the right for this selection.

Figure 14-7: The straight lines in the image make the Polygonal Lasso tool the right choice for this selection.

✔ **Inverse:** Sometimes you're going to want to make a selection of an image area that is just tough to select. If you're lucky, the rest of the image may be easier to select. If that's the case, select the easier area and then choose Select ➪ Inverse. The inverse command takes your selection and reverses it to the unselected portion of your image.

✔ **Feather:** Choose this command, and then indicate the number of pixels. A feather of two or three pixels provides a smooth realistic edge for your selections in many photos. Experiment with setting the feature to different pixels until you find the right setting for your photo. To feather a selection, choose Select ➪ Feather or press Ctrl+Alt+D (⌘+Option+D on the Mac).

✔ **Grow:** When you choose the Grow command, you can increase the contiguous areas of your selection to areas that are similar in color. To grow a selection, choose Select ➪ Grow.

✔ **Similar:** The Similar command increases your selection to all like colors of the current selection, regardless of their place in the image. To expand a noncontiguous selection with similar colors, choose Select ➪ Similar.

In order to use the Select commands, you must have actual selections made in your image. Make sure you duplicate the background layer before making selections.

Creating Fill Layers

Fill layers are layers that affect the entire image. Fill layers create a layer that contains a solid color, gradient, or pattern.

The following steps illustrate how to replace part of an image by first making a selection in the image and then replacing the selected part of the image with a fill layer:

1. **If you haven't already, make a duplicate of the background layer by pressing Ctrl+J (⌘+J on the Mac).**

2. **Make your selection of the subject of your image.**

   Right-click the selection and choose Layer Via Copy. This isolates the intended foreground from the new background you'll create in Step 5.

3. **Choose Select ➪ Inverse to select the background of the image.**

4. **Click the background layer to make that layer active.**

5. **Create a Gradient fill layer by choosing Layer ➪ New Fill Layer ➪ Gradient.**

6. **Click OK in the New Layer dialog box.**

   If you prefer, you can rename the layer.

7. **Choose the type of gradient you want to use for the new background of your image.**

8. **Experiment with different gradient types and options.**

   You can experiment with the different gradient types in the Gradient dropdown list (see Figure 14-8). Or click the arrow to view the flyout menu.

Figure 14-8: Selecting a gradient type.

Figure 14-9 shows several gradient types, and how you can change the appearance of your backgrounds.

Figure 14-9: Different backgrounds.

Experiment with changing the opacity and fill of the layer by clicking an adjustment layer in the Layers palette. Click the Opacity field in the palette and use the slider to decrease the opacity of the layer. Decreasing the opacity changes the tone of the background. Click the Fill field in the palette and use the slider to decrease the fill amount. Decreasing the fill fades the foreground.

Creating Layer Masks

One of the more advanced features of Photoshop separates the casual user from the serious user: *layer masks*. Layer masks simply let you hide or expose parts of a layer by painting the portions you want to hide or expose with the Paintbrush tool.

You have many ways to accomplish the same task in Photoshop. Using layer masks is just one of many techniques you can use to hide portions of images and replace with other effects, layers, or adjustments. Examples of uses of layer masks, explained later in this chapter, include:

- **Creating a layer in a portrait to blur or soften the subject's skin (a portrait editing technique).** With most portraits, the subjects don't want to see their wrinkles, pores, or blemishes! Many photographers use a technique to blur the image, such as a Gaussian blur, but paint in the sharpened portions of the portrait, such as hair and eyes, that they do not want blurred.

- **Creating a layer mask to selectively paint in the effects of an overall adjustment, blur, or sharpening.** Using layer masks is a common technique used in retouching photographs where you want to make adjustments selectively.

- **Selectively darkening a background.** Darken the entire image using Brightness/Contrast command to the level where the background is darkened to your liking. Don't worry! You can create a layer mask and then paint back in the areas that you don't want darkened.

- **Replacing the background of an image by masking that selection from an image.**

To better provide an example of the power of using layer masks, the following steps show you how to use a layer mask to hide the sharp portions of a blurred image and then selectively paint back in the parts of the image you want to remain sharp.

1. **Make a duplicate of the image's background layer**.

   Choose Layer ⇨ Duplicate Layer or press Ctrl+J (⌘+J on the Mac) to create a new copy of the background layer.

   Provide descriptive names to your layers when you create them. You can change the layer name by clicking the layer name in the Layers palette and typing the new text.

2. **Blur the image.**

   Choose Filters ⇨ Blur ⇨ Gaussian Blur. Try a blur setting from one to four, as shown in Figure 14-10.

Adjust the amount of blur

Figure 14-10: Applying a Gaussian Blur to the image.

3. Create a layer mask by choosing Layer ⇨ Layer Mask.

Choose the Reveal All option in the flyout menu to fill the layer with white, allowing the effects of the layer adjustment to show through. Choosing the Hide All option in the flyout menu paints the layer with black to hide the effects of the Gaussian Blur layer adjustment. For this example, I've chosen Reveal All.

The Reveal All option lets the effects of the Gaussian Blur continue to show in the image. Choose this option to paint the areas to hide the Gaussian Blur effect. Choosing the Hide All option hides the Gaussian Blur effect, allowing you to use a paintbrush to paint in the areas of the image where you want to have the Gaussian Blur effect.

4. Click the Paintbrush tool in the Photoshop Toolbox.

Press the D key to set the foreground color to white and the background color to black. The D key always changes these back to the Photoshop default colors of white for foreground and black for background. Press the X key to reverse these colors.

Paintbrush head

Painting with black as the foreground color in the Reveal All mode paints away the layer mask. Painting using white as the foreground color paints the layer back in.

5. Lower the opacity to around 70 percent in the Opacity field on the Paintbrush Option bar.

Lowering the opacity reduces the "strength" of your painting, resulting in a more realistic transition between the masked and the painted areas of the layer.

Figure 14-11: Softened portrait after painting in the sharp areas of the image hidden by the layer mask.

6. Paint in the areas of the image you want to sharpen.

Painting areas of the image hides the Gaussian blur and reveals the sharper image that is behind the Gaussian blur mask, leaving the unpainted areas still blurred.

Painting reveals the sharper details of the hair, eyes, and eyebrows in the portrait, but leaving a softened look otherwise, as shown in the image's final form in Figure 14-11.

To selectively sharpen an image, use the same procedure described to blur the image. Create a layer and merge the previous layers. Sharpen the entire image, and create a layer mask to hide the sharpening. Paint the areas you want to sharpen, and that's it!

Editing Techniques

Selections, fill layers, and layer masks are all good tools for making edits. Selections are important when you want to change only certain portions of an image. Fill layers provide a quick means of creating a solid color, gradient, or patterned layer to use to blend in with your image. Using layer masks to reveal or hide effects made to a layer and then painting in the hidden portion has been a secret technique long-used by professionals in their retouching efforts.

When you take photos, there are often imperfections that you don't notice while shooting. When you view the photos later on a computer, you may want to change the imperfections that nag you. With portraits, most people don't want the sharpness today's digital cameras can deliver. After all, who wants to see the all the pores or wrinkles on someone's face? Most people would rather see shining hair and glistening eyes. Yellow teeth? You can help that. Red spot on someone's face? You can fix that. Want that flower petal brightened up a bit and the background darkened in only some spots? You got that covered, too.

Get the red eye out

One of the most common complaints I hear about photos of people is the red eye effect. Photoshop now offers a new tool to eliminate red eye, as shown in Figure 14-12. Getting rid of those devilish eyes is now literally one click away:

1. **After opening your image, duplicate the background layer by choosing Layer ⇨ Duplicate Layer or pressing Ctrl+J (⌘+J on the Mac).**

2. **Zoom in on the subject's eyes by pressing Ctrl+ (⌘+ on the Mac) a few times until the eyes are large enough to edit.**

3. **Click the Red Eye tool in the Toolbox.**

Before

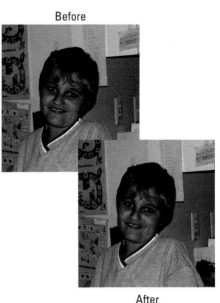

After

Figure 14-12: Original image and then corrected with the Red Eye tool.

4. Drag a box around the red portion of the eye to remove the red.

If all the red is not removed, drag the marquee over the eye again and let go of the mouse button. Repeat the process for both eyes.

Retouching using the Spot Healing Brush

Finding a photograph to use as an example of how the Spot Healing Brush eliminates blemishes was hard to do. Not many models would approve of a page or two about their imperfections! A landscape can't argue, and I use a landscape to show you how to fix dust spots on an image with the Healing Brush.

You may think that with today's digital cameras, dust spots are a thing of the past. That's not necessarily so. Digital SLRs use interchangeable lenses. When you change these

Dust

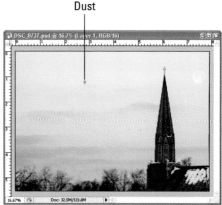

Figure 14-13: Dust on a digital SLR sensor can show up in photos.

lenses, dust can sneak into the camera and onto the image sensor, and you have digital dust spots. Figure 14-13 shows a photo that contains a dust spot that needs to be removed.

To remove a portion of the image such as a blemish or a dust spot:

1. Complete overall color adjustments using an overall adjustments workflow, such as the one shown in Chapter 13.

2. Create a new layer to edit your image.

Create the new layer by choosing Layer ⇨ New ⇨ Layer or by pressing Ctrl+Shift+Alt+N (⌘+Shift+Option+N on the Mac).

3. Combine all previous layers into the new layer.

Merge the existing layers by pressing Ctrl+Shift+Alt+E (⌘+Shift+Option+E on the Mac).

4. If needed, zoom in on the portion of the image that includes the blemish, dust spot (as in the example shown), or unwanted pixels.

Press Ctrl+ (⌘+ on the Mac) to zoom in on your images. Press Ctrl– (⌘– on the Mac) to zoom back out.

5. **From the Photoshop Toolbox, right-click the Healing Brush tool and choose the Spot Healing Brush tool.**

6. **Adjust the size of your brush so it's just larger than the spot you want to remove.**

   Enlarge the brush size by pressing the right-bracket key (]) or reduce the brush size by pressing the left-bracket key ([).

7. **Drag the brush over the dust spot while holding down your mouse button, and then let go of the mouse button, as shown in Figure 14-14.**

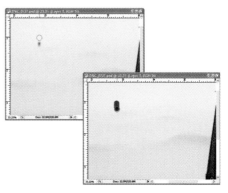

Figure 14-14: Removing a dust spot with the Spot Healing Brush tool.

Figure 14-15 shows the image after overall corrections were made, the moon was darkened, and the dust spot removed from the sky.

The Healing Brush works the same way as the Spot Healing Brush with one exception: When using the Healing Brush tool, you can pick the sample of pixels it uses to replace the area you paint. To select an area to clone pixels *from,* press Alt+click (Option+click on the Mac) that area.

Figure 14-15: The final image after completing the overall image and image editing workflows.

Dodging and burning to make your images pop

Going back to the old days of printing in a darkroom, one of the *only* tricks I had up my sleeve to edit prints was to dodge and burn. Dodging was the process of blocking out light to certain portions only of the photographic paper as it was being exposed, thus reducing light to that part of the image. The result was a lightening of the area.

Burning was a technique used to *add* light to certain areas of the image that I wanted to be *darker* than the rest of the image. If I wanted part of the background darker, I burnt it. If I wanted a petal of a flower lighter, I dodged it.

It wasn't an exact science, and I couldn't see the results of my efforts until the print came out of the chemical process, washed and dried. Worse yet, I had to dodge or burn each print individually to have the same effect across all prints. Multiple copies of the same print meant multiple dodging and burning. This was a long, hard process. With Photoshop, you can edit your images, dodge and burn each image once, and print as many as you want.

To dodge and burn your images:

1. **Complete overall color adjustments using an overall adjustments workflow, such as the one described in Chapter 13.**

2. **Create a new layer to edit your image.**

   Create the new layer by pressing Ctrl+Shift+Alt+N (⌘+Shift++Option+N on the Mac).

3. **Combine all the previous layers into the new layer.**

   Combine the existing layers by pressing Ctrl+Shift+Alt+E (⌘+Shift+ Option+E on the Mac).

4. **Evaluate the image.**

   Look at the photo and evaluate which areas you want to darken and areas you want to lighten.

   If you haven't noticed yet, one of my favorite subjects to photograph is flowers. Flowers don't get bored with posing, they don't complain, and they make the house livelier, especially in the winter months.

5. **If needed, zoom in on the portions of the image you need to darken or lighten with the zoom tool. Click the Zoom tool in the Photoshop Toolbox and then click the image.**

   Press Ctrl+ (⌘+ on the Mac) to zoom in on your images. Press Ctrl- (⌘- on the Mac) to zoom back out.

6. **Click and hold the mouse button over the Dodge tool or press Shift+O a few times to click the tool you want to use.**

   Use the Dodge tool to lighten areas or use the Burn tool to darken areas.

7. **Make your brush larger by clicking the] key to enlarge the brush or the [key to reduce the size of the brush.**

8. **Choose the Burn tool to make the light areas you want to darken.**

9. From the Option bar, experiment with different Brush and exposure settings.

I usually accept the defaults and make sure my Exposure setting is around 35 percent. You can dodge and burn Highlights, Midtones, and Shadows by making those individual selections in the Option bar, as shown in Figure 14-16.

10. Choose the Dodge tool to make the dark areas of the image brighter.

Figure 14-17 shows the original image and then how dodging and burning can make the colors in your image pop out.

Adjust Highlights, Midtones, or Shadows

Brush options

Option bar

Figure 14-16: Adjust brush and exposure settings.

After applying your filter in Photoshop, don't be afraid to further enhance your effects by adding contrast, color saturation, or other adjustments.

Figure 15-12 shows the original image and the same image with a number of filters applied. If you have the time, grab some of those old images you've never processed in Photoshop and see how you can bring them back to life.

Original

Canvas

Charcoal

Colored Pencil

Fresco

Glass

Splatter

Sprayed strokes

Stained glass

Underpainting

Watercolor

Waterpaper

Figure 15-12: Applying a filter gives a whole new look to your photo.

9. **From the Option bar, experiment with different Brush and exposure settings.**

   I usually accept the defaults and make sure my Exposure setting is around 35 percent. You can dodge and burn Highlights, Midtones, and Shadows by making those individual selections in the Option bar, as shown in Figure 14-16.

10. **Choose the Dodge tool to make the dark areas of the image brighter.**

    Figure 14-17 shows the original image and then how dodging and burning can make the colors in your image pop out.

Adjust Highlights, Midtones, or Shadows

Brush options   Option bar

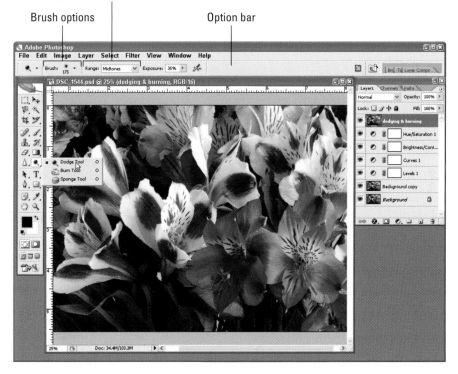

Figure 14-16: Adjust brush and exposure settings.

Before

After

Figure 14-17: Comparing the images before dodging and burning and after dodging and burning.

Creating Artistic and Black-and-White Images from Color

Many amateur and professional photographers at times prefer to work either exclusively in black-and-white or in color. It's a matter of taste to the photographer. Many art schools seem to drill into their students' heads that the only true "fine art" photograph is in black-and-white. I say that's a bunch of garbage. Hogwash. Bogus. The truth is, it's a narrow-minded way of thinking. Art is what *you* see it as.

Personally, I like color. I also like black-and-white. Black-and-white gives me creative options and a whole new way of looking at photographs. Life's too short, why limit the artistic possibilities? There has to be a middle ground. I say, why not do both?

I do a lot of reading and Web surfing regarding digital photography. Once in a while, I'll come across an article on using Photoshop to create black-and-white photographs out of color digital images. To this day, I have not seen a consensus on how to do it, so I came up with my own technique.

The technique I developed is a simple process of creating a new layer in a color image after I complete my entire color correction and image editing workflows. No messing around with saving files to another version, working with the red channel, using this plug-in, and so on. The last thing I do before resizing, sharpening, and printing is to create my black-and-white layer:

1. **After your final image editing process, create a new layer by pressing Ctrl+Shift+Alt+N (⌘+Shift+Option+N on the Mac).**

2. **Combine the previous layers into the new layer by pressing Ctrl+Shift+Alt+E (⌘+Shift+Option+E on the Mac).**

   Name your layer "Black & White."

3. **Choose Image ⇨ Adjustments ⇨ Hue/Saturation (as shown in Figure 14-18) or press Ctrl+U (⌘+U on the Mac).**

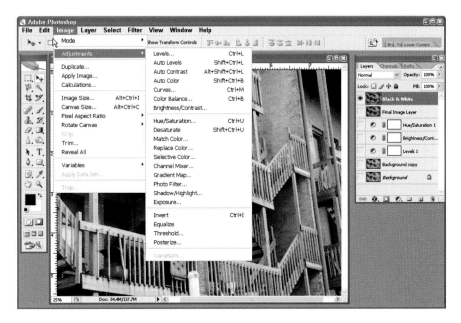

Figure 14-18: Making a Hue/Saturation adjustment to the black-and-white layer.

4. **From the Edit dropdown list, choose Reds.**

5. **Move the Saturation slider all the way to the left until the amount reads –100, as shown in Figure 14-19.**

6. **Repeat the same procedure for all the colors, yellows, greens, cyans, blues, and magentas.**

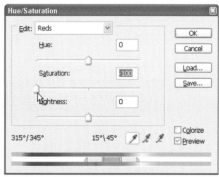

Figure 14-19: Eliminating the saturation amount for each color.

For a little artistic toning, adjust the reds to the right just a tad until a little tone shows in the photograph. You can also try adjusting all colors down to –100 except for blues, greens, or magentas for some cool special effects. Experiment with the color saturation settings and lightness with different photographs. You'll be surprised what gems you come up with.

Figure 14-20 shows the color, black-and-white, and selective color version of the same image.

If you want to create some simple black-and-white images from color originals without adding any additional colors for effects or for tones, choose Image ➪ Adjustments ➪ Desaturate or press Ctrl+Shift+U (⌘+Shift+U on the Mac). Desaturate changes your image to black-and-white in one command!

Create new layers every time you want to see a different version of your image, retaining all previous layers. It's easier to keep one image to contain all your different versions.

Color

Black-and-white

Selective color

Figure 14-20: Artistic touches to the same image.

Image Editing Workflow Recap

Editing images can involve a lot of tweaks and processes to photos. Nailing down one workflow to handle image editing is like mapping out an entire step-by-step process for life itself. Though it sounds like it can't be done, there are some basic steps to keep in mind to reinforce best practices. Consider this your image editing workflow:

1. **After your final overall adjustment workflow, create a new layer by pressing Ctrl+Shift+Alt+N (⌘+Shift+Option+N on the Mac).**

2. **Combine the previous layers into the new layer by pressing Ctrl+Shift+Alt+E (⌘+Cmd+Option+E on the Mac).**

3. **For each edit you make, create a separate layer.**

   Separate layers for each edit enable you to go back at a later time and remove the edit or change it.

4. **Name each layer.**

   Click the layer name in the Layers palette and type the new name for the layer. Name the layer to indicate the type of edit made using that layer, such as "Healing Brush," "Dodge," "Burn," Black-and-White," or "Red eye Removal."

You'll find by practicing these three basic steps for each edit, your files will be more organized, making it easier to track changes for editing at a later time.

Other best practices to keep in mind when planning to edit your images:

- ✏ **Layer masks can be a powerful tool when making edits to your images.** You can make a global change to an image, such as applying a blur, sharpening, or adjusting brightness, contrast, and then only selectively apply these changes to your image.

- ✏ **Making selections is an art in itself.** Practice using the various selection tools. Making precise selections allows for more precise editing.

- ✏ **Fill layers offer an easy way to use patterns, solid colors, or gradients for your backgrounds, foregrounds, or individual selections.**

- ✏ **The Healing Brushes and Red Eye tools are quick and easy methods to correct the oopsies in your image files.**

- ✏ **For every color image, create separate black-and-white layers.** It only takes a few minutes to create and actually doubles the number of images in your portfolio at the same time! Best of all, you don't have to double the amount of files you store on your hard drive. Make a habit of creating selective color and black-and-white layer versions of your images.

- ✏ **Experiment with Photoshop tools and have fun!**

Chapter 15

Changing Images Using Photoshop Filters

*W*ouldn't it be great to change history? Change something after it happens? Think of the possibilities for a moment. Changing the outcome of any event you choose. Now *that* can be interesting. You can change the way you look, change who won last year's World Series or *any* year's World Series. You can do anything you want.

Changing history probably wouldn't work out so well. Everybody's hometown team would win the championship. Everybody would wind up with an instant makeover. The world would become topsy-turvy, or at least more topsy-turvy than it already is!

In reality, no one can change anything that has already happened, but with some really neat Photoshop filters, you can change photos, totally or partially transforming their appearance. It may not seem like much compared to changing history, but for photographers, artists, and changers of images, transforming images is kind of a big deal.

Filters Can Be Fun

Photoshop filters allow you to change the appearance of an image. You can take a photo and, by applying one filter, transform it into a painting, a stained glass window, a mosaic, or a sketch. Figure 15-1 shows a photo of some fall color transformed into an abstract using the Distort Glass filter. Adobe offers a number of these filters in Photoshop, and you can add a number of filters called plug-ins from third party developers.

Figure 15-1: An abstract created from a fall color landscape using the Distort Glass filter.

There are a number of special effects and editing tools that you can purchase and add to Photoshop. These add-on programs are called *plug-ins,* and installing them is as easy as copying the plug-in files to the Adobe Photoshop CS2/Plug-Ins folder on your computer. After installing plug-ins, Photoshop automatically displays them at the bottom of the Filter menu.

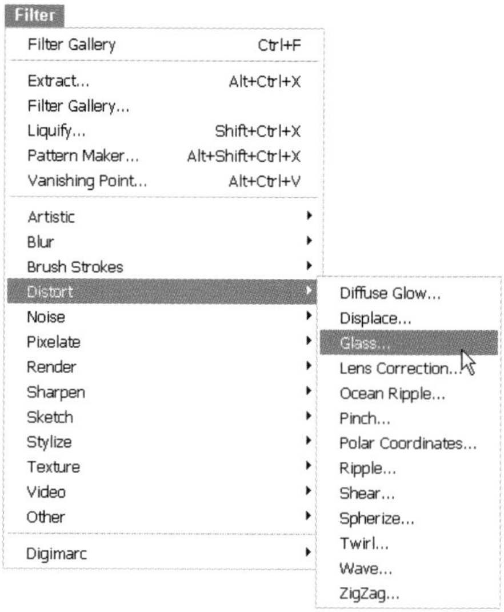

Before diving into the filters in Photoshop, a few points are important to know:

✔ Filters are located in the Filter menu, as shown in Figure 15-2.

✔ You can apply filters to active layers and selections only. Make sure you create a new layer and merge the existing layers into it by pressing Ctrl+Shift+Alt+N (⌘+Shift+Option+N on the Mac). Merge the existing layers by pressing Ctrl+Shift+Alt+E (⌘+Shift+Option+E on the Mac).

Figure 15-2: The Photoshop Filter menu.

✓ Many filters only work in 8-bit/channel mode, though some work in 16-bit/channel mode. Convert your image to 8-bit/channel mode by choosing Image ➪ Mode ➪ 8 Bits/Channel.

✓ Most filters require a lot of RAM on your computer: 384MB of RAM is recommended for running Photoshop CS2, but 512MB is really the minimum you should be running on your computer. If your Photoshop experience is slow, double the amount of memory on your computer; you'll be glad you did!

Morphing Using the Liquify Filter

This filter is so cool it deserves its own section. The Photoshop Liquify filter is one of the features that made Photoshop famous. This is a filter that can be dangerous in the hands of the digital photographer who knows how to use it. In other words, people get mad if you make them look like space aliens in your photos.

The Liquify filter is used to warp parts of your image: You can warp, twirl, pucker, bloat, push, mirror, and disrupt pixels with the tools shown in Figure 15-3. Imagine the possibilities!

To use the Liquify filter:

1. **Open an image and make your overall adjustments and edits.**

2. **Create a new layer to make your Liquify edits in, or make a copy of the background layer.**

3. **Choose Filter ➪ Liquify or press Ctrl+Shift+X (⌘+Shift+X on the Mac).**

I used a photo of a photographer friend of mine who had no problem with my using his portrait to show you what the Liquify filter is capable of. Figure 15-4 illustrates what some of the Liquify brushes can do to an image.

— Forward Warp tool
— Reconstruct tool
— Twirl Clockwise tool
— Pucker tool
— Bloat tool
— Push Left tool
— Mirror tool
— Turbulence tool
— Freeze Mask
— Thaw Mask
— Hand tool
— Zoom tool

Figure 15-3: The Liquify tools.

To get the effects I wanted in the photo, I first used the Forward Warp tool to lengthen the ear and teeth. I then used the Pucker tool to narrow the nose and eyes just a bit. The opposite of thinning with the Pucker tool is fattening with the Bloat tool, which I applied to the eyes. The result? An image of a pretty disturbing looking vampire worthy of the front cover of any supermarket tabloid.

Original

A few pointers to think about when using the Liquify filter:

Forward Warp tool

- The Forward Warp tool is used most often to drag changes to parts of the image.

- Increase or decrease the size of your tool brushes by pressing the bracket keys: the [key to reduce the brush size or the] key to increase the brush size.

- The Twirl Clockwise tool distorts parts of an image as you drag your mouse over the area.

Pucker tool

- The Pucker tool narrows the area you drag the brush over.

- The Bloat tool expands the area you drag the brush over. Enlarge the brush to the diameter of an area you want to distort and hold down the mouse button for a circular bloat.

- You can reset your image if the edits you make don't work out. Click Restore All to change your view of the image back to the original.

Bloat tool

Experiment with the different tools, brush sizes, and density. Going overboard with the Liquify filter is easy. I find that subtle changes are better than drastic changes; subtly makes the effect you're trying to achieve more believable. Surprisingly, some professional retouchers use this tool to touch up photos of models: thinning noses, lengthening legs, and so on.

Figure 15-4: Effects using the Liquify filter tools.

Adjust Lighting in an Image

Photoshop offers an often overlooked tool that you can use to add lighting effects to your images. Using the Lighting Effects filter, you can dramatically change an image by adding lighting effects, such as directional lighting, spotlighting, soft lighting, or mixed lighting. Figure 15-5 shows an example of a lighting effect you can add to an image. This dark forest photo was enhanced using the Lighting Effects filter Spotlight effect.

Before   After

Figure 15-5: Applying the Lighting Effects filter can give a different look to your image.

The steps for adding the Lighting Effects filter to a photo are:

1. **Choose an image to add the Lighting Effect filter to.**

   Make your overall image adjustments and merge all the previous layers into a new layer. Create a new layer by pressing Ctrl+Shift+Alt+N (⌘+Shift+Option+N on the Mac). Merge the other layers by pressing Ctrl+Shift+Alt+E (⌘+Shift+Option+E on the Mac). Name the layer according to the lighting effect, such as "Spotlight."

If you made your overall adjustments in 16-bits/channel mode, change to 8-bits/channel mode. The Lighting Effects filter works only in 8-bits/ channel mode. Choose Image ⇨ Mode ⇨ 8 Bits/Channel.

2. Choose Filter ⇨ Render ⇨ Lighting Effects.

The Lighting Effects window appears, as shown in Figure 15-6.

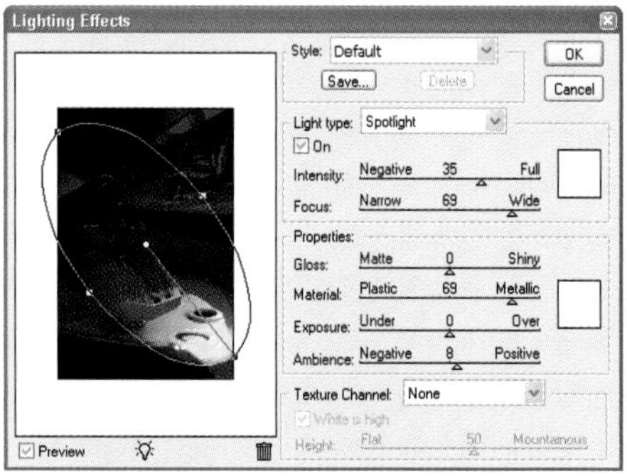

3. Choose Style.

Choose the type of lighting effect you want to add to your image from the Style dropdown menu, shown in Figure 15-7. You can view each one in the image preview.

Be careful not to delete any of the default lighting effects in the Style dropdown menu. The Delete button is next to the Save button; normally, you'd use it to delete any styles *you* define. However, if you're not careful, you can delete the default styles that Photoshop CS2 provides.

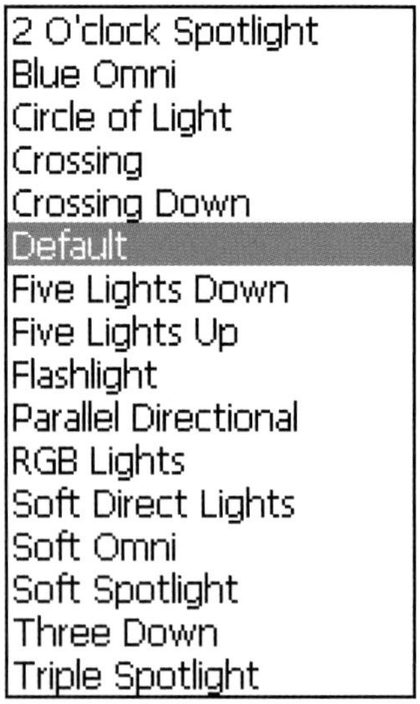

4. Apply lighting types.

The Lighting Effects filter lets you make a number of adjustments to the style selected in the Light type area of the Lighting Effects window. For each style, you can apply a different type, such as Omni, Directional, and Spotlight. Omni applies the lighting from all directions to a circular area in an image. Directional shines the light from a distant source, imitating the sun. Spotlight projects a beam of light.

5. Adjust lighting focus points.

Click and drag the lighting focus points in the image preview until you get lighting direction you want, as shown in

Figure 15-6: The Lighting Effects window.

2 O'clock Spotlight
Blue Omni
Circle of Light
Crossing
Crossing Down
Default
Five Lights Down
Five Lights Up
Flashlight
Parallel Directional
RGB Lights
Soft Direct Lights
Soft Omni
Soft Spotlight
Three Down
Triple Spotlight

Figure 15-7: Lighting effects.

Figure 15-8. Click over the anchors and then drag the anchors to expand and narrow.

6. **Adjust Intensity, Focus, and Properties.**

Adjust the Intensity and Focus sliders to make changes to the amount of light and its focus on the portions of the image you are applying the lighting effects to. Experiment with changing settings in the Properties area, such as Gloss and Material. Gloss and Material change the way surfaces reflect light. Exposure increases or decreases the amount of light, while Ambience diffuses the light source.

Figure 15-9 shows the image before lighting effects were applied and then after adjustments were applied to the image. The Lighting Effects filter can be a powerful tool to make lighting adjustments to images that you may

Figure 15-8: Dragging anchor points to change the direction of the light style.

not have normally even bothered processing. You can use it as a special effects tool or an image correction tool to enhance lighting in any number of subjects you photograph.

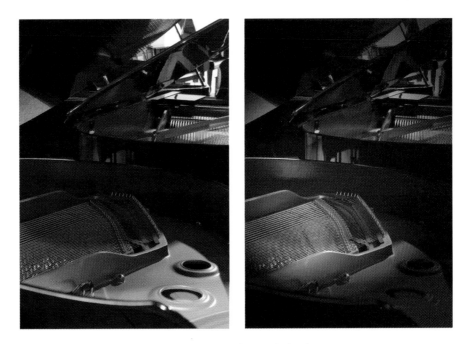

Figure 15-9: Lighting Effects can change the entire mood of an image.

When viewing images in Bridge, take a second look at images that look dull and not very interesting. Evaluate these images to see if they can be helped with a little creativity. The photo illustrated in Figure 15-9 never would have made it to my "images to edit" list without my thinking about applying some creative lighting effects to it. From the result I achieved, I'm glad I did.

Create Artistic Masterpieces

Photoshop is packed with a number of artistic filters you can apply to your images. You have endless possibilities to transform ordinary images into pencil drawings, frescoes, oil paintings, and so on. Like I stated before, Photoshop filters offer you a method to salvage photos you normally wouldn't bother with.

There are two ways you can work with filters in Photoshop. The first way is simply to choose the Filter menu and cruise through the different submenus and filters, applying one at a time if you want. The second way is much easier; choose the Filter Gallery from the Filters menu.

You're not limited to just one filter per image. You can apply multiple filters to an image for even more special effects.

Using the Filter Gallery

Follow these steps to use the Filter Gallery to apply Photoshop filters to your photos and create works of art:

1. **Choose an image to apply a filter to.**

   Make your overall image adjustments and merge all the previous layers into a new layer. Create a new layer by pressing Ctrl+Shift+Alt+N (⌘+Shift+Option+N on the Mac). Merge the other layers by pressing Ctrl+Shift+Alt+E (⌘+Shift+Option+E on the Mac). Name the layer according to the type of filter, or filters, you are applying.

2. **Choose Filter ⇨ Filter Gallery.**

   Figure 15-10 shows the Filter Gallery window.

3. **Preview the different filters by clicking any of the six filter menus and choosing filters within those menus.**

4. **After choosing a filter that you prefer for your image, make adjustments to the filter using the adjustment sliders and choosing options available for that filter, as shown in Figure 15-11.**

   To expand the image preview, click the arrow to the left of the OK button. This hides the Filter menus while expanding the image preview, as shown in Figure 15-11.

5. **Click OK to save your filter settings.**

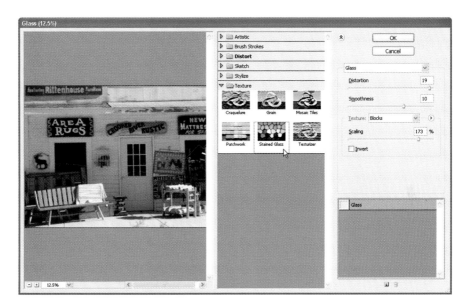

Figure 15-10: The Photoshop Filter Gallery offers you all the artistic filters to preview, apply, and adjust.

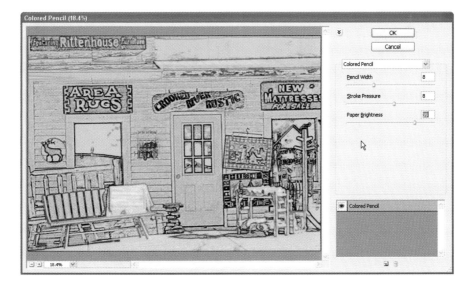

Figure 15-11: Each filter has its own set of adjustment sliders and options that allow you to be more creative.

After applying your filter in Photoshop, don't be afraid to further enhance your effects by adding contrast, color saturation, or other adjustments.

Figure 15-12 shows the original image and the same image with a number of filters applied. If you have the time, grab some of those old images you've never processed in Photoshop and see how you can bring them back to life.

Original

Canvas

Charcoal

Colored Pencil

Fresco

Glass

Splatter

Sprayed strokes

Stained glass

Underpainting

Watercolor

Waterpaper

Figure 15-12: Applying a filter gives a whole new look to your photo.

Show your artistic side with Artistic filters

Bring out your artistic self, and show the artist that has always been hiding within you with the Artistic filters.

You've heard the saying that one person's trash is another person's treasure. Figure 15-13 shows some of the Artistic filters you can pull out of your hat to transform some otherwise plain images into artistic expressions.

Original

- **Colored Pencil.** Provides the effect of an image drawn using colored pencils.
- **Cutout.** Create an image that looks like it was made up of cutup pieces of colored paper.
- **Dry Brush.** Simulates simple colored airbrush techniques. Reduces the number of colors that are contained in the image.
- **Film Grain.** For some photographers, film grain was something to avoid, for others it adds an artistic touch. The Film Grain filter applies an even grain-like pattern to shadow and midtones.
- **Fresco.** Creates a coarse, daub-like pattern, like a Fresco painting.
- **Neon Glow.** Adds glows to an image in a softening manner. Using different brushes achieves various effects.
- **Paint Daubs.** Applies a number of different painting effects using 50 different brush sizes in a number of brush types.
- **Palette Knife.** Transforms the image into a thinly painted scene with texture underneath.
- **Plastic Wrap.** Creates a plastic wrap-like texture over the entire image. Great for creating abstracts.
- **Poster Edges.** Reduces the number of colors in an image (posterizing) while drawing black lines around edges.
- **Rough Pastels.** Applies chalk strokes to the image and creates a textured background.
- **Smudge Stick.** Like the name implies, smudges backgrounds while highlights become brighter with less detail.
- **Sponge.** Simulates the sponge painting technique used by artists.
- **Underpainting.** Applies the image to a textured background.
- **Watercolor.** Simulates a watercolor painting. Reduces detail while watering down the highlights.

Paint Daubs

Palette Knife

Plastic Wrap

Figure 15-13:
Going bonkers
with Artistic filters.

More artsy filters to transform your photos

Photoshop's artsy filters don't end with the Artistic filters. Expand your horizons even more and become the next hot artist using the Sketch and Brush Strokes filters.

The best effects can be obtained by applying filters to a duplicate layer, and then adjusting the Opacity or Fill in the Layers palette. Duplicating the background layer retains the original image and allows you to go back and delete the duplicate if you don't like the effect you're applying.

With 37 Artistic, Sketch, and Brush Stroke filters to play with, a photographer can get lost for days at his desk experimenting and combining the effects of all these filters. Use layer masks to hide or expose parts of a layer that a filter is applied to and you have some real industrial-strength image editing capabilities.

Figures 15-14 and 15-15 show you some of the effects of the Sketch filters.

A list of the Sketch filters follows:

- **Bas Relief.** Dark areas and light areas swap color while the image is transformed into a carved looking plate.

- **Chalk and Charcoal.** Transform your image into a monochrome chalk or charcoal drawing.

- **Charcoal.** Reduced color with drawn highlights, like a charcoal drawing.

- **Chrome.** Transforms the drawing as if it were molded in shiny chrome.

- **Conté Crayon.** Conté crayons create the effect of a monochromic drawing with a textured background such as canvas, sandstone, or brick.

- **Graphic Pen.** Swaps foreground and background color while creating a grainy black-and-white image.

Original

Chrome

Conté Crayon

Figure 15-14: Sketch filters can help you create some innovative yet simple effects to your images.

✔ **Halftone Pattern.** Creates a halftone version of the image while adding a dot, circular, or horizontal pattern.

✔ **Note Paper.** Produces a toneless grayscale embossed version of the image.

✔ **Photocopy.** Like the name says, the results of this filter look like you made a photocopy of your photo.

Reticulation

✔ **Plaster.** Similar to the Note Paper filter, this filter creates a grayish embossed version of the image.

✔ **Reticulation.** Applies a textured look to a monochromic version of the image.

✔ **Stamp.** Like the name says, your image looks as if it were printed using a rubber stamp. Black and white are the only two colors.

Stamp

✔ **Torn Edges.** Similar to the Stamp filter effect but with smoother edges.

✔ **Water Paper.** Provides a fine-art look to the photograph; the colors look like they were poured on and merged.

Figure 15-15: More Sketch filters.

A list of the Brush Stroke filters follows:

✔ **Accented Edges.** Changes the edges of the image simulating either dark or light edges. Gives the photo a soft painted look.

✔ **Angled Strokes.** Paints the image using angled strokes.

✔ **Crosshatch.** Transforms the image as if it were painted with a cross-hatch pattern.

✔ **Dark Strokes.** Similar to the Water Paper Sketch filter, it can provide a fine-art look to portraits.

✔ **Ink Outlines.** Simulates a pen and inkwell drawing effect to the image. Creates a surrealistic look.

✔ **Spatter.** Gives your image the appearance that ink was shot through a small nozzle.

✔ **Sprayed Strokes.** Similar to the Spatter filter only you can change the direction the strokes are made.

✔ **Sumi-e.** Presents an eerie feeling to the image.

Art Project: Creating Abstracts with Filters

I often use Photoshop filters to create abstracts. Abstracts are photos that don't show a true representation of a scene. Instead, an abstract is an unusual angle or just a portion of a subject that may leave you guessing as to what you're looking at. One technique I use to get an abstract effect is to zoom in on a small portion of an image, crop, and then apply the filters from there. The results I get are something I could never do in a darkroom.

Figure 15-16: Original image with oversaturated colors.

To create an abstract:

1. **Open an image and zoom in a portion of the image you want to turn into an abstract.**

2. **Create any overall adjustments that may be needed.**

   Make your overall image adjustments and merge all the previous layers into a new layer. Create a new layer by pressing Ctrl+Shift+Alt+N (⌘+Shift+Option+N on the Mac). Merge the other layers by pressing Ctrl+Shift+Alt+E (⌘+Shift+Option+E on the Mac). Name the layer according to the type of filter (or filters) you are applying.

 TIP

   For some abstracts I create, I first make the overall adjustments I discuss in Chapter 13 to over-saturate colors and add contrast, as shown in Figure 15-16. I then apply the abstract effects.

Figure 15-17: Making a crop from the middle of the image.

3. **Crop the portion of the image you want to turn into an abstract.**

   Figure 15-17 shows a small portion cropped from the middle of the original image.

Make sure to use the Crop tool while cropping from the original image, and set the print size and resolution for the output you want, such as 300 pixels/inch. You want to make sure you are giving yourself enough image data to print after you have applied the filters.

4. **Choose Filter ⇨ Filter Gallery.**

   Choose your desired filter. For my abstract, I chose the Glass filter shown in Figure 15-18.

Figure 15-18: Using the Glass filter to create abstracts.

5. **Make the necessary filter adjustments to create the effect you want for the abstract.**

6. **Click OK to save changes.**

7. **Make any necessary overall adjustments to the image.**

   I often add additional contrast and color saturation after the filter effects are applied, if needed.

8. **If needed, perform final cropping.**

   After my image was modified using the Glass filter and then adjusted for further contrast and color saturation, I picked a portion of the image that I wanted to use for the final image. Figure 15-19 shows the original image and the final abstract I created from it.

Original   Abstract

Figure 15-19: Original image and the final abstract created using the Glass filter.

Using Filters to Correct Images

Photoshop filters can be used for more than applying artistic effects to completed images. Some filters serve a specific function, such as sharpening an image, or correcting for lens distortions. These filters can be a critical tool in your image editing workflow. Four groups of filters can be used to edit images: lens correction filters, noise reduction filters, blur filters, and sharpen filters. Sharpen filters are explained in Chapter 17.

Correcting lens imperfections with the Lens Correction filter

I covered lens correction in Chapter 11, because Camera Raw allows for lens corrections before converting raw images into Photoshop. New in CS2 is the Lens Correction filter (see Figure 15-20). Like the Camera Raw function, the Lens Correction filter fixes common lens shortcomings, such as chromatic aberration and vignetting. A few more corrections were added to the filter as a bonus for those who don't shoot in raw format but want the ability to correct for lens shortcomings.

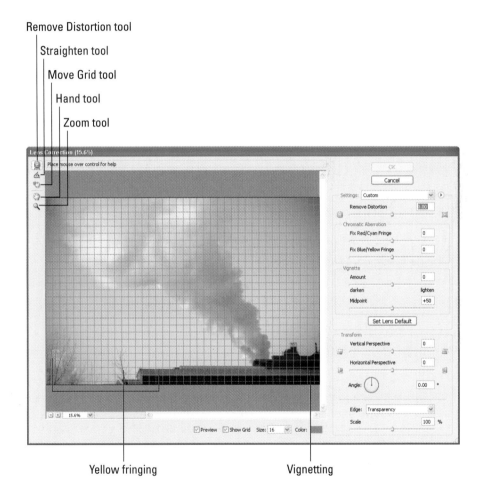

Remove Distortion tool

Straighten tool

Move Grid tool

Hand tool

Zoom tool

Yellow fringing Vignetting

Figure 15-20: You can use the Lens Correction filter to correct distortion, vignetting, and chromatic aberration.

The Lens Correction filter allows you to correct the following in your images:

- **Remove Distortion:** Increase or decrease lens barrel or pincushion image distortion.
- **Chromatic Aberration:** Fix red/cyan or blue/yellow fringing that occasionally occurs in the edges of images.

- **Vignette:** Correct darkened edges that appear in some lenses or when lens shades are attached to a lens.

  Burning in the edges of portraits is an effect used by some photographers. You can use the lens correction filter to *introduce* vignetting into your images.

- **Vertical Perspective:** Change the perspective of the top and bottom of the image.

- **Horizontal Perspective:** Change the left side and right side perspective of the image.

  Use the Vertical and Horizontal perspective corrections to add drama to ordinary photographs. The tools are there for you to make corrections, but who says you can't use them to change the way images were taken? Be creative and have a good time!

- **Angle:** Rotates the image clockwise or counterclockwise.

To make corrections to an image using the Lens Correction filter:

1. **Choose Filter ⇨ Distort ⇨ Lens Correction.**

2. **Make necessary corrections to your image.**

   The image shown needs some correction to compensate for vignetting and chromatic aberration. You can make the corrections by using the sliders provided in the Chromatic Aberration and Vignette areas of the Lens Correction window.

3. **Click OK to save your changes.**

   Figure 15-21 shows the original image and the corrections made using the Lens Correction filter.

Reducing noise in your images

One of the problems with digital cameras is the image noise that can plague your photos, preventing you from blowing up these images to 8×10 prints. Image noise can be described as random pixels that appear in your image when you shoot at a high ISO setting or use slow shutter speeds. Image noise can be evident as that grainy look in the grayscale part of your image, or those multicolored specks of color that appear in shadow areas. Either way, noise doesn't look good.

Original

Corrected

Figure 15-21: Original image and the corrected image using the Lens Correction filter.

To reduce image noise in your photos, use the Reduce Noise filter:

1. **Open an image that you want to reduce the image noise in.**

2. **Make any necessary overall adjustments to the image and then merge all the previous layers into a new layer.**

   Create a new layer by pressing Ctrl+Shift+Alt+N (⌘+Shift+Option+N on the Mac). Merge the other layers by pressing Ctrl+Shift+Alt+E (⌘+Shift+ Option+E on the Mac). Name the layer accordingly, using a name such as "Noise Reduction."

3. **Choose Filter ➪ Noise ➪ Reduce Noise.**

   Figure 15-22 shows the Reduce Noise filter window and an image that contains image noise.

Figure 15-22: The Reduce Noise filter window.

4. **Zoom in on the image to get a better view of image noise.**

5. **Adjust Strength.**

   Moving the Strength slider to the right reduces the noise present in the red, green, and blue channels. Figure 15-22 shows the slider moved all the way to the right to get the maximum noise reduction.

6. **Adjust the Preserve Detail percent.**

   The higher you adjust this, the more image detail is preserved; however the less noise is reduced. Balance this adjustment with the Strength adjustment for the best results

7. **Adjust the Reduce Color Noise slider to reduce random color pixels.**

   You may not notice a difference increasing the value of this adjustment, that's okay! The Reduce Color Noise slider removes these pesky pixels as you move the slider to the right.

I'd suggest not using the Sharpen Details slider. I save sharpening for the last step before printing and do not sharpen during noise reduction.

8. **Click OK to save changes.**

Figure 15-23 shows the results of reducing noise in an image using the Reduce Noise filter.

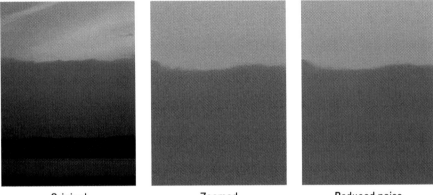

Original   Zoomed   Reduced noise

Figure 15-23: Reducing image noise using the Reduce Noise filter.

Blurring photos with the Blur filter

Believe it or not, some photographers intentionally blur portions of photos. Not all a photographer's efforts are aimed at shooting and processing sharp images; there are some situations where a little blur can go a long way. Case in point? Portraits. Many times, people looking at their portraits will say "I didn't realize my wrinkles would show up so much, can you somehow remove them?" Or, "I sure do need a face lift!" I'm not a plastic surgeon, but I do have a few tricks up my sleeve to smooth out some of those imperfections. No injections, just a few creative Photoshop retouching techniques.

Photoshop provides a number of different filters that you can use to blur selections of images or entire images, as listed here. Blur filters are useful for retouching portraits but are also used to enhance parts of images with a blurred effect.

- **Average.** Finds the average color of an image and then fills the entire image with that color.

- **Blur and Blur More.** These two filters smooth edges by averaging pixels on hard edges.

✔ **Box Blur.** Blurs the image based on the size of neighboring pixels. You can increase the radius to increase the blur effect.

✔ **Gaussian Blur.** Blurs the image based on the Gaussian bell curve.

✔ **Lens Blur.** Simulates lens blurring by providing a number of lens blur adjustments. By establishing the depth of field in an image, also referred to as depth map, you can blur the foreground while maintaining a sharp background or vice versa.

To add a blur to selected sections of an image:

1. **Open an image you want to apply a blur to.**

2. **Make any necessary overall adjustments to the image and then merge all the previous layers into a new layer.**

   Create a new layer by pressing Ctrl+Shift+Alt+N (+Shift+Option+N on the Mac). Merge the other layers by pressing Ctrl+Shift+Alt+E (+Shift+Option+E on the Mac). Name the layer according to the type of filter (or filters) you are applying.

3. **Choose Filter ➪ Blur and choose the Blur filter you want to apply.**

   Figure 15-24 shows the Gaussian Blur filter being applied to a portrait.

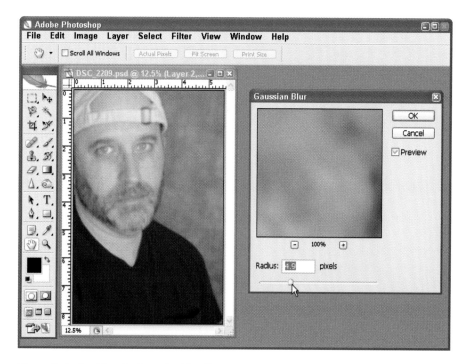

Figure 15-24: Applying the Gaussian Blur filter.

4. To remove the Gaussian Blur filter effect to parts of the image you want to remain sharp, click the Eraser tool.

Adjust the brush size by pressing the [key to reduce the brush or the] key to enlarge the brush. Paint over the sections of the image where you want to erase the Gaussian Blur effect.

For retouching portraits, add a Gaussian Blur with a Radius setting between 3 and 6. Selectively remove the blur using the Layer Mask technique shown in Chapter 14 or by simply using the Eraser tool to paint in the sharp portions of the image you want to show.

Figure 15-25 shows the original image and the edited image with the Gaussian Blur selectively applied.

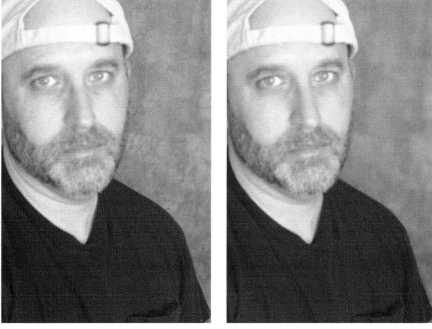

Before   After

Figure 15-25: The original and edited portraits.

Chapter 16

Getting Efficient with Automation

*M*any would argue that the most-sought-after resource isn't money, fame, cars, boats, or cameras. If you're anything like me, time is the scarcest resource. Jobs, books, Friday night sci-fi, some photography here and there, and, most importantly, family and friends: I always need more time.

In your everyday work, anything that saves time becomes important. If you spend a lot of your day at your computer, shortcuts are always welcome. Macros are a good shortcut, whether you're crunching numbers in Excel or automatically formatting text in Word.

In the Photoshop world, automating repetitive processes can save you a lot of time. Just the task of sharing a dozen photos over e-mail can be chore, but Photoshop can put the whole thing into a PDF slideshow in a heartbeat. Creating a Web page to show off your images on the Web is only a few clicks away. Save yourself some time using the automated features in CS2, and then use that time to see a ballgame or to take the kids out for some ice cream!

Using Bridge and Photoshop to Batch Process Files

A photographer may have to process tens or hundreds of images at a time. I can shoot hundreds of images just in one day on one subject or assignment! A person can literally fall asleep at the keyboard renaming files and applying Raw conversion settings to all those files.

Bridge and Photoshop bring some industrial-strength tools to drive those repetitive blues away. Though most of these tools are available in the Photoshop File menu, it's better to run these utilities in Bridge, so you don't have to process images one at a time, like you do in Photoshop:

- **Batch rename any number of files in a folder.** If you're submitting images to a client or just don't like the filenames your digital camera blesses you with, now is your chance to rename a group of files in a folder all at the same time.

- **Create a contact sheet.** Back in the days of the film and chemical dark-room, a photographer would line up his negatives on photo paper, expose it to light, and develop the paper like any other photo. I used these contact sheets to take a quick look at the photos I shot, and I didn't have to hold each negative up to light and guess how the photos turned out.

- **Process images using the Image Processor.** This is one powerful com-mand that lets you perform processes on a group of files without having to go through the hassle of creating Photoshop Actions (more on actions later in this chapter). The Image Processor allows you to:

  - Batch process a group of images to convert them from raw format with a single set of raw adjustments.

  - Convert files to TIF, JPEG, or PSD formats or to all three at the same time.

  - Resize a group of files to a single set of pixel dimensions.

  - Convert a set of files for use on the Web.

  - Assign a color profile, such as sRGB, to a group of files.

- **Create a PDF slideshow.** One of the easiest ways to share photos on the Internet is to e-mail a group of photos arranged in a slideshow. Photoshop CS2 provides the function to easily create a slideshow that contains any number of images you want.

✐ **Construct panoramas using Photomerge.** Photomerge lets you choose images that you want to stitch together into a panoramic image.

✐ **Create a set of photos using Picture Package.** Picture Package arranges one or more photos on a sheet in groups of different sizes. You can create picture packages just like they do for school photos. You see how to create Picture Packages in Chapter 17.

✐ **Create a photo Web site using Web Photo Gallery.** Take it from someone who's created many Web sites since the world was turned loose on the Internet: This is one easy-to-use *and* cool photo site generator.

✐ **Photoshop Actions:** Actions are the macros of Photoshop. Record repetitive tasks and replay them on images to save time.

Rename a whole bunch of files at the same time

One of the biggest timesavers is the Batch Rename function in Bridge. You really don't have control over the naming conventions your digital camera uses. From an image management standpoint, you're better off if you can name the files according to how you want to file them, rather than have the camera name them. With Bridge, you can rename files in groups or in folders according to how you tell Bridge to name them.

To rename files in a folder recently downloaded from my memory card, I follow these steps:

1. **Start Bridge by choosing File ➪ Browse in Photoshop or by clicking the Go To Bridge button on the Photoshop Option bar.**

2. **Choose a folder that contains images you want to rename, such as the folder shown in Figure 16-1.**

3. **Select the files you want to rename.**

   If you want to select all the files in the folder, press Ctrl+A (⌘+A on the Mac). To pick only some of the files in the folder to rename, click each file while holding down the Ctrl key (⌘ key on the Mac).

4. **Choose Tools ➪ Batch Rename or press Ctrl+Shift+R (⌘+Shift+R on the Mac).**

   The Batch Rename window appears.

5. **Designate a folder to copy the renamed files to.**

   To select the destination folder, select the Copy to Other Folder option. Click the Browse button to choose a folder to copy these renamed files to or to create a new folder.

Figure 16-1: Bridge and selected folder.

 Be careful not to use the same folder original images are stored in as the folder to save renamed image files to. When designating a folder for your renamed files, always choose another folder you have already created, or create a new folder as suggested in Step 4.

 Make a backup of your new folders twice, one a working CD or DVD and one CD or DVD to put in your safety deposit box or fire safe. Keeping one backup on-hand and one backup offsite ensures that your images are safe from any unfortunate incident, such as computer or hard disk failure, theft, fire or nat-ural disaster. Keeping a copy offsite ensures that you always have copies of your original images.

6. **In the New Filenames section, type the text in the textbox next to the selection box (named "Text" in Figure 16-2) you want to have all the selected files' filenames start with, as shown in Figure 16-2.**

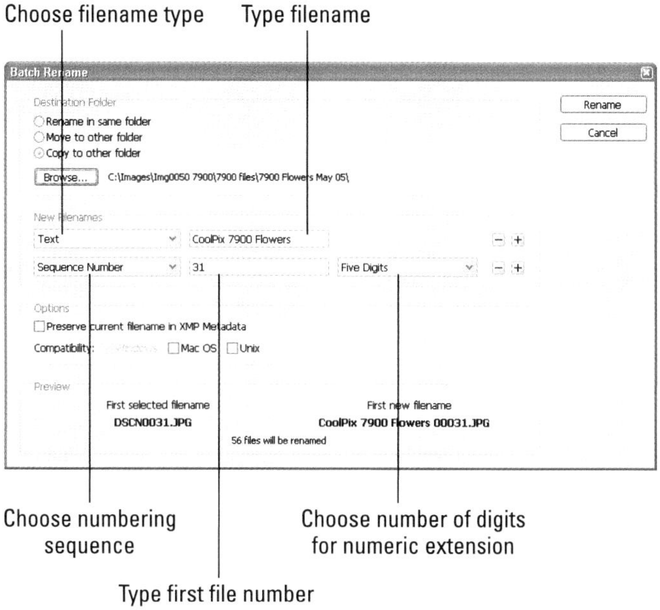

Choose filename type   Type filename

Batch Rename

Destination Folder
○ Rename in same folder
○ Move to other folder
○ Copy to other folder

Browse...   C:\Images\Img0050 7900\7900 files\7900 Flowers May 05\

New Filenames
Text   CoolPix 7900 Flowers   – +
Sequence Number   31   Five Digits   – +

Options
☐ Preserve current filename in XMP Metadata
Compatibility: ☐ Mac OS ☐ Unix

Preview
First selected filename   First new filename
DSCN0031.JPG   CoolPix 7900 Flowers 00031.JPG
                  56 files will be renamed

Rename
Cancel

Choose numbering   Choose number of digits
sequence   for numeric extension

Type first file number

Figure 16-2: Creating a naming convention for your files.

For this example, I've typed CoolPix 7900 Flowers.

You can use a filename type other than text you enter by selecting a different filename type from the New Filenames Text dropdown list.

7. **Type the text you want all your filenames to include in the New Filenames text field.**

   Include a descriptive name (like CoolPix 7900 Flowers) that defines the types of photos included in the folder. Flowers, portraits, landscapes, or family are all good names to describe a group of photos.

8. **Type the number that the sequential file numbering should start with in the Sequence Number text field.**

   I've typed 31.

9. **Indicate the number of digits to include in the filename.**

   Choose four or five digits for number sequences; you can actually shoot thousands of images with your digital camera. I like to keep all the photos taken with my cameras kept in numeric sequence as much as possible.

10. **Click the Rename button to rename your selected files.**

   Photoshop proceeds to rename and copy the files to the folder you specified in Step 4.

We have contact: Creating contact sheets

When I deliver images on CD to a client, I like to include a neatly folded contact sheet that includes thumbnails of all the images the CD contains. Bridge offers a great utility to create a contact sheet of images that can be printed, folded, and stuffed in the CD sleeve.

To create a contact sheet:

1. **Start Bridge by choosing File ⇨ Browse in Photoshop or by clicking the Go To Bridge button on the Photoshop Option bar.**

2. **Choose a folder that contains images you want include in your contact sheet.**

3. **Select the files to include in the contact sheet.**

    If you want to select all the files in the folder, press Ctrl+A (⌘+A on the Mac). To pick only some of the files in the folder, click each file while holding down the Ctrl key (⌘ key on the Mac).

4. **Choose Tools ⇨ Photoshop ⇨ Contact Sheet II, as shown in Figure 16-3.**

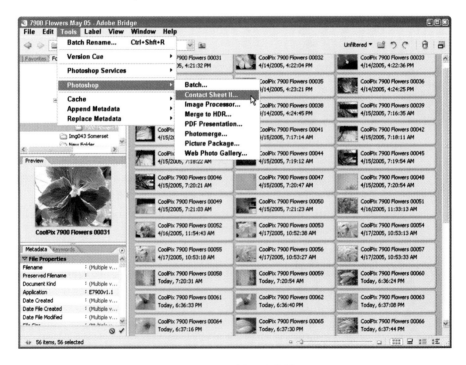

Figure 16-3: Creating a contact sheet of selected files in Bridge.

The Contact Sheet II window appears, as shown in Figure 16-4.

5. **Choose to create the contact sheet from images you selected in Bridge or from a specific folder in the Source Images section.**

6. **Specify the paper size and resolution in the Document section.**

For most printers, specify a Resolution setting of 300 pixels/inch.

7. **Specify Thumbnails settings.**

I usually leave the default settings at 5 columns and 6 rows for an 8½×11 inch sheet.

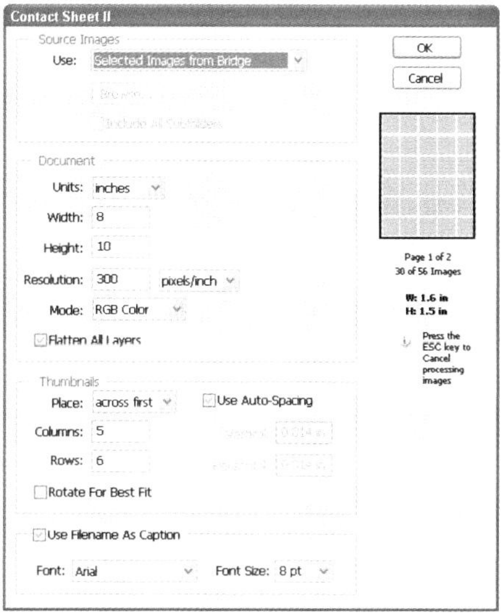

8. **Set the Font and Font Size.**

This setting is for the filenames printed below each photo.

I usually shrink the Font Size down to 6pt to allow for my long filenames.

9. **Click OK to create your contact sheet.**

If you selected more than 30 images, Photoshop creates multiple contact sheets that hold 30 thumbnails per page.

Figure 16-5 shows a completed contact sheet.

10. **Save and print the contact sheets.**

Contact sheets are Photoshop image files and can be printed, converted to another file format, or saved like any other image file.

Figure 16-4: Setting up the contact sheet in the Contact Sheet II window.

Showing off photos with a PDF slideshow

E-mail can be a blessing or a curse. The curse is the junk mail that floods everyone's inbox on a daily basis. The good things about e-mail are the jokes (still my favorite part of the Internet), and the messages from friends and family. Another positive aspect of e-mail is that it can be a great way to share photos with others by attaching them to a message.

Photoshop offers a quick way to group together a number of photos into one file that presents a slideshow of your photos. The PDF slideshow can be stored on your computer or e-mailed to others for viewing.

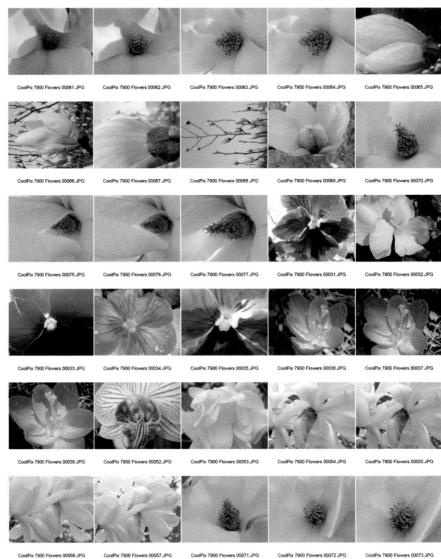

Figure 16-5: A contact sheet includes image thumbnails and filenames.

The steps to create a PDF slideshow are:

1. **Start Bridge by choosing File ⇨ Browse in Photoshop or by clicking the Go To Bridge button on the Photoshop Option bar.**

2. **Choose a folder that contains images you want to include in your PDF slideshow.**

3. **Select the files to include in the PDF slideshow.**

   If you want to select all the files in the folder, press Ctrl+A (⌘+A on the Mac). To pick only some of the files in the folder, click each file while holding down the Ctrl key (⌘ key on the Mac).

4. **Choose Tools ⇨ Photoshop ⇨ PDF Presentation.**

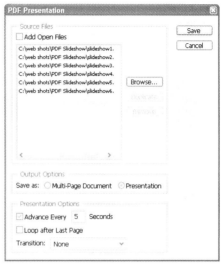

Figure 16-6: Files selected for your PDF slideshow.

   The PDF Presentation window appears, as shown in Figure 16-6. The files you chose in Step 3 are listed in the Source Files section. Click the Browse button to select files in another folder.

   Choose a transition from the Transition drop-down menu at the bottom of the PDF Presentation window, as shown in Figure 16-7. A transition is a special effect used when switching from one slide to another. Adding a transition to your presentation makes it more fun to watch.

5. **Select Presentation in the Output Options section.**

   This creates a PDF presentation instead of a PDF multi-page document. (Multi-page documents are intended mainly for business documents and don't include as many features for the Web as presentations.)

6. **Click Save.**

Blinds Horizontal
Blinds Vertical
Box In
Box Out
Dissolve
Glitter Down
Glitter Right
Glitter Right-Down
None
Random Transition
Split Horizontal In
Split Horizontal Out
Split Vertical In
Split Vertical Out
Wipe Down
Wipe Left
Wipe Right
Wipe Up

Figure 16-7: Choosing a transition for your PDF slideshow.

7. Select a folder and type a filename in the Save window.

8. Click the Open button.

The Save Adobe PDF window appears.

9. Select the output quality for your PDF presentation from the Adobe PDF Preset dropdown menu, as shown in Figure 16-8.

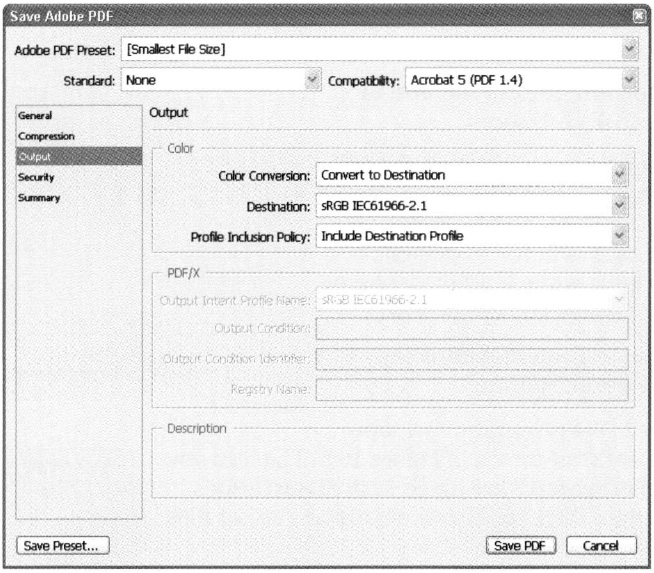

Figure 16-8: Making final settings for the PDF slideshow.

For PDF presentations I create that are to be viewed on the Web or on a computer display, I choose Smallest File Size, because high resolution files are not needed for computer displays or the Web.

Selecting Smallest File Size automatically sets the compression to 100 dpi for display viewing and the color space to sRGB, which is the best for viewing on computers.

10. Click General in the left side and the window and type a description of your presentation in the Description field.

This helps provide a description of the PDF Presentation for later reference.

11. Click Save PDF.

Photoshop generates the PDF Presentation and saves it to the location you specified in Step 7. To view the presentation, double-click the PDF file in the folder you saved it to. The presentation automatically starts running, as shown in Figure 16-9. (You will need to have Acrobat Reader installed on your computer.)

Figure 16-9: Viewing the PDF slideshow in Acrobat Reader.

Getting photos to the Web

The World Wide Web has revolutionized how photography is displayed. In the old days, you either had to purchase a book or go to a gallery to view a photographer's work. Now it's as easy as typing an address in your browser's address bar. There are thousands and thousands of photographer Web sites on the Internet today, and that list just keeps growing.

Photoshop gives you the capability of making a simple photography gallery Web site. You can access the Web Photo Gallery in either Bridge or from the Photoshop File menu.

To create a photo Web site using Photoshop CS2:

1. Start Bridge by choosing File ➪ Browse in Photoshop or by clicking the Go To Bridge button on the Photoshop Option bar.

2. Choose a folder that contains images you want to include in your Web site.

3. Select the files to include in the Web Photo Gallery.

If you want to select all the files in the folder, press Ctrl+A (⌘+A on the Mac). To pick only some of the files in the folder, click each file while holding down the Ctrl key (⌘ key on the Mac).

4. **Choose Tools ⇨ Photoshop ⇨ Web Photo Gallery.**

   The Web Photo Gallery window appears, as shown in Figure 16-10.

5. **Choose a style from the Styles dropdown menu.**

   You can see what each site looks like in the Web style preview.

6. **Select a folder to save the Web Photo Gallery to.**

   Click the Destination button, and the Browse For Folder window appears. You can select an existing folder or create a new one. If creating a new folder, type the name of your new folder in the Folder field. Click OK.

Web style preview

Figure 16-10: Setting up your Web site using the Web Photo Gallery window.

7. **Click OK in the Web Photo Gallery window to create your Web site.**

   Figure 16-11 shows the Web site created using the Web Photo Gallery. You are now an official Web-head!

Figure 16-11: A Web site created with the Web Photo Gallery.

Loading your Web Photo Gallery to the Web

After you create your Web Photo Gallery, you still need to get that gallery on the World Wide Web so others can see it. A number of free Web hosting sites are on the Internet, but the best place to start your search is with your own Internet provider. Whether you have an Internet dial-up, DSL, or a broadband connection through your cable TV provider, most ISPs offer free Web hosting to their subscribers. Check with your Internet service provider to see how you can load your new Web Photo Gallery and share your photographs across the Internet.

Stitch 'em together with Photomerge

Panoramas are wide-format photos that are equal to three, four, or more images put together side-by-side. You shoot each image in succession from left to right, allowing some of the image to overlap with the one next to it.

Some digital cameras come with panoramic assist features. Look up the feature in your owner's manual to see if your digital camera has this feature. If your camera doesn't, that's okay! Geeks like me like to do things the hard way anyway.

My technique for shooting panoramas is right out of the textbook. I attach the camera to the tripod, shoot my first shot, lock the exposure, pan to the right two-thirds of a frame and click the shutter again, pan to the right two-thirds of a frame and click the shutter again. Three photographs, each overlapping the next by a third of a frame, exposure the same for all three. The makings of a potentially great panorama.

Figure 16-12 shows a panorama of a sunset I took just a half mile from my home, stitched together in Photoshop using Photomerge.

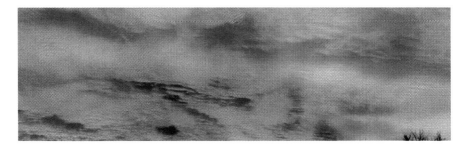

Figure 16-12: Panoramic stitched together in Photoshop using Photomerge.

To create a panoramic photo using Photomerge:

1. **Start Bridge by choosing File ⇨ Browse in Photoshop or by clicking the Go To Bridge button on the Photoshop Option bar.**

   Though you can start Photomerge from the Photoshop File menu, I find it easier to start Photomerge from Bridge so I can see the images for my panorama in Bridge.

2. **Choose three or four images that were taken in succession.**

   Press the Ctrl key (⌘ key on the Mac) while clicking each of the three images.

   If you want to stitch together raw images, all three images should match each other with the same exposure, white balance, saturation, and contrast. Before you select the images, apply raw settings to the first image, copy those settings, and then apply them to the next two images.

3. **Choose Tools ⇨ Photoshop ⇨ Photomerge, as shown in Figure 16-13.**

   Photoshop begins to stitch the selected images together.

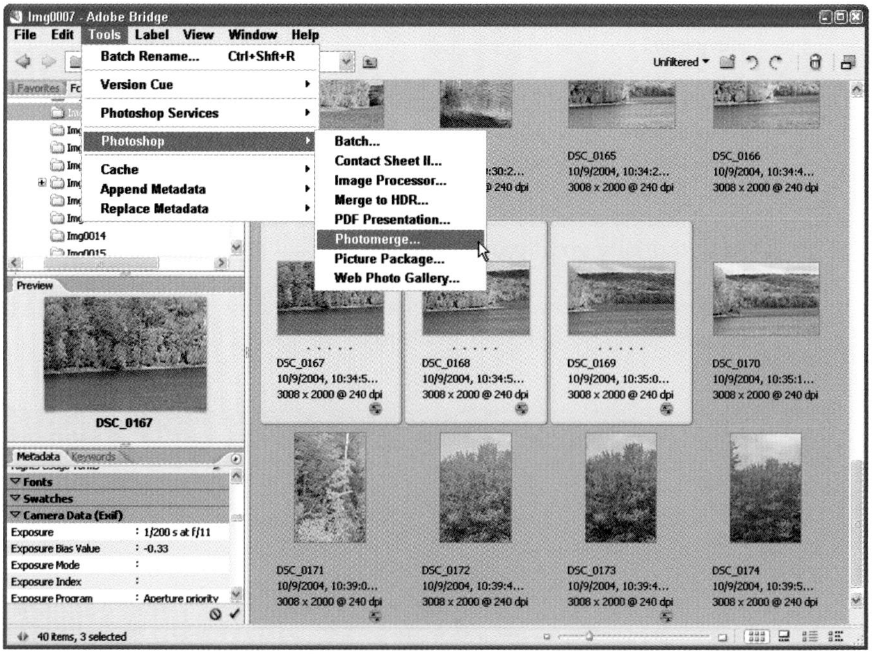

Figure 16-13: Choosing images in Bridge to stitch together using Photomerge.

Some images are easier for Photoshop to stitch (merge) together than others. Images, such as the sunset shown in Figure 16-12, can be difficult to merge due to the lack of straight lines, which Photoshop uses as references to determine what to merge together. If Photoshop can't determine how to merge an image, it allows you to manually merge the image yourself to the other images selected by dragging the separate images together in the Photomerge window yourself.

4. Make final edits to the merged panorama in the Photomerge window.

To fine-tune the panorama, you can rotate each of the images separately, zoom in and out of the image, and change the perspective of the image. Figure 16-14 shows the Photomerge window and controls.

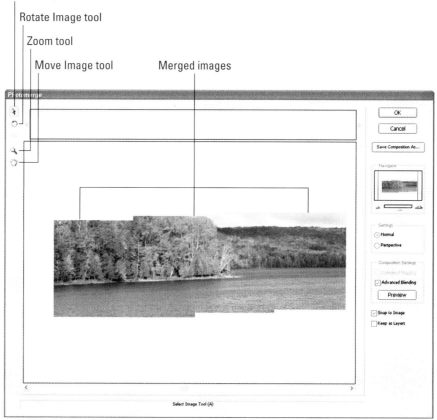

Figure 16-14: The Photomerge window.

5. **Click OK to open the image in Photoshop.**

6. **Using Photoshop, make any necessary overall adjustments to the image.**

   You can adjust Levels, Curves, Brightness/Contrast, or Saturation.

7. **Crop the panorama to eliminate any jagged edges.**

8. **Save the image.**

   Figure 16-15 shows the final adjusted and cropped panorama. I know you'll have a blast using this feature!

Figure 16-15: The adjusted and cropped final panoramic image.

Who said panoramas always need to be horizontal? Try creating a panoramic image of a tall building from the bottom up. Shooting in a portrait orientation, get three frames overlapping each other by about a third. Make sure to rotate the images on their sides with the rotate commands in the Bridge Edit menu and then select them for Photomerge. Photomerge cannot do vertical panoramas so you have to stitch the separate images together on their sides in the Photomerge window. Dare to be different!

Lights, Camera, Photoshop Actions!

Do you ever get sick and tired of doing the same mundane tasks over and over and over again? Wouldn't it be nice if you could automate doing the laundry with one click of a button? Load the dirty clothes into the washer, add soap, turn it on, put the washed clothes in the dryer, turn it on, fold the dried clothes, and put them away. That would sure make *my* family happy!

Nothing exists that I know of to take the drudgery out of everyday chores, but in Photoshop, I can streamline processes I use often that have a lot of steps. Photoshop Actions are series of commands that you can record and then play back on an image or a series of images. Think of an action as a *macro* for Photoshop. There are three types of actions: Actions that are pre-defined in Photoshop, actions that you record, or actions that you can purchase from a third party. If you have a number of files you want to size and sharpen for viewing on the Web, you can create an action that applies the Image Size command to resize all the images, and then uses the Unsharp Mask filter to sharpen all the images. You can add the save command to save all the images in JPEG format. Automating all those steps can save you a ton of time compared to resizing and sharpening each image individually.

Some Photoshop functions can't be recorded in an action. Painting, cropping, and erasing are examples of tools that cannot be recorded, for obvious reasons. How does Photoshop know what part of the image to paint? As a rule of thumb, keep in mind that actions are best used for overall adjustments.

Actions ready to go

Photoshop comes loaded with a number of actions that are predefined for you. These actions contain Photoshop commands and give you one more way to do these commands without having to find them in the Photoshop menus. Some of these actions include:

- **Commands:** A number of commonly used Photoshop commands such as Rotate, Crop, and Flatten Image.

- **Frames:** Lets you create virtual picture frames around images that you want to display on the Web or print.

- **Image Effects:** A number of Photoshop filters ready to be run, such as Oil Pastel and Neon Glow.

- **Production:** A number of image sizing and save options used when preparing images for final output such as the Canvas sizes and Save commands.

- **Text Effects:** A number of goofy effects used to create text. These actions are great for creating graphics for the Web.

- **Textures:** A slew of textures, such as wood, asphalt, bricks, and lava to apply to an image as special effects.

Loading and running an action

I'm picky about how I display my images on the Web, so I found a Photoshop Action at the Web site fredmiranda.com to create mattes and frames around my images. You can find them too at www. fredmiranda.com. After paying for the action, I downloaded it to my computer and copied to the Photoshop Actions folder, Adobe Photoshop CS2/Presets/Photoshop Actions. To load and run a Photoshop Action:

1. **Open an image (see Figure 16-16) that you want to run the action on.**

2. **Open the Actions palette by choosing Window ⇨ Actions or by pressing Alt+F9 (Option+F9 on the Mac).**

   Figure 16-17 shows the Actions palette.

3. **From the Actions palette, click the arrow to open the flyout menu and then choose Load Actions.**

4. **Choose the action you want to run in the Load window.**

Figure 16-16: Image before running the FM_Frames_V1.2 action.

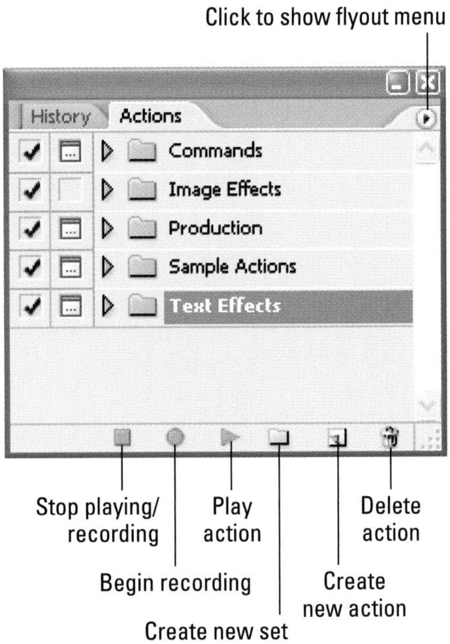

Click to show flyout menu

Figure 16-17: The Actions palette.

5. Click the Action step you want to run.

An action can contain many steps that you don't necessarily use. In the FM_Frames_V1.2 action, there are many frames and mattes to choose from. Figure 16-18 shows the Emboss Large Matte part of the action that I want to apply to my image.

6. Click the Play Action button on the bottom of the Actions palette.

Figure 16-19 shows the finished product after running the FM_Frames_V1.2 action. Using the Text tool, I added a signature to the image for that final touch.

Recording an action

The final step to knowing all there is to know about actions is actually recording and saving one for later use. To record and save a Photoshop Action:

1. Click the Create New Action button on the bottom of the Actions palette.

2. Type a name for the action in the New Action window.

3. Choose a set to include the new action in from the Set dropdown menu.

4. Click the Record button.

5. Perform the commands you want to record in the action.

In this example, using the Image ⇨ Image Size command, I reduced the horizontal size to 6 inches at 72dpi by typing these values into the Image Size window, making the framed image I just created more browser friendly.

6. Click the first step recorded in the Actions palette.

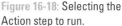

Figure 16-18: Selecting the Action step to run.

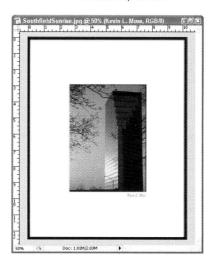

Figure 16-19: Image after running the FM_Frames_V1.2 action.

7. **Open the Actions palette flyout menu and choose Save Actions, as shown in Figure 16-20.**

8. **Type the name of the action you want to save to the Actions folder.**

Congratulations! You just created your first Photoshop Action on an image!

You can apply your own action, or the resizing action I've used as an example, to multiple files by selecting the files in Bridge and then choosing Tools ⇨ Photoshop ⇨ Batch. In the Batch window, select the set you chose in Step 3 from the Set dropdown menu and then choose the action from the Action dropdown menu. Click OK to run the action on the selected photos.

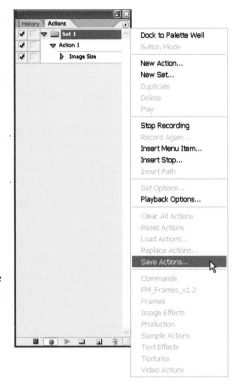

Figure 16-20: Saving the newly created action.

Chapter 17

Preparing for Final Output

Y ou've gone through just about everything you need to know about Photoshop CS2 in your quest for image-editing perfection. You've figured out your color management, overall color correction, and image editing work-flows. Your images are breathtaking in Photoshop, as they should be. Just when you thought it was safe to go back into the water, there's more!

After getting your images adjusted in Photoshop, one more little item needs attention: getting your photos ready for output. Looking at photos in Photoshop is great, but the whole purpose is to *get* those images printed, viewed on the Web, or submitted to *someone* for *some purpose*.

Getting ready for the final destination of your images means that a few more step-by-step proce-dures are needed. Organizing output files, sizing, and sharpening images are all important steps to take before your photo arrives at its final destination.

Organize Your Image Files for Output

You were introduced to organizing files in Chapter 12 where you were shown the importance of keeping your original image files separate from your work-ing files. The reason? Dealing with thousands of image files is a curse that plagues anyone who works in the graphic arts field. It's important to keep all these images organized.

Whether you create photos for the Web or photos for inkjet prints, for publication, or for display on a Web site, managing thousands of files can become a chore. When you prepare your edited photos for output, you can wind up with even more versions of the same image.

To keep all your image files organized, start by figuring out what you are going to do with your edited images.

Figure 17-1: Photos are meant to be printed and displayed.

- ✔ **Are your photos going to be printed?** Printing is the top destination for photos, so I'll assume you'll be printing your images, like the 8×10 coming off the printer in Figure 17-1.

- ✔ **Are your photos going to be displayed on a Web site?** Many photographers post their best images on their personal Web sites to show off their work. Photographers, amateur or pro, like to show off their photos!

- ✔ **Are your photos going to be submitted for the press or for printing?** Photos are often displayed in books, magazines, newsletters, and business documents.

- ✔ **Are you going to send your photos to a Web photo service for printing?** In the past few years many Web sites specializing in processing digital images have emerged. You set up an account and e-mail your images, and the service in turn mails you prints. In Figure 17-2 I'm ordering prints from photos I uploaded to Yahoo! Photos.

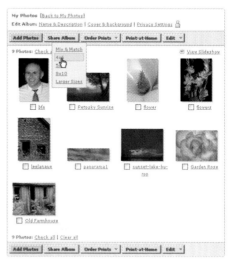

Figure 17-2: Sharing photos and ordering prints on the Web using sites such as Yahoo! Photos.

After you determine the type of output you want to produce, set up your folders accordingly. Depending on how many images you work with in Photoshop and prepare for output, consider setting up output folders.

I have one folder on my hard disk named Digital Images where I manage all my files. Digital Images contains three subfolders:

- **Original Images:** This subfolder contains original images downloaded from my digital cameras. Each time I download a memory card filled with images, I create a new subfolder in the Original Images folder and give it a sequential name, such as Img0045. I copy the next card of images to Img0046, and so on.

  For added protection, flag all your original images as read only; that way, you can be assured that you won't mistakenly overwrite these files with the edited versions.

  To make your images read-only in Windows, choose Start ➪ Windows Explorer. Select the folder to flag as Read Only, choose File ➪ Properties, and then select the Attributes Read Only option.

  If you're a Mac user, select images in the folder to flag as read only, choose File ➪ Get Info (or press ⌘+I). Scroll down to Ownership and Permissions, and choose Read Only from the You Can dropdown menu. Click the Details disclosure triangle, and change Access Permissions to Read Only. The Owner may be locked. If you're the owner, you can double-click the padlock icon to make the changes. If you aren't the owner, you don't have permission to change access.

- **Working Images:** When you choose an image in Bridge to edit, save the file in Photoshop PSD format to the Working Images folder.

- **Output Files:** If you're going to re-purpose the same image for different types of output, consider creating Output folders for each type. For example, save your files intended for print to a Print folder. Save photos sized for viewing on a Web site in a folder called Web Site Images.

Sizing Things Up

When working with your photos, you eventually have to re-size your images. I usually save this step until after my overall color corrections and image edits are made. Depending on the type of output you have planned for your photos, you have to determine two factors:

1. **Determine the document size.**

   The document (or photo) size is the dimensions you specify for width and height. Do you want an 8×10, a 5×7, or a 4×6 photo? If your photo's destined for the Web, you may want something smaller.

2. **Determine the resolution.**

   If you are targeting the file for the Web, you'll want to set the resolution to 72 pixels/inch. Anything more would be a waste: a resolution of 72 pixels/inch is all that's needed. If you are preparing the image for printing, set the resolution to 300 or 360 pixels/inch. More on image sizing later in this chapter.

The larger the ppi setting you specify, the larger the file. For example, a 4-inch wide photo set to 72ppi takes up around 29K of disk space, while the same file optimized for printing at 8 inches wide with a ppi setting of 360 can be around 2 megabytes. If you're e-mailing photos, make sure they're optimized at 72ppi: You want to e-mail smaller files.

Explaining those little pixel thingies

Before you dive in and resize your images, you want to understand pixels and resolution so that you can make correct decisions in Photoshop when you resize your photos. The first step is getting familiar with the basic terms:

- **Pixels:** Pixels are those little square dots that make up an image. Each pixel is uniform in size and contains one color. If your digital camera is, say a 5 megapixel camera, each image captured has the capability to contain 5 *million* pixels. I say potential because you always have the option to capture images at smaller resolutions, such as 3.2 megapixel or less. In any case, that's *a lot* of pixels.

- **Image resolution:** Resolution is the setting used to size an image for output. For example, images to be viewed on screen or on the Web should be set to a resolution of 72ppi (pixels per inch, sometimes referred to as dots per inch or dpi). Images targeted for printing should be set to around 300ppi.

Image resolution is relative. Different digital cameras produce differently sized images, but it's the number of pixels per inch that actually count: More pixels per inch means better image quality when printing large photos. My 7 megapixel compact digital camera captures images at 300ppi where the image dimensions are 10.24×7.68 inches. My older 5 megapixel compact digital camera captures images at 72ppi, but the dimensions are 35.5×26.6 inches!

If you change the resolution of the image from the 5 megapixel compact digital camera from 72ppi to 300ppi, the dimensions then shrink to 8.5×6.4 inches. You really haven't changed the actual size of the image; you have just shrunk the image to achieve a desired output resolution that matches your printer's optimum printing conditions. If you had a 35-inch-wide printer, you could change the ppi setting back to 72 to achieve that image output size, but the image quality at that huge print size would be very poor.

- **File Size:** For digital images, the best way to describe the size of a file is by the number of pixels it contains. The 7 megapixel file my compact digital camera produces is 3,072×2,304 pixels. Multiply those two pixel dimensions together and you have 7,077,888 pixels, also referred to as 7 megapixels.

- **Image Dimension:** Image dimension is the actual physical size of an image when it's printed or sized for display. Image dimension should not be confused with resolution or file size.

Why resolution matters

If you print large prints, 11×14, 13×19, or even 16×24, the more resolution your digital camera can produce without interpolation, the better. *Interpolation* is the process of increasing the resolution of an image, or a section of an image when cropping to increase the pixels per inch. A 5 megapixel digital camera should be able to produce 8×10 prints without a problem. If you do a lot of cropping, the image quality may noticeably decrease at that print size unless you interpolate by indicating a higher resolution in the Crop tool Option bar when you crop. More information on interpolating images is available later in this chapter. Some photographers, me included, often crop out small portions of a photograph, sort of like creating a photo from a photo, but indicating a higher resolution in the Option bar may degrade the quality somewhat, depending on how much of the image you're eliminating in your crop. Images from 7 or 8 megapixel cameras can provide enough resolution to produce high-quality large prints even if you do some extreme cropping, like I've done in this example.

Resizing images using the Crop tool

One easy way to size your images is to use the Crop tool. The Crop tool allows you to specify the exact width, height, and output resolution of an image. Figure 17-3 shows the Crop tool used to crop and size an image.

Crop tool

Figure 17-3: Using the Crop tool to crop and size images.

To use the Crop tool:

1. **Open an image that you want to edit.**

2. **Click the Crop tool in the Photoshop Toolbox.**

3. **Type the width in the Width field in the Option bar.**

   This measurement is how wide you want your output file to print or to appear on the Web. I've chosen a width of 7 inches.

4. **Type the height in the Height field.**

   I've chosen a height of 5 inches.

5. **Type the resolution you want for your file.**

   If you're preparing an image for printing, enter 300ppi to 360ppi in the Resolution field. If the file is destined for the Web, enter 72ppi. I've chosen a resolution of 360ppi.

6. **Click and drag the area in your image that you want to crop, as shown in Figure 17-4.**

Figure 17-4: Cropping the image.

Release the mouse button. When you do, the crop area you selected remains bright while the area you want to eliminate is darkened.

7. Resize or move the crop area to the position you like best.

Click the crop area and, while holding down the mouse button, move the highlighted crop area around until you position the crop where you want it.

Click any of the corners of the crop box and drag the corner up or down to resize the crop area. Click just outside any corner to rotate the crop area.

8. Click the check mark icon in the Option bar to complete the crop.

Figure 17-5 shows the image after cropping. The image is sized exactly as selected at 5×7 at 360ppi. Does the male half of the couple look familiar? He's also the vampire in Chapter 15. He looks much better now, posing with his better half!

Figure 17-5: The final cropped portrait.

Resizing using the Image Size command

Instead of using the Crop tool to size images, you can use the Image Size command to change the size of images that do not need cropping.

To change the size of an image using the Image Size command:

1. Choose Image ⇨ Image Size or press Ctrl+Alt+L (⌘+Option+L on the Mac).

Figure 17-6 shows the Image Size window.

2. Deselect the Resample Image option.

3. Type the width of the image.

If you are printing an 8×10, type 8 in the Width field if the image is in portrait orientation or 10 if the image is in landscape orientation.

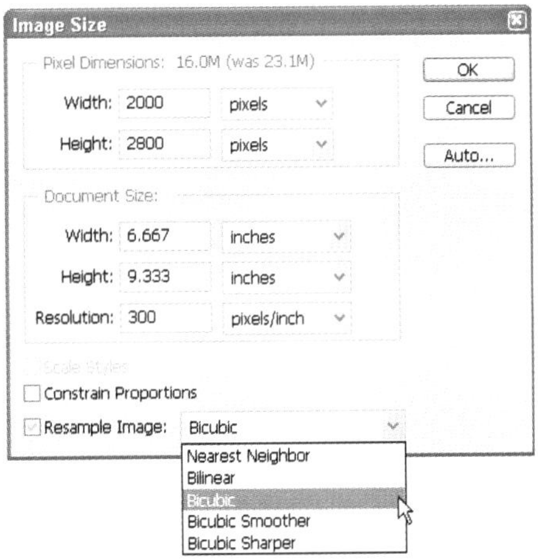

Figure 17-6: The Image Size window.

If you type the width first, the height and resolution automatically change to accommodate the new width. The Image Size adjustment automatically changes the height and resolution as long as the Resample Image check box is not selected.

4. Select the Resample Image option.

Selecting this option now locks the width and height so that those dimensions don't change when you enter the resolution you want.

5. Type the resolution for the photo.

Leave the default resampling method, Bicubic, which is the best setting for photographs.

6. Click OK to close the window and save your changes.

Interpolating images

One of the most confusing details about resizing images is what method to use. The default in the Image Size window is Bicubic, but what about those other ones? What does Nearest Neighbor or Bicubic Sharper mean? To help explain the resampling choices, I'll first explain the term *interpolation*.

When you choose the resample method, Photoshop actually assigns an *interpolation method*. Interpolating is the process used to assign color values to the new pixels that are created when you enlarge an image. Photoshop bases these color values on a sample of neighboring pixels: hence the term *sampling*. The resampling method you choose helps preserve the quality of the image when you size an image larger than its native (original) resolution.

The resampling choices the Image Size window are

- **Nearest Neighbor:** Used for basic illustrations when quality isn't an issue. Not recommended for photos.

- **Bilinear:** Another method not recommended for use with photos but that can be used for some illustrations.

- **Bicubic:** The preferred method of resampling photos. This method uses the values of surrounding pixels to interpolate. Leave Bicubic as your default resampling method because it provides the highest quality interpolation method in Photoshop.

- **Bicubic Smoother:** This method is similar to the bicubic method and is used for *increasing* the size of an image with smoother results than with other resampling methods. May be good for some images and portraits.

- **Bicubic Sharper:** This resampling method is used for *reducing* the size of an image while enhancing sharpness.

Because sharpening is a step that should come after resizing, Bicubic Sharper really isn't needed.

Sharpen Up!

The final step in an output preparation workflow is making photos more sharp. Digital camera photos need some sharpening before you print the image or save it for use on the Web Digital cameras take sharp pictures, but digital images need to be sharpened after you make adjustments to them.

Sharpening enhances the edges in an image and increases contrast. Different photos need different amounts of sharpening applied; there is no standard amount that works for all images.

Because sharpening is the last step in running an image through Photoshop, running your image through noise reduction is a good idea if it's needed. Noise reduction using the Noise Reduction filter is explained in Chapter 15.

Other tips for sharpening images include

- **Sharpening does not help photos that are out of focus or blurred.** Sharpening only benefits photos that have been properly focused in the camera when you shoot.

- **Sharpening should be done only after an image has been sized for final output.**

- **Create a separate layer to sharpen the image.** If you resize the image later, you can always delete the original sharpening layer. Re-create the sharpening layer and sharpen the image with the new size. Create a layer by pressing Ctrl+Shift+Alt+N (⌘+Shift+Option+N on the Mac). Merge the existing layers into the new layer by pressing Ctrl+Shift+Alt+E (⌘+Shift+Option+E on the Mac).

- **Sharpen images using the Unsharp Mask or Smart Sharpen filters located in the Filter ➪ Sharpen menu.**

- **The Smart Sharpen filter offers enhanced sharpening capabilities not found in the Unsharp Mask filter.**

- **Use sharpening as a tool to evaluate the quality of images.** When you first open an image in Photoshop, duplicate the background layer and sharpen the image as described in the next steps. When you're through evaluating the image, choose Edit ➪ Undo Unsharp Mask.

By now you may wonder why Adobe called the best sharpening tool for photos Unsharp Mask. It doesn't make too much sense, does it? Unsharp Mask is a term used in sharpening processes back in the darkroom days. I'm not sure why Adobe just didn't change the name to Photo Sharpening, or to Use this Filter to Make Your Photos Sharp. For now, just remember that Unsharp Mask is the best tool to use to sharpen your images.

You can selectively sharpen only portions of your image by using the layer mask techniques explained in Chapter 14.

To sharpen a photo using the Unsharp Mask filter:

1. **Open the image that you want to sharpen.**

   Figure 17-7 shows an image before sharpening.

   Make sure that you have resized the image for final output. If you sharpen an image and then resize it, the quality of the image decreases.

2. **Zoom in on the image to better see the effects when you sharpen.**

3. **Choose Filter ➪ Sharpen ➪ Unsharp Mask.**

   The Unsharp Mask filter window appears.

4. **Click a part of the image that contains straight lines or contrast.**

   Straight lines or contrast may help you judge the amount of sharpening to apply. It's easier to see the effects of using too much sharpening when you view zoomed sections that include straight lines or contrast between areas of the image.

5. **Move the Amount slider to the right, as shown in Figure 17-8.**

   The amount to set depends on the image. For portraits, settings around 100 to 150 may be

Figure 17-7: Original image before sharpening.

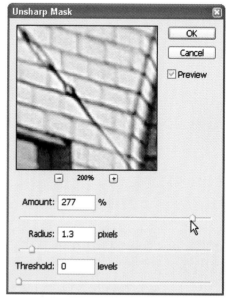

Figure 17-8: The Unsharp Mask filter window.

sufficient. For landscape photos, 200 to 300 may produce results the results you want.

6. **Move the Radius slider to the left.**

    Move to the slider to the range of 1.3 pixels to 1.5 pixels. Beyond 1.5 can mean poor results. View the image in the Unsharp Mask window and the image window to judge the results.

7. **Move the Threshold slider to the right until the zoomed preview shows a reduction of sharpening artifacts.**

    Sharpening increases unwanted artifacts that appear as noise in your image. Moving the Threshold slider to the right to a setting of four to seven reduces those artifacts in your image after you set the Amount and Radius. Increasing the threshold reduces some sharpening. Judge the amount of threshold you use. Like other things in life, sharpening and threshold have a give-and-take relationship!

Figure 17-9 shows the image before and after the Unsharp Mask filter was applied.

Before   After

Figure 17-9: Before and after applying the Unsharp Mask filter.

Reviewing an Output Preparation Workflow

Just as you can apply color management, overall color correction, and image editing workflows, you can also apply a workflow when you output images. Using an output preparation workflow enables you to produce consistently better photos. Practice makes perfect, and sticking to best practices *will* make you a better photographer.

A review of an output preparation workflow:

1. **Organize your output photos.**

   When you edit images in Photoshop, keep those versions of your image files in a folder named to indicate that you've edited those images. When you prep your photos for output, set up folders to save separate versions of the images in folders for prints, Web, or press.

2. **Properly resize your images.**

   Use the Crop tool or the Image Size command to resize your images according to your output needs. Make sure you specify the correct output resolution, such as 72ppi for Web images or 300ppi for prints. Resize your images using the Bicubic resampling method (for enlarging photos) or the Bicubic Smoother resampling method (for reducing the size of photos).

3. **Sharpen your photos.**

   Almost all digital photos look better when you sharpen them in Photoshop. To sharpen photos, use the Unsharp Mask or the new Smart Sharpen filters available in the Filter menu. For best results in most photos, first increase the amount to 100 to 300, set the Radius around 1.3 or 1.4, and then slide the Threshold slider to about 5 to 7 to reduce sharpening artifacts.

Chapter 18

Printing Workshop

Spending years acquiring photo gear is a tough job, but somebody's got to do it! Photo geeks (like me) seek out all variety of digital cameras, lenses, compact cameras (to carry everywhere), color management tools, software, printers, ink, paper, magazines, and books. Taking long trips to get those fall color or waterfall shots is another part of the job. All right, it's really not a job: It's a quest.

All the gadgets, trips, and photos lead to one thing only: the final print. Many photographers make a living or a hobby out of taking photos. Many don't print anything themselves; they send it out or have their assistants do the printing. Other photographers personally do all of their shooting, editing, and printing on their own. That's how I do it. After going through this chapter, that's how you may want to do it, too. Using a simple but structured printing workflow can help you get to the ultimate destination, the final print.

Printing and Handling Photos for the Long Term

Remember all those photos taken when you were a kid? I bet a lot of them are turning orange and fading. Color photographs typically don't last that long. Depending how they are stored, maybe five or 10 years before they begin to fade. That doesn't seem like a long time for photos intended to be treasured for many years.

Image permanence is the life of a photographic print before it starts to deteriorate. When I say deteriorate, I mean that photos start to lose their color definition: They begin to fade and change colors.

The question for you is how important image permanence is in your digital photography work. If a print fades after 10 years, you can just print another one! I have to admit, that argument does have merit, but I can't help thinking that if I'm busy printing today, the last thing I'll want to do is print my photos all over again in a few years! Figure 18-1 shows a print I made 10 years ago. I'm sure I'll be reprinting this one because the ink and paper combinations used at that time didn't have the permanence that today's ink jet printer ink and paper have.

When it comes to longer lasting prints, inkjet printers have come a long way in the past 10 years or so. The first photo-quality inkjet printers produced prints with an image permanence rated at about 30 or 40 years, if you used the right paper. That length of time is pretty good, often surpassing the permanence of prints received from the corner drugstore.

As a digital artist, I want my prints to last 100 to 200 years without any noticeable deterioration. Fine art prints should last as long as technically possible. A few desktop inkjet printers on the market today offer papers and inks that have an image permanence rating of 100 to 200 years, depending on the paper you use.

Figure 18-1: Prints made 10 years ago may have to be reprinted sooner rather than later.

To make prints that last for the next several lifetimes, keep these facts in mind:

✔ **Choose a printer that produces good photo quality images and offers paper and ink options that are rated to last at least 100 years.**

✔ **Only use ink cartridges and paper intended for your particular brand of printer.** Be very careful with using third party inks in your printers. The printer wasn't designed with third party inks in mind. Manufacturers, by the way, make their money off of selling supplies, not hardware. They have a monopoly on the supply market for their printers, but I still recommend sticking with your manufacturer's brand of inks.

✔ **Use papers manufactured for your printer model.** Your printer wasn't engineered to work with most third party papers. Image permanence ratings are sometimes non-existent for these papers. You'll get the best results using the printer manufacturer's brand.

✔ **Adhere to the manufacturer's suggested storing and displaying standards for your photographs.** Typically photographic paper/ink combinations are rated with the assumption that the photographs are stored in *archival* conditions.

Archival is a term used mostly by museum curators, librarians, and classic book dealers to mean long lasting. In the photographic area, archival means specific handling of photographs and media using papers, mounting boards, gloves, and special glass that encourage preservation. A whole industry is out there for archival supplies!

Wilhelm Imaging Research

Wilhelm Research is the photographic permanence gold standard when it comes to rating photographic output materials for image permanence. The company is the closest the imaging industry has to a standard governing body. Wilhelm Imaging Research conducts research on the stability and preservation of traditional and digital color photographs, and publishes brand name-specific permanence statistics for inkjet printers and other imaging devices. Printer manufacturers advertise their printing products permanence ratings using data acquired from Wilhelm Imaging Research. When you're in the market for an inkjet printer, check out the printer's permanence rating from Wilhelm

Imaging. Visit the Wilhelm Imaging Research Web site at www.wilhelm-research.com, shown here.

To preserve the life and quality of your prints, consider using the following for storing and displaying your prints:

⌐ **Archival matte and backing boards:** Whether you cut your own mattes or have a professional framer do the work, make sure you're using 100 percent acid-free materials. Adhesives, tapes, and photo corners also need to be acid free.

⌐ **Archival photo storage boxes:** Store unframed and photos in archival boxes. Any light and air pollutants such as dust or pollen can quickly degrade the permanence of photos. Make sure you store your prints in boxes specifically sold as archival quality.

⌐ **Display mounted photographs in frames and behind UV protected glass (or plexiglass).**

For more information regarding archival photo supplies, visit Light Impressions at `www.lightimpressionsdirect.com`. Light Impressions is a good mail order or online supplier of archival quality photo materials.

Fundamentals of Printing

Printing in Photoshop is all about color management. I discussed color management in Chapter 9, and I'll review several of those concepts now discussing printing. Specifying color management options tells Photoshop how to handle your images so that your printer prints images that look like what you see on your computer monitor.

A tale of two printing workflows

The two basic workflows for printing in Photoshop that I suggest are

1. **Print letting Photoshop determine colors.**

   Photoshop can perform all the color conversion of your images specific to your chosen printer and paper. Photoshop uses assigned color profiles to convert colors to the output device's gamut and then sends the data to the printer.

   This workflow is usually preferred for printing photos, but is dependent on the quality and accuracy of the printer driver and profiles provided by your printer manufacturer.

2. **Print letting the printer determine colors.**

   In this workflow, Photoshop doesn't perform the necessary conversion of image data, but sends all necessary conversion data to the printer. I discuss this workflow later in the chapter.

You won't find too many experts in the digital photography field that recommend this second workflow for printing. However, letting the printer determine colors does work well in many inkjet and paper combinations. If you're having trouble getting good color results with the first workflow described, try letting the printer determine colors.

Understanding working space versus printing space

Confusing as things can be, when it comes to printing with accurate colors you need to be familiar with *spaces.* To avoid spacing you out with all this jargon, I'll try to keep this simple:

- ✔ **Printer space refers to the settings that tell Photoshop what printer, paper, and quality you are printing to.** Hey, to make great prints, Photoshop needs to know the printer and paper you're using so it can convert your photo's data over correctly when you tell it to print.

- ✔ **Working space is defined as the color area Photoshop uses to work with colors.** Images are edited in Photoshop using the working space color settings and *then* converted to the printer space during printing. Figure 18-2 shows the Photoshop CS2 Color Settings window, where your working space is applied in Photoshop. See Chapter 9 for more information on color settings.

For photographers, there are only two working spaces to consider using, Adobe RGB (1998) and ColorMatch RGB. Deciding which color space to use in Photoshop depends on the type of printer you have. In my case, ColorMatch RGB best matches the colors my Epson r1800 or Epson 870 Photo printers can produce. Choosing either working space produces excellent results.

To set your Photoshop color space:

1. **Choose Edit ➪ Color Settings.**

   The Color Settings window is where you set up your working space for editing photos.

2. **Choose U.S. Prepress Defaults in the Settings field.**

   This selection provides the best options for photographers.

3. **Choose Adobe RGB (1998) or ColorMatch RGB in the Working Spaces RGB field.**

   You get great results using either choice for photos. ColorMatch RGB may provide more accurate color for use with some inkjet printers.

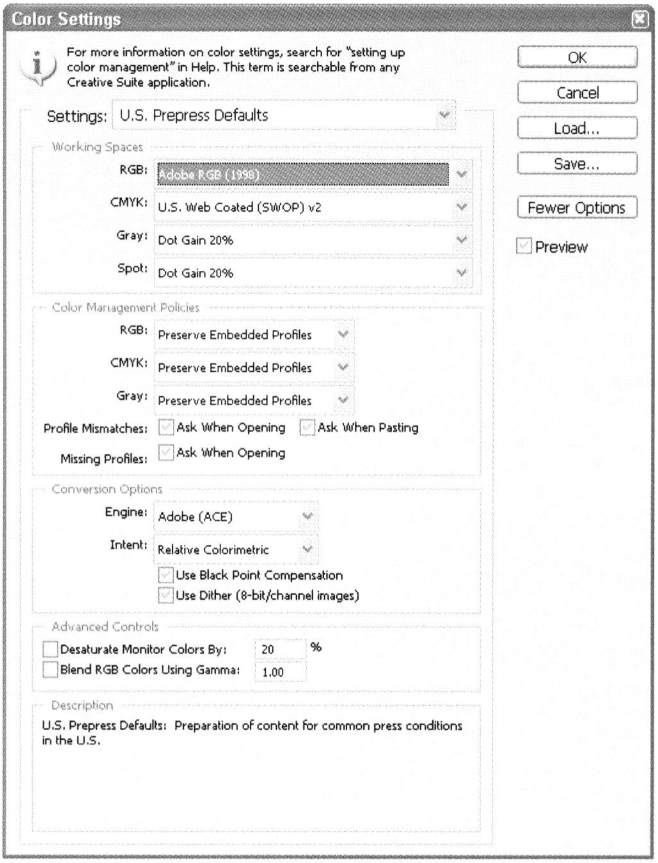

Color Settings

For more information on color settings, search for "setting up color management" in Help. This term is searchable from any Creative Suite application.

Settings: U.S. Prepress Defaults

Working Spaces
RGB: Adobe RGB (1998)
CMYK: U.S. Web Coated (SWOP) v2
Gray: Dot Gain 20%
Spot: Dot Gain 20%

Color Management Policies
RGB: Preserve Embedded Profiles
CMYK: Preserve Embedded Profiles
Gray: Preserve Embedded Profiles
Profile Mismatches: ☑ Ask When Opening ☑ Ask When Pasting
Missing Profiles: ☑ Ask When Opening

Conversion Options
Engine: Adobe (ACE)
Intent: Relative Colorimetric
☑ Use Black Point Compensation
☑ Use Dither (8-bit/channel images)

Advanced Controls
☐ Desaturate Monitor Colors By: 20 %
☐ Blend RGB Colors Using Gamma: 1.00

Description
U.S. Prepress Defaults: Preparation of content for common press conditions in the U.S.

OK
Cancel
Load...
Save...
Fewer Options
☑ Preview

Figure 18-2: Photoshop color settings.

4. Choose Preserve Embedded Profile in the Color Management Policies RGB field.

When you open a file that has an embedded working space other than what you have specified in the Working Spaces RGB field, Photoshop either converts those files to your working space or preserves the embedded profile.

I keep the default Preserve Embedded Profiles. That way, I'll be notified of any mismatches (see Figure 18-3) when I open the file, and have the opportunity to

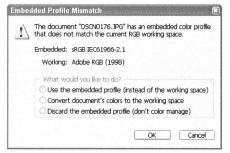

Embedded Profile Mismatch

The document "DSCN0176.JPG" has an embedded color profile that does not match the current RGB working space.

Embedded: sRGB IEC61966-2.1

Working: Adobe RGB (1998)

What would you like to do?
○ Use the embedded profile (instead of the working space)
○ Convert document's colors to the working space
○ Discard the embedded profile (don't color manage)

OK Cancel

Figure 18-3: The Embedded Profile Mismatch window.

convert the file to my working space at that time. By leaving the Profile Mismatches Ask When Opening option selected, Photoshop prompts me to either leave the image in its embedded working space or convert the image to the working space I have specified in the Color Settings window.

5. **Set Conversion Options.**

   Make sure to choose Adobe (ACE) (Adobe Colorimetric Engine) in the Engine field, and Relative Colorimetric in the Intent field, as shown in Figure 18-2. Adobe (ACE) is the engine used to convert colors, and Relative Colorimetric is the best choice for rendering intent for photographers.

6. **Keep the Use Black Point Compensation option selected.**

   Black point compensation ensures that your black points are set in the shadow areas of your photos.

7. **Click OK to save your changes.**

With your color settings ready to go and a color management workflow in place, it's safe to move along to printing!

A-Printing We Go!

Finally! You've gotten through everything you need to do to a photo to get it ready for printing. You've set up color management, made overall corrections and edits, sized, and sharpened. Time to get down to the final step in kicking out those stunning prints!

Choosing papers

Assuming you are printing using a photo quality printer, you have a slew of paper choices. There is no right or wrong paper to use; follow your personal taste.

When choosing papers, keep these ideas in mind:

- ✔ **Choose photo quality papers manufactured for your printer model.** There are a lot of papers on the market, but choosing papers that were intended for your model of printer works best.

- ✔ **If available, choose papers where individual profiles for that specific paper type are available.** For some printers and papers, you can install files on your computer that tell your printer driver and Photoshop how to handle colors. These files are called ICC or ICM files, also referred to as paper profiles. Check your printer manufacturer's Web site for the latest printer drivers and paper profiles to load on your computer.

✏ **Make sure the paper type is compatible with your printer.** There are two different types of inkjet printers: printers that use dye-based inks, and printers that use pigment-based inks. For best results, make sure the paper you choose is compatible with your printer and the type of ink it uses.

Dye-sub printers work only with papers made for those types of printers, and they use printing technology different from that found in inkjet printers.

Letting Photoshop do the printing

I mentioned in the previous section that there are two workflows you can use for printing: The first choice is letting Photoshop handle color management, and the second choice is letting the printer handle color management.

To print letting Photoshop handle the color management for your image:

1. **Open the file you want to print.**

   If the Embedded Profile Mismatch window appears (see Figure 18-3), select the working space that you set up in the Color Settings window.

2. **Indicate the print orientation.**

   Choose File ➪ Page Setup and select Portrait or Landscape orientation, depending on your image. Figure 18-4 shows the Page Setup window.

3. **Choose File ➪ Print with Preview or press Ctrl+Alt+P (⌘+Option+P on the Mac).**

   The Print window appears, with a preview of your image.

4. **Click Show More Options to view all the settings shown in Figure 18-5.**

5. **Choose Color management from the dropdown list below the print preview.**

6. **Select the Document option in the Print area to indicate the image's color space.**

   The color space should be listed as Adobe RGB (1998) or ColorMatch RGB, depending on what you chose in the Color Settings window.

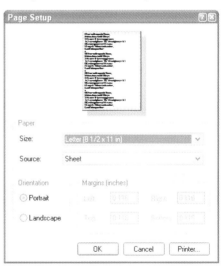

Figure 18-4: Selecting Portrait or Landscape in the Page Setup window.

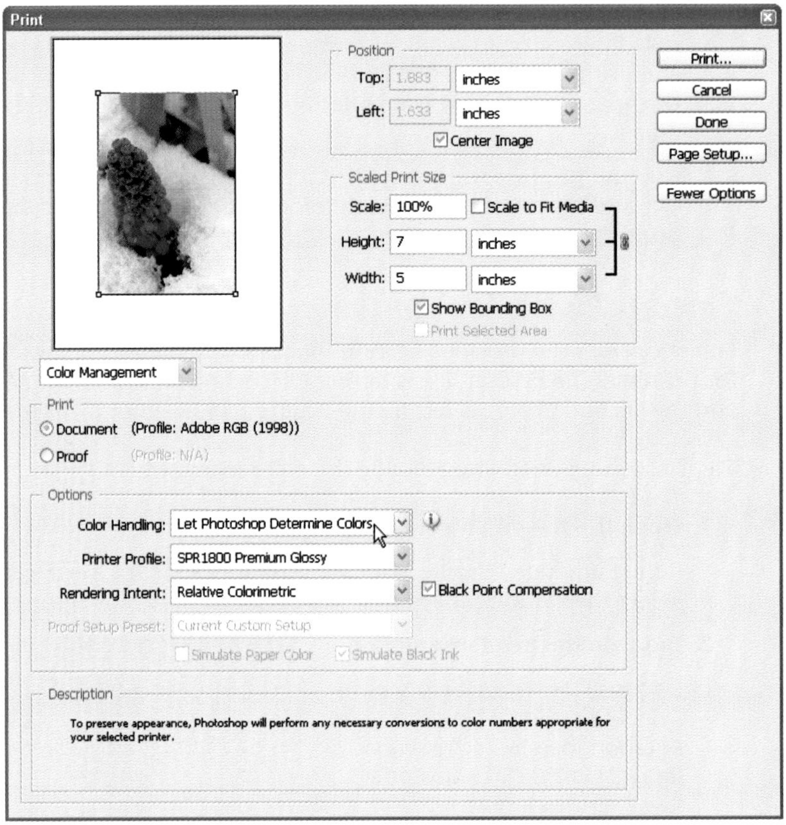

Figure 18-5: The Print window, with a preview of your image.

7. **Choose Let Photoshop Determine Colors in the Options Color Handling field.**

8. **Choose Relative Colorimetric in the Rendering Intent field.**

   Make sure the Black Point Compensation option is selected. This setting ensures that the black point is correctly set in the image's shadow areas.

9. **Click Print.**

   The Print window shown in Figure 18-6 appears.

Click to view printer driver window

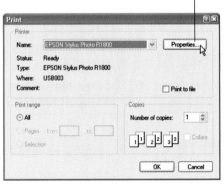

Figure 18-6: The Print window.

10. **Choose the correct printer from the Print window Name dropdown list.**

11. **Click Properties in the Print window.**

    The printer driver window appears, as shown in Figure 18-7.

The printer driver window is different for different printers. A driver is the software that is loaded on your computer when you install a new printer. The printer driver window shown in Figure 18-7 is for the Epson r1800 printer.

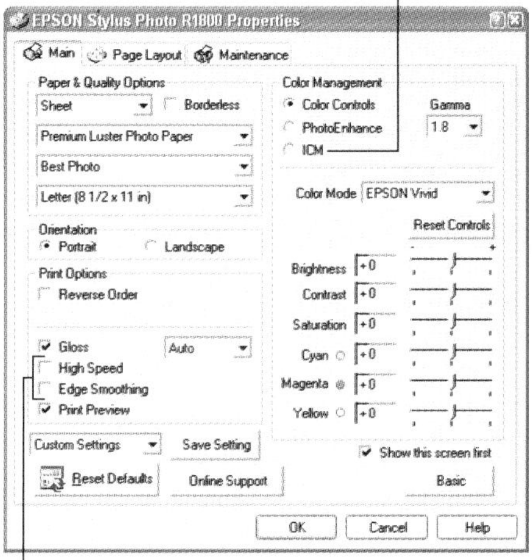

Deselect to turn off printer color management

Figure 18-7: The printer driver window.

Deselect for better quality

12. **In the printer driver window, select the appropriate paper feed type in the Paper and Quality Options area.**

    You can usually use the default setting for this selection.

13. **Select the paper type.**

    This selection is important because the printer prints differently according to the type of paper you have loaded.

If the paper you are using is not listed in the Paper and Quality area of the printer driver window, try downloading the latest printer driver from the printer manufacturer's Web site.

14. **Select the quality you want to print your photo with.**

    I usually use the highest quality setting, Best Photo.

15. **Select the paper size.**

Make sure you select the paper size you have loaded in the printer.

16. **For better print quality, make sure High Speed and Edge Smoothing are *not* selected in the Print Options area.**

17. **Select ICM in the Color Management area.**

Figure 18-8 shows how the printer driver window changes when you select ICM.

18. **Select Off (No color adjustment) in the ICC/ICM Profile section.**

This turns off printer color management and lets Photoshop convert colors.

Selecting the Off (No color adjustment) option is important. This prevents color management from being applied twice to the photo, which would make your photo too dark and too red.

19. **Click OK.**

You're ready to print!

If you selected the Print Preview option in the Print Options area of the printer driver window, you'll next see the Print Preview window shown in Figure 18-9. The Print Preview window gives you a quick peek at the photo before you send it to the printer. Click OK in the printer driver window to send the image to the printer.

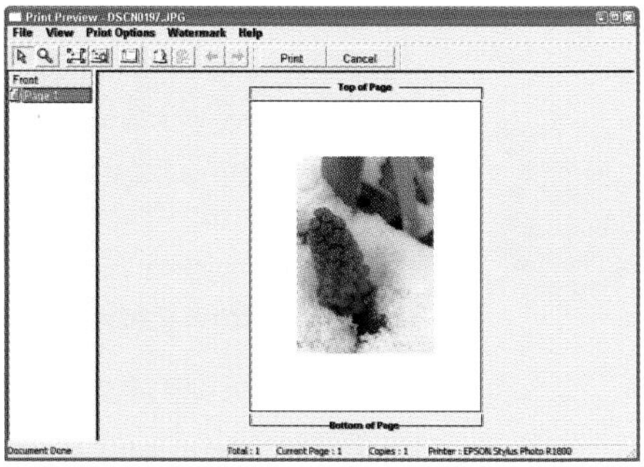

Prints need typically 24 hours to dry after coming out of the printer. Lay the prints on a flat surface and let them dry overnight. If necessary, you can stack prints with tissue paper in between.

Don't count on the Print Preview to give you a good representation of how your print is going to come out on the printer. Color, tone, brightness, and contrast may not appear correctly in the preview. Use Print Preview as a "sanity" check to make sure that you selected the right orientation, size, and so on.

Select to turn off printer color management

Select to turn on printer color management

Figure 18-8: Select ICM in the printer driver window.

Figure 18-9: The Print Preview window.

Letting your printer do the printing

If letting Photoshop handle the color management doesn't work out for you, you can choose the second workflow and let your printer handle the color duties.

As mentioned in the previous section, letting Photoshop handle the printing is the preferred method. Use this workflow *only* if your printer's paper profiles or driver produce unacceptable results.

This method is also best used to print when printer profiles aren't available or when you don't know what type of paper you're using. This method may also be best if the paper profiles provided for your printer don't print with accurate color using the Photoshop printing workflow.

To print letting the printer handle the color management for your image:

1. **Open the file you want to print.**

   If the Embedded Profile Mismatch window appears (see Figure 18-10), select the working space that you set up in the Color Settings window.

2. **Indicate the print orientation.**

   Choose File ➪ Page Setup and select Portrait or Landscape orientation, depending on your image.

Embedded Profile Mismatch
⚠ The document "DSCN0176.JPG" has an embedded color profile that does not match the current RGB working space.
Embedded: sRGB IEC61966-2.1
Working: Adobe RGB (1998)
What would you like to do?
○ Use the embedded profile (instead of the working space)
○ Convert document's colors to the working space
○ Discard the embedded profile (don't color manage)
[OK]   [Cancel]

   Figure 18-10: The Embedded Profile Mismatch window.

3. **Choose File ➪ Print with Preview or press Ctrl+Alt+P (⌘+Option+P on the Mac).**

   The Print window appears, with a preview of your image.

4. **Click Show More Options to view all the settings shown in Figure 18-11.**

5. **Choose Color Management from the dropdown list below the print preview.**

6. **Select the Document option in the Print area to indicate the image's color space.**

   The color space should be listed as Adobe RGB (1998) or ColorMatch RGB, depending on what you chose in the Color Settings window.

7. **Choose Let Printer Determine Colors in the Options Color Handling field.**

   With this choice, you are telling Photoshop to let the printer convert the image color information to the printer, not Photoshop.

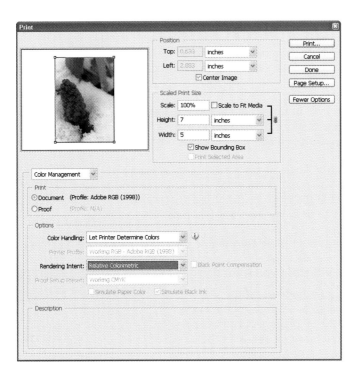

Figure 18-11: The Print window, with a preview of your image.

8. **Select Relative Colorimetric for the Rendering Intent selection.**

9. **Click Print.**

   The Print window shown in Figure 18-12 appears.

10. **Choose the correct printer from the Print window Printer Name dropdown list.**

11. **Click Properties.**

   The printer driver window appears, as shown in Figure 18-13.

 The printer driver software is loaded when you install your printer. Different manufacturers have their own versions of these utilities. I am

Click to view printer driver window

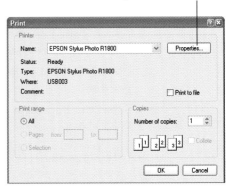

Figure 18-12: The Print window.

demonstrating using the Epson r1800 printer driver, as shown in Figure 18-13. The printer driver windows may be different printer-to-printer, but the concepts are still remain the same.

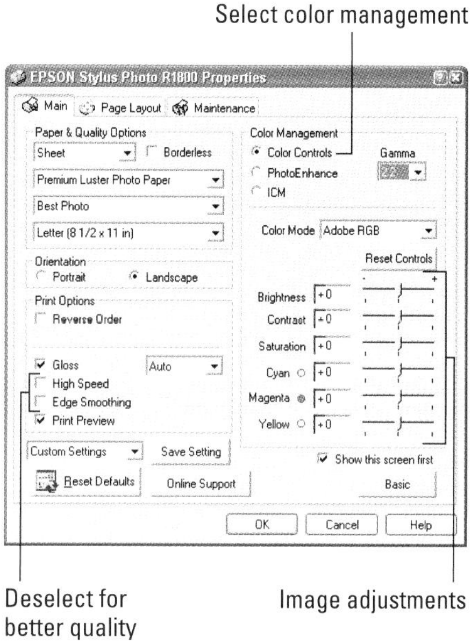

Select color management

12. **In the printer driver window, select the appropriate paper feed type in the Paper and Quality Options area.**

    You can usually use the default setting for this selection.

13. **Select the paper type.**

    This selection is important because the printer prints differently according to the type of paper you have loaded.

14. **Select the quality you want to print your photo with**.

    I usually use the highest quality setting, Best Photo.

Deselect for better quality

Image adjustments

Figure 18-13: The Print window.

15. **Select the paper size.**

    Make sure you select the paper size you have loaded in the printer.

16. **For better print quality, make sure High Speed and Edge Smoothing are *not* selected in the Print Options area.**

17. **Select the Color Controls option in the Color Management area.**

    This turns *on* printer color management and lets the printer convert colors.

18. **For the first print, leave the image adjustments set to their defaults.**

    These adjustments can be used later to fine-tune your prints if color or brightness need to be adjusted.

19. **Click OK.**

    You are ready to print!

Prints need typically 24 hours to dry after coming out of the printer. Lay the prints on a flat surface and let them dry overnight. If need be, you can stack prints with tissue paper in between.

Printing Packages

Remember back to your school days when you had your picture taken every year for the class picture or for the yearbook? If you have children who are school age, you have to shell out a few bucks, but you get those classic picture packages of your darlings. You get an 8×10 inch print, a 5×7 inch print or two, and a couple of sheets with a bunch of wallet sized pictures.

Photoshop offers a nifty utility to produce your own picture packages, just like the ones your kids bring home from school or the ones that are available at the local department store portrait studio. To produce picture packages:

1. **Choose File ➪ Automate ➪ Picture Package.**

   The Picture Package window appears, as shown in Figure 18-14.

Figure 18-14: The Picture Package window.

2. **Choose a page size in the Page Size field in the Document area.**

3. **Choose a picture package in the Layout field in the Document area.**

   Picture Package has 16 different packages that combine multiple pictures ranging from 2×2 inches to 5×7 inches.

4. **Add text to each photo in the picture package.**

   Picture Package gives you the option to add text to each photo. Choose Custom Text from the Label Content field, and then type your text in the Custom Text field. Some photographers like to add their signature to each photo.

5. **Click OK to create the picture package.**

   Photoshop creates each photo in the picture package separately and then assembles all the photos into one PSD document, like the one shown in Figure 18-15.

6. **Print the Picture Package.**

7. **Save the picture package by choosing File ⇨ Save and typing a file-name for the file.**

That's a wrap!

Figure 18-15: The completed picture package.

Part V
The Part of Tens

The 5th Wave   By Rich Tennant

"Why don't you try blurring the brimstone and then putting a nice glow effect around the hellfire."

The Part of Tens gives you 10 really great Web sites that provide wonderful resources for the digital photographer. I show you some of the most helpful places for digital photographers on the Internet, such as the Digital Photography Review site, as well as some off the beaten path sites that you'll find interesting and informative. Saving the best for last, in this part I provide 10 cool ways to make your photos even better using Photoshop. Creating art posters, adding frames to photos, and painting the sky are a few of the 10 quick techniques I show in this part.

The number 10 seems to be a theme. Do yourself a favor; spend 10 minutes going over the Part of Tens!

Chapter 19

Ten Great Digital Photography Web Resources

In This Chapter

- Digital Photography Review
- Digital Camera Resource Page
- Fred Miranda
- Rob Galbraith Digital Photography Insights
- PBASE
- photo.net
- Adobe
- National Association of Photoshop Professionals
- spaceweather.com
- Dummies.com

*A*s an early adopter of the World Wide Web, I'm still convinced it's the greatest thing since, well, digital photography. I bet you thought I was going to say "sliced bread," but that has too many carbs. I could have said "canned beer," but to tell you the truth, it's better in a bottle.

Getting back to the Web. You have the world at your fingertips with the Web. Where else can you do a search on just about anything *ever* thought of and then receive more results than you can possibly view? If you haven't already, do a search on your own name and see what you come up with.

As a user of the Web, my tastes are pretty simple. I frequent only a dozen or so Web sites on a regular basis. Fantasy football, news, For Dummies, and my absolute favorite, digital photography sites!

www.dpreview.com

One of my daily rituals after brushing my teeth and drinking my first cup of coffee is to check my e-mail and then view the Digital Photography Review site for the latest digital camera news and announcements. The site, at `www.dpreview.com`, has been a staple in my browser favorites for years. Recently, Digital Photography Review hit a huge milestone. According to the Web site, its discussion forums have become the largest online digital photography community with over 10 million messages posted in its forums.

Figure 19-1: Research nearly any model camera at the Digital Photography Review site.

The discussion forums are the fun part of this site. If you own a particular model camera, for example the Nikon Cool Pix 8800 shown in Figure 19-1, there's a specific forum just for that model. Log on to the forum and view (you're "lurking" if you don't contribute) the ongoing discussions on subjects related to that camera model. You can also find forums for professionals and for printing and software tools.

www.dcresource.com

One of the top four digital camera resources on the Net, the Digital Camera Resource Page has been around since 1997. Now that's staying power. Go to www.dcresource.com for unbiased reviews of digital cameras as they hit the market.

Photo courtesy of Sony Electronics, Inc.

Figure 19-2: You can find reviews of many Sony Cyber-shot models at the Digital Camera Resource Page.

One of the things I like most about the site is its simple presentation. For example, click Reviews and Info, and you get a great digital camera model database that gives you a quick view of features of 650 digital cameras, including the Sony Cyber-shot shown in Figure 19-2. A well-written buyer's guide and forums are also available on the site. Click News to see galleries of images taken with the reviewed cameras, as well as a reader submitted gallery of Forth of July fireworks photos.

www.fredmiranda.com

One day while searching the Web for a Photoshop action that would help me create a virtual matte and frame to present my photos on the Web, I came across Fred Miranda's site at www.fredmiranda.com, shown in Figure 19-3. Fred's site is unique. He's set up forum areas, contests, user reviews, and an assortment of Photoshop plug-ins to purchase.

Figure 19-3: Fred Miranda offers some useful Photoshop plug-ins.

The site offers camera-specific software utilities and plug-ins. If you own a digital SLR, take a gander to see what Fred Miranda may have available for your model of camera.

www.robgalbraith.com

Rob Galbraith started this site in 1996 as a self-publishing venture to provide photo documentary stories. You can find it at www.robgalbraith.com. Rob Galbraith Digital Photography Insights offers forums, articles, and industry news of interest to both pro photojournalists and hobbyists.

Figure 19-4: Find Nikon software updates at Rob Galbraith Digital Photography Insights.

As a bonus, the site also boasts a comprehensive software update section. Take a look to see if there are any updates to your existing arsenal of raw converters or Photoshop add-ons and drivers. Rob's Quick Links section takes you to interesting photography stories around the Net — find the latest news about your Nikon (see Figure 19-4).

www.pbase.com

I'm amazed at the quality of photography I see on PBASE. Shown in Figure 19-5, PBASE is an online community at www.pbase.com where photographers from around the world show off their photography. I highly recommend viewing as many of these galleries as you can. The best way to learn about photography is to view the work of others. Viewers have the chance to rate and review photos.

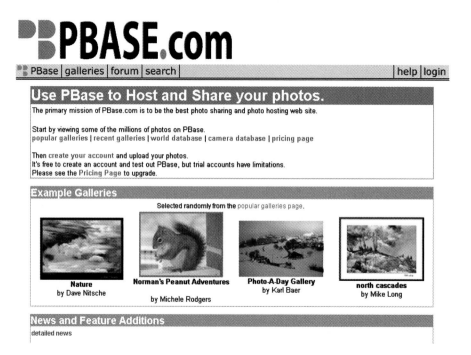

Figure 19-5: PBASE is an online photo community to show off your work and to browse the photography of others.

The content of some of the galleries may not be suitable for viewing by children. Nude photography is considered art by some and offensive by others. Just giving you a heads-up that some of the galleries contain images of models who may not be wearing much as far as clothing goes.

www.photo.net

Visit another great photo-sharing site, photo.net, to search and browse galleries from amateur photographers from around the world. The site, found at www.photo.net and shown in Figure 19-6, also offers some interesting articles and product reviews.

Content of some of the galleries may not be suitable for viewing by children. Nudity ahead: See my previous warning.

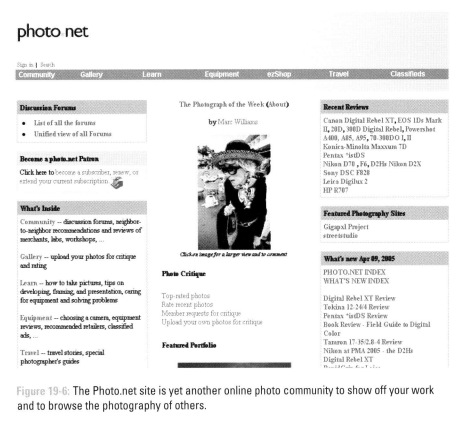

Figure 19-6: The Photo.net site is yet another online photo community to show off your work and to browse the photography of others.

www.adobe.com

Where should you go for information, updates, tutorials, and tips about Photoshop but to the original source? The Adobe Web site, shown in Figure 19-7, is a great resource for information, tips, and tutorials on using Photoshop. Downloads for the latest versions of plug-ins and converters as well as trial versions of all Adobe software products are available at www.adobe.com.

Figure 19-7: Adobe provides resources for Photoshop users.

www.photoshopuser.com

You can find the National Association of Photoshop Professionals (NAPP) site at www.photoshopuser.com. I like the acronym, too. The NAPP refers to itself as "a dynamic trade association and the world's leading resource for Photoshop education, training, and news." Their Web site, shown in Figure 19-8, is a great resource for Photoshop users.

Figure 19-8: The site of the National Association of Photoshop Professionals.

Some of the world's leading educators, writers, and Photoshop evangelists head up this group. You'll recognize many of the NAPP contributors. Membership to the NAPP provides discounts to educational and trade events and a subscription to its magazine, *Photoshop User*.

www.spaceweather.com

The other site I view every morning while enjoying my cup of java is spaceweather.com, shown in Figure 19-9. Astronomy is a passion of mine, primarily because of the great photographic possibilities the subject offers. I visit www.spaceweather.com to stay current on the solar winds, upcoming meteor showers, and eclipses.

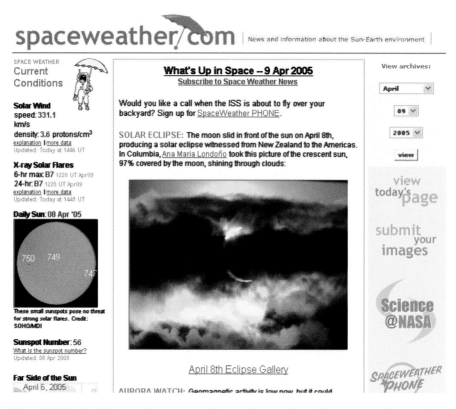

Figure 19-9: Celestial happenings, news, and great photography at the spaceweather.com site.

One of the coolest parts of the site are the galleries. During aurora season, amateur astrophotographers from around the world post their digital photos to the site. It's a lot of fun and I bet a lot of you are going to get hooked, just like I did. Next time an eclipse rolls around, view the site for all the great photos that are posted, as fast as just a few hours after the eclipse.

www.dummies.com

I know it's hard to believe, but there are actually other things in the world to read about besides digital photography! Check out the Dummies.com site, at `www.dummies.com` and shown in Figure 19-10, and you discover the world of possibilities the *For Dummies* series offers. Gardening, religion, sports, travel, and even Dr. Ruth are all included in this ever-growing library of excellent reference books.

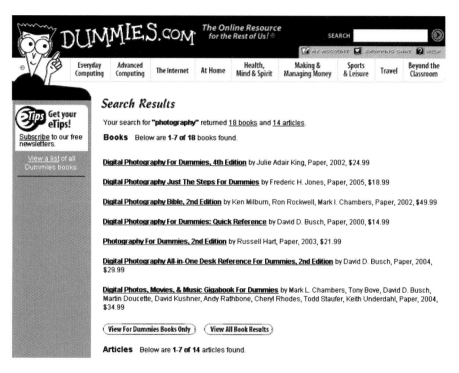

Figure 19-10: Everything's at the Dummies.com site.

Chapter 20

Ten Cool Things to Do with Your Photos

*W*orking with photos and seeing the results come out on the printer is still a thrill for me. Most of my body of work over the years has been straight prints with minor modifications in Photoshop, work purists would approve of. There are plenty of purists out there who believe that you shouldn't mess with your photos, or change what was captured in the camera. I think they just don't use their imagination; I'd rather have some fun!

Throughout the book I touch on some cool things you can do to photos, such as applying filters, blurring portraits, creating a slideshow, and so on. I reserved this chapter for a little more creative fun.

If you sit and play with your photos in Photoshop, you'd be surprised how much fun you can have being a little creative. It sure beats the same old purist approach; sometimes you just need to take the goofy approach!

Dragging Selections to Other Photos

Everyone's seen the kooky images with someone's head pasted on a monkey or something. I guess I should show you how to do things like that. After all, photography is *supposed* to be fun!

1. **Open an image to make a selection from.**
2. **Open an image to make a selection to.**
3. **Make the selection in the photo you want to paste to the other photo.**

   Use the Magnetic Lasso or other selection tool that works best for you.
4. **Click the Move tool in the Photoshop Toolbox.**
5. **Drag your selection to the photo you want to paste it to.**

   Figure 20-1 shows dragging the selection to the target photo.

Figure 20-1: Dragging a selection from one photo to another.

Figure 20-2 shows your new work of art!

After you make a selection, you can drag the selection any number of times to the same photo or to different photos. Experiment and have fun!

Figure 20-2: Successful Photoshop surgery.

Box and Glow

Once in awhile I like to take a photo that I'd normally do nothing with and start experimenting on it using common Photoshop commands. I came up with an effect that I like to use every now and then: creating an inner frame in a photo.

To create an inner frame:

1. **Open an image to apply the inner frame effect to.**

2. **Make a copy of the background image.**

   Choose Layer ➪ Duplicate Layer or press Ctrl+J (⌘+J on the Mac).

3. **Using the Rectangular Marquee tool, click and drag a box around the area you want to frame, as shown in Figure 20-3.**

4. **Choose Select ➪ Inverse to change your selection to the outer frame of the section of the image you just selected.**

   You can also press Ctrl+Shift+I (⌘+Shift+I on the Mac) to inverse your selection.

5. **Press Ctrl+J (⌘+J on the Mac) to duplicate the selection into a new layer.**

Figure 20-3: Making a selection using the Rectangular Marquee tool.

6. **Choose Image ⇨ Adjustments ⇨ Brightness/Contrast and lower the brightness of the outer frame, as shown in Figure 20-4.**

7. **Press Ctrl+J (⌘+J on the Mac) to duplicate the layer for the next step.**

Creating new layers for each added effect you are about to apply is always a good habit. With each effect in a separate layer, you can always go back and make changes or deletions.

8. **Choose Image ⇨ Adjustments ⇨ Color Balance.**

Try moving any of the sliders left or right to get a color cast you like.

9. **Press Ctrl+J (⌘+J on the Mac) to duplicate the layer for the last step.**

10. **Choose Filter ⇨ Blur ⇨ Gaussian Blur.**

Move the Radius slider to about 10 to 15.

Figure 20-5 shows the finished product.

Effects to selections aren't limited to what I've just shown. Instead of applying a Gaussian blur, try a different technique, like converting the selection to black-and-white, or using a filter. There are unlimited possibilities you can try.

Figure 20-4: Using Brightness/Contrast to darken the outer frame.

Figure 20-5: Finished photo with new inner frame.

Applying Virtual Lens Filter Effects to Your Photos

Photographers acquire a collection of filters they put over their lenses to add effects or to block out different levels of light. Photoshop CS2 packs a new tool that lets you simulate the effects of camera lens filters.

1. **Open a photo to apply a Photo Filter to.**

2. **Choose Image ⇨ Adjustments ⇨ Photo Filter.**

   The Photo Filter window is shown in Figure 20-6.

3. **Choose a filter from the Filter dropdown menu.**

4. **Adjust the filter effect by moving the Density slider to the right.**

Figure 20-6: The Photo Filter window.

Figure 20-7 shows the effects of several of these filters on your photos.

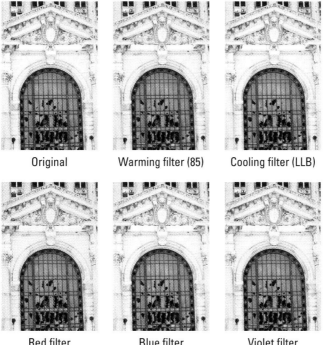

Original	Warming filter (85)	Cooling filter (LLB)
Red filter	Blue filter	Violet filter

Figure 20-7: Photo Filter effects.

Deeply Colored Sky Effects

This is another one of those "rescue the blah photo by applying effects" techniques. You're going to liven up a dull photo by coloring the sky. To change the sky in an image:

1. **Pick a photo that shows the subject in the photo with a backdrop of a cloudy sky.**

2. **Using the Magic Wand or Magnetic Lasso tool, make a selection around the sky portion of the photo.**

3. **Choose Layer ⇨ New ⇨ Layer via Cut.**

   You can also press Ctrl+Shift+J (⌘+Shift+J on the Mac).

4. **Choose Image ⇨ Adjustments ⇨ Channel Mixer.**

   Experiment with changing the settings for the red, green, and blue amounts, or use the Constant slider to get an unlimited color effect for your sky area.

Try using the Brightness/Contrast or Saturation adjustments to further enhance the sky.

Figure 20-8 shows the rather dull image compared to the image where I enhanced the sky.

Before   After

Figure 20-8: Original image and image with new sky.

Using the Channel Mixer to Convert to Black-and-White

One quick method to see how your images will look if converted from color to black-and-white is to use the Channel Mixer adjustment. This is an alternative method to converting to black-and-white from what I showed in Chapter 14. To use the channel mixer to convert to black-and-white:

1. **Open a photo to convert to black-and-white.**

2. **Duplicate the background layer.**

   Choose Layer ➪ Duplicate Layer or press Ctrl+J (⌘+J on the Mac).

3. **Choose Image ➪ Adjustments ➪ Channel Mixer.**

4. **Select the Monochrome option.**

5. **Move each Red, Green, and Blue slider to change the effects in the image.**

   Try making adjustments to each Red, Green, and Blue channel.

Figure 20-9 shows the original image and the image converted to black-and-white using the Channel Mixer adjustment.

Figure 20-9: Original image and image converted to black-and-white.

Cool Abstract Art with Extreme Cropping of Flowers

One of the things I like to do with photos, especially with photos of flowers, is to crop a small portion of the image to create a fine art abstract. I especially like strong colors on my abstracts with simple subject matters, so I choose colorful subjects for my abstracts of flowers. Like I described in Chapter 15, an abstract is a photo that really doesn't represent a scene in a realistic way. To create an extreme abstract:

1. **Choose a photo where a small portion would make for an interesting abstract.**

2. **Click the Crop tool in the Photoshop Toolbox.**

   Don't forget to type in the Width, Height, and Resolution for the image you are cropping.

3. **Crop a portion of the image.**

4. **Apply overall image adjustments.**

Figure 20-10 shows the original image and the abstract created from it.

Original   Abstract

Figure 20-10: Original photo and abstract created from it.

Making Power Lines Disappear

One of the most disappointing things when shooting photos is when you get a great shot, only to find out there's a power line or a streetlight in the way. You may not have noticed when taking the photo, but those power lines sure appear when you're browsing through your photos with Bridge. Many times things that you didn't notice can ruin a shot. No more! To make these pesky lines go away:

1. **Open a photo where something ruined the shot.**

2. **Click the Spot Healing Brush tool in the Photoshop Toolbox.**

3. **Enlarge or reduce the size of the brush by pressing the [key or the] key.**

4. **Click and drag the Spot Healing Brush over the lines.**

Figure 20-11 shows the original photo and the corrected photo.

Before   After

Figure 20-11: Original photo and photo with power lines removed.

Creating an Art Poster

You've seen them hanging up in office buildings, doctor's offices, and in galleries. Gallery prints, also called art posters, are photos with white mattes that include the name of the photographer, gallery, or even motivational text. Creating art posters in Photoshop only takes a few steps; all you need is a great photo!

To create an art poster:

1. **Open one of your favorite photos that has been corrected and edited in Photoshop.**

2. **Add the virtual matte by adding white space around your photo by choosing Image ⇨ Canvas Size.**

   Figure 20-12 shows the Canvas Size window.

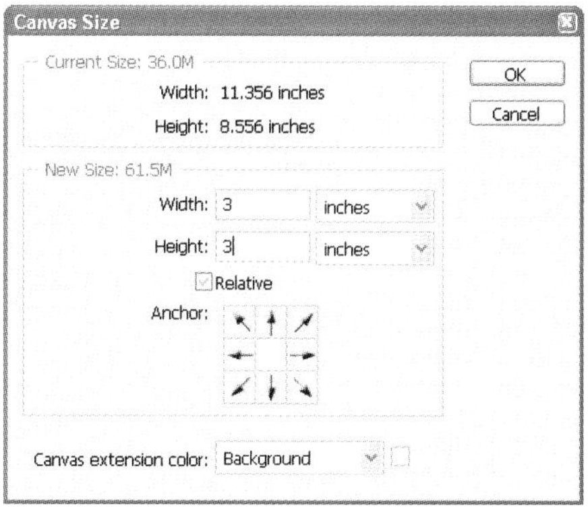

Figure 20-12: The Canvas Size window.

3. **Select the Relative option, and type 2 or 3 inches in the Width and Height fields.**

   Click OK to save changes. The measurements you added are added as white space surrounding the image, as shown in Figure 20-13.

   The amount of white space to add to the photo is up to you. If you have a 5×7 inch photo, add two or three inches. If the photos are larger in size, add *more* inches to make the white space bigger.

4. **Make a selection around the photo using the Rectangular Marquee tool.**

5. **Add a thin black line to the photo by choosing Edit ⇨ Stroke.**

   Figure 20-14 shows the Stroke window.

6. **Enter a Width of 4 to 7 px.**

7. **Select the Outside option in the Location section.**

8. **Click OK.**

9. **Click the Text tool in the Photoshop Toolbox.**

   Choose the font and size of your type. Type the text you want under the photo, as shown in Figure 20-15.

Figure 20-13: Adding a few inches of white space around the image.

Figure 20-14: Adding a thin black line around the photo.

Click the Move tool and drag the photo up if you need more white space on the bottom of the photo.

Chances are your printer can only print up to 8×10 inch prints. If that's the case, you can create your poster in a large size anyway, sizing up to 11×17 inches or 16×20 inches. There are plenty of companies that can print your digital file on large format printers. Check local printing companies such as Kinko's or other service bureaus on the Web.

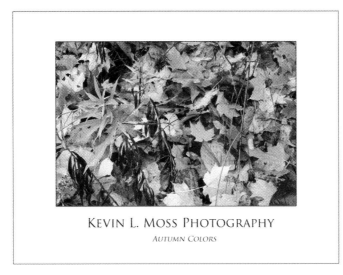

KEVIN L. MOSS PHOTOGRAPHY

AUTUMN COLORS

Figure 20-15: An art poster.

Creating a Collage

Another cool thing you can do to show off your photos is to create a collage. A collage is where you combine a number of photos into one. The creative possibilities are endless.

To create a collage:

1. **Open four or five photos in Photoshop.**

   Make sure your photos are sized at approximately two or three inches wide.

2. **Create a new file in Photoshop by choosing File ➪ New.**

   Figure 20-16 shows the New File window.

3. **Specify a file size of 5×7 inches or 8×10 inches at 300ppi.**

4. **Choose White from the Background Contents drop-down menu.**

5. **Click OK.**

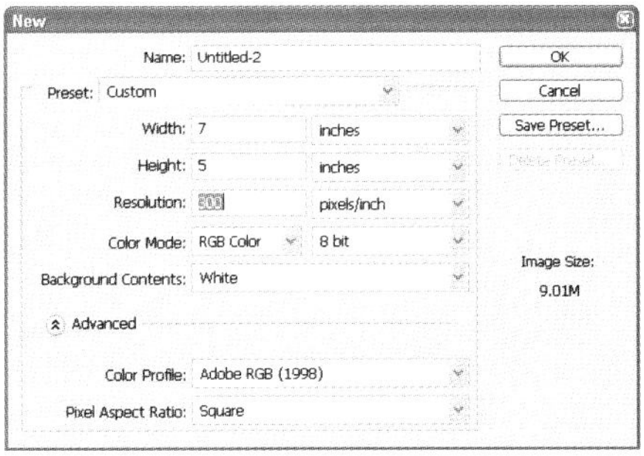

Figure 20-16: The New File window.

6. **Open the Layers palette by choosing Window ⇨ Layers.**

7. **Click an image and drag the background layer to the new file.**

Repeat the procedure for each of the photos you opened.

Figure 20-17 shows an example of a photo collage.

Figure 20-17: The completed collage.

Holding an Exhibition

All the fruits of your digital photography efforts deserve a showing. Photographs are meant to be displayed and enjoyed by others, so what better way to show off your work than to hold an exhibition! Invite your friends, family, and co-workers, and show them the artist that you truly are.

To hold an exhibition:

✔ **Print, mount, matte, and frame 10 or 20 of your best photographs.**

✔ **Find a location for your photography exhibit.** Local bookstores, community centers, places of worship, or neighborhood art centers are all good places to start. There probably won't be a fee involved, and these organizations like it when you bring people into their establishment.

✔ **Set a date and time for a reception to launch your exhibit.**

✐ **Send out personal invitations.** Print your invites on photo paper with a sample of your work.

✐ **Advertise your exhibit by contacting your local newspaper.** Many newspapers will list your notice for free in their weekly or daily art-exhibit section.

If you intend on selling your framed photos at the exhibit, make sure you keep a few extra prints of each photo in the exhibit on hand. You may be surprised how well your art will sell! Check with the establishment you are exhibiting your photos in to see what their policy is regarding selling your work.

Index

Don't forget about these bestselling For Dummies® books!

From sign-up to selling —
the bestselling guide to online auction success!

eBay®
FOR DUMMIES®

4th Edition

Expert advice on bidding to win and successful selling

A Reference for the Rest of Us!®

FREE eTips at dummies.com®

Marsha Collier
Author of Starting an eBay Business For Dummies

0-7645-5654-1

The bestselling Windows XP book, fully updated to better answer your XP questions

Windows® XP
FOR DUMMIES®

2nd Edition

Revised with expanded e-mail, security, and upgrading answers

A Reference for the Rest of Us!®

FREE eTips at dummies.com®

Andy Rathbone
Expert author of Upgrading & Fixing PCs For Dummies and TiVo For Dummies

0-7645-7326-8

Available wherever books are sold. Go to www.dummies.com or call 1-877-762-2974 to order direct.

Don't forget about these bestselling For Dummies® books!

The bestselling PC book—completely updated and revised!

PCs
FOR
DUMMIES®

10th Edition

Updates on the Internet, wireless networking, and managing info

A Reference for the Rest of Us!®
FREE eTips at dummies.com®

Dan Gookin
Author of Troubleshooting Your PC For Dummies, 2nd Edition

0-7645-8958-X

Get started, get savvy, and get things done with the Internet

The Internet
FOR
DUMMIES®

10th Edition

Revised to cover broadband, wireless, blogging, and more

A Reference for the Rest of Us!®
FREE eTips at dummies.com®

John Levine
Margaret Levine Young
Carol Baroudi

0-7645-8996-2

Available wherever books are sold. Go to www.dummies.com or call 1-877-762-2974 to order direct.